Philosophy of the Family

Also available from Bloomsbury

Animal Dignity, edited by Melanie Challenger
Introduction to Applied Ethics, by Robert L. Holmes
Nussbaum's Politics of Wonder, by Jeremy Bendik-Keymer
Practicing Empathy, by Mark Fagiano
Reconceiving Medical Ethics, edited by Christopher Cowley
The Moral Philosophy of Maria Montessori, by Patrick R. Frierson

Philosophy of the Family

Ethics, Identity and Responsibility

Teresa Baron and Christopher Cowley

BLOOMSBURY ACADEMIC
LONDON • NEW YORK • OXFORD • NEW DELHI • SYDNEY

BLOOMSBURY ACADEMIC
Bloomsbury Publishing Plc
50 Bedford Square, London, WC1B 3DP, UK
1385 Broadway, New York, NY 10018, USA
29 Earlsfort Terrace, Dublin 2, Ireland

BLOOMSBURY, BLOOMSBURY ACADEMIC and the Diana logo
are trademarks of Bloomsbury Publishing Plc

First published in Great Britain 2024

Cover design: Ben Anslow
Cover image: Gypsies at a funeral, Jarabina, Czechoslovakia, 1963.
(© Josef Koudelka / Magnum Photos)

A catalogue record for this book is available from the British Library.

ISBN: HB: 978-1-3503-7362-4
PB: 978-1-3503-7363-1
ePDF: 978-1-3503-7365-5
eBook: 978-1-3503-7364-8

Typeset by Integra Software Services Pvt. Ltd.

To find out more about our authors and books visit www.bloomsbury.com
and sign up for our newsletters.

TB – To Lucy and her family.
CC – Františce a Elišce, samozřejmě.

Contents

Introduction

Almost all of us live in families: some larger, some smaller. Even if we do not live *with* any family members. or even communicate with them, most of us understand ourselves as part of a family in some sense of that word. At the very least, most of us have a story to tell about how we came into the world and grew up, with our parents, perhaps with siblings, perhaps with extended branches of cousins, aunts, uncles, grandparents. In that minimal sense, our families will always be part of our identities.

The problem is that the concept of the family is at once so *familiar* – we know our own family well, perhaps we know our partner's family, we recognise family tropes on television sitcoms – and at the same time the concept of the family is so *diffuse*. There are so many different kinds of families, of family relationships, of family duties, of family rituals. The way one person understands her family and her place in it might have nothing in common with how the person next to her on the bus understands his family and his place in it. At first glance, it's even difficult to define what a family is, beyond a group of at least two individuals who decide to call themselves a family. Some family members will be connected by biology, but this is no longer either necessary or sufficient; and of course, the two people who 'start a family' will not normally be biologically related. Colloquially, I might be more inclined to call my neighbour 'family' than a faraway cousin. Close friends of parents might be called 'Auntie X' or 'Uncle Y' and have more contact with that child than the relevant biological relations.

This is a fundamental tension in any discussion of family ethics, family law and social policy: we have very confident opinions about our own family, and yet – unless we're a family therapist or social worker, say – we have very little knowledge or opinions about other families. Even when I observe another family in action from up close (e.g., my partner's parents), I may form opinions but be reluctant to express them, except in more extreme situations. There is a basic kind of polite non-interventionism, exacerbated by a fundamental opacity about other people's marriages and families. Indeed, there might be an opacity in my own relationship with my parent, sibling or partner: I know the 'ground rules' of the dynamic, but I don't know their rationale.

Despite such diversity, we should not forget that we have enough shared ideas of what 'healthy' family relations are, and they will be closely linked to our ideas of what a healthy friendship is, or a healthy collegial relationship at work. We share a basic understanding of what respect, fairness, loyalty, kindness and equality are, for example – no society could hold together for long without such a shared understanding. And these shared ideas are enough to make the humour in a television sitcom broadly intelligible to most, even if not laugh-out-loud funny to all. We can recognise classic characters such as the evil stepparent, and we can understand the other characters' condemnation of him/her. We can distinguish the relevant from the irrelevant issues in a divorce drama. The aforementioned social worker and family therapist will have studied at a university, where there is enough agreement on the core material, principles, and paradigms of their specialization. The interventions of the social worker and the therapist will be guided by the idea of an 'unhealthy' family *benefiting* from the intervention. Some of these shared ideas of 'healthy' and 'unhealthy' family relations are what we are exploring in this book.

We hesitate to speak of a 'good' family because of the connotations of class – the intersection of class and family will be a theme throughout the book. In the same way, we hesitate to speak of a 'good' mother because of the connotations of oppressive patriarchal norms on girls and women. But there will be better and worse 'mothering' and 'parenting', and we will be looking at such roles; just as the participation in and resistance to patriarchal structures will be a recurring theme in the book.

This book is mainly a work of philosophy, but it is also broadly interdisciplinary. Many of the traditional university disciplines are interested in families and also presuppose an understanding of what a 'healthy' family is. Psychology and psychiatry are interested, for example, in the interplay between childrearing practices and family dynamics on the one hand, and wellbeing and mental health on the other. Political science examines the family as a locus of power relationships and injustice, and discusses 'family-friendly' state policies. Sociologists will tend to look at the larger patterns within and between families across a society. Historians might look at how our understanding of the family has changed through the years, especially with regard to the status of women and children. There is a whole area of law called 'family law' (including matrimonial law and child law, and part of property law). And the family is of course one of the main lenses through which to look at literary works.

There are plenty of books about families in all these disciplines – academic monographs and textbooks and popular works – and we are not trying to compete with any of them. Despite our frequent interdisciplinary accommodation, we have not attempted to present anything rigorous or systematic from these other disciplines. Sociologically minded readers should not be dismayed by the scarcity of data, for example; legally minded readers should not be dismayed by the scarcity of discussions about statutes and cases. We do think that our book can complement these other disciplines, however.

Our approach and method are mainly philosophical. But we are assuming a reader who has never studied philosophy before. For our purposes, philosophy concerns the *analysis of concepts*. And of course, the first concept is 'family'. What does it mean, exactly? How might two people disagree on their understanding of the concept? What are they each assuming in using the concept?

Imagine that Anna is talking to her friend Bethany about her (Anna's) sister Charlotte. And Anna says, 'Oh but of course, Charlotte is family!' What does Anna mean? A lot will depend on the context of the discussion; but maybe Anna means that Charlotte always gets away with outrageous behaviour, since she knows that she will always be forgiven by Anna and other family members *in virtue of* being 'family'. This would certainly be a plausible interpretation, and one familiar to many people. Already we can see how much is packed into the concept of 'family' in this short dialogue, and how much Anna expects Bethany to understand – even if Bethany has never met Charlotte. So more accurately, our philosophical approach is about analysing concepts in action, almost as if we were theatre directors working with actors (though with less unilateral control over their choreography).

Other central concepts that we will be examining include 'marriage' and 'partner', together with the concept of 'intimacy'. We all know what these concepts mean, and we use them regularly and correctly; yet it is the philosopher who will demand to know what *exactly* they mean, both in general and in particular contexts. Think about the concept 'child', which has a straightforward legal definition based on chronological age. But of course, a one-year-old child is very different from a seventeen-year-old child, and the main differences are not about physical size. The concept 'child' is directly linked to a special *status* in society: certain things that are and are not expected of children of a certain age, for example. Similarly, 'parent' is not just about a relationship to a child, but it involves a role, partly constituted by parental duty – but what's a parental duty, exactly? What's the relationship between parental duty and parental love? And suddenly we've got a quite complicated discussion.

Insofar as we are interested in duty and love, then, this will be a book about ethics, which is itself one of the main areas of academic philosophy. Another area of philosophy is called metaphysics, and this concerns things that we cannot see or touch. For example, 'time' is a metaphysical concept. But more importantly for this book, the 'self' and 'identity' are metaphysical concepts. We know what the concepts mean, we use them frequently. But the philosopher will ask: what *exactly* is identity? Where does it come from? How does an identity become fixed, or change? What is a healthy identity, if there is such a thing?

Another concept central to this book is 'autonomy'. Most people think that autonomy is all about an individual being free to do what she wants. But it's not that simple. Consider an alcoholic, standing before a glass of wine. She wants to drink it, that's clear. And there are no obstacles to her taking it and drinking it. But when she does so, would we really say she is acting autonomously? Or would it be better to say that she is being *driven* by her alcoholism? That whilst she wants the wine on a superficial level, she does not want, at a deeper level, to be an alcoholic? This talk of 'levels' is also metaphysical.

Clearly, we are not allowed to act entirely autonomously: criminal law is there to prevent us from harming or risking harm to other people. But the long-term battle between parents and their growing teenage child will often be couched in terms of autonomy. The same can be said of some disagreements between intimate partners. There is also a question about the relationship between my duties and my autonomy: if I have a duty to do X, then I must do X, regardless of what I want to do (perhaps I do not want to do X because it is costly or inconvenient). That would seem to be a restriction of my autonomy; but when the duty is grounded in a longer-term family relationship, a relationship that itself partly constitutes my identity, then my very autonomy relies on that relationship, which relies on the acceptance of certain duties. (We discuss this in Chapter 2.)

In a similar way that an *individual* can be autonomous, so too a *family* can be autonomous: 'In our family, we do it this way.' But how much autonomy should families be allowed to have? The most obvious limits on family autonomy have to do with taxation and compulsory education. However, in the UK (unlike in other countries), vaccination against diseases such as measles, tetanus and polio is not compulsory. Why not, when it is clearly to the benefit of both the child and other citizens? The state tests applicants before giving them a driver's licence, based on the real harm that unskilled drivers can cause; why does the state not test applicants before giving them a *parenting* licence, on the same grounds? When one looks at the statistics of abuse and neglect of children, are we deferring too much to family autonomy? (We discuss parental licensing in Chapter 1, and domestic abuse in Chapter 9.)

When we foray into relevant research from other disciplines, we will tend to focus on the UK: UK law, UK social data, UK social policy. This is not a matter of chauvinism, but mainly a practical decision based on our own expertise and knowledge, as well as a matter of focusing the book. However, the issues we discuss should be familiar to readers from other countries, even where social policy or statistics vary greatly. Now and then we will offer international comparisons, but our primary aim there is to make a critical point about some aspect of family law or politics: for example, we may argue that a particular point of Swedish policy is better than its British counterpart, and why.

We should mention the existence of other important philosophical work on the family. Some of this other work focuses on what might be called the 'political philosophy' of the family, the most famous recent exemplar being Brighouse and Swift's 2014 book *Family Values*. (We discuss that book's central thesis in Chapter 1.) In addition, there is plenty of philosophical work in applied ethics on some of the big debates that relate to reproduction – abortion, assisted reproduction, surrogacy – and these obviously relate to the family. (We will discuss these in Chapter 6.) There is a huge literature in the philosophy and psychology of education that concerns children learning both at school and at home (Chapter 4). There is work in feminist philosophy and queer theory that looks at the development of the self and concepts of identity inside and outside family relationships. Feminist philosophy also has a lot to say about state policies that have better or worse impacts on women and on mothers, whether single mothers or those co-parenting (Chapters 3 and 9). Our book is unique in touching on all these issues in a single volume, although given the length of the book we do not make any claim to comprehensiveness. Instead, our aim is to introduce our readers to a number of interesting philosophical issues, and to steer them towards the above literatures and disciplines in case of further interest.

Some starting assumptions

Any book about the family risks being controversial along one particular axis – the axis between social liberalism and social conservatism. Frankly, we want to avoid this controversy, because we worry that it involves more *cultural* disagreements than *philosophical* disagreements. There is nothing wrong with cultural disagreements, but our concern is that they too often collapse into irreconcilable viewpoints, with little potential for engagement. Genuine engagement with, and understanding of, all such disagreements would require more space than we can devote, given our aim of introducing a broad philosophical field in relatively concise bites.

Take the issue of same-sex marriage, for example. This is legally recognised in many Western countries. There are, however, also a lot of Westerners who oppose it because it 'degrades' marriage, or because they believe that homosexuality is itself 'wrong'. Rather than investigating what 'degrade' and 'wrong' mean when deployed by social conservatives, and evaluating the foundations of their position in order to take on their arguments, we hereby declare ourselves to be social liberals from the start, with no interest in engaging in the debate over same-sex marriage. We will therefore be taking same-sex marriage as *obviously* legitimate, and *obviously* something that should be recognised alongside heterosexual marriage. We will not spend any time arguing in favour of same-sex marriage, and we will not discuss or respond to the arguments against. Partly this has to do with the book's length and our need to be selective, but partly it has to do with our belief that there are many other debates that are simply much more philosophically interesting and fruitful. There is still a lot to say about marriage itself (between people of whatever gender), as we do in Chapter 8.

Similarly, we have no objection to same-sex couples or single women being parents, and do not engage in the normative debate over the 'true' nature of a nuclear family – rather, we critique the ideals and stereotypes associated with this idea. We will take it as obvious that a woman does not have any fundamental, gender-determined duty to look after her spouse, her children and her house, *beyond* the equal duties that a man might have in this regard. Likewise, we take it as obvious that a woman's career can be as important to her as a man's career to a man. We acknowledge that a particular couple (regardless of their gender) might allocate different parenting tasks to one another, just as they might allocate different money-earning roles to each other, but we will worry about the effect of patriarchal norms on the negotiations behind the allocations. However, the main point is that we will not spend any time arguing for this egalitarian position, just as we will not consider any 'traditionalist' arguments against it. As much as possible we will talk about 'parents' rather than 'mothers' or 'fathers', and will only take gender-specific detours when necessary – for example, when considering the role of gender stereotypes in reproducing disparities in the distribution of care work.

We want to avoid the abortion debate, partly because it is too distracting, partly because we assume the main arguments are familiar enough to most readers, but mainly because the main context of our discussions is the UK in 2023, where abortion has not been a major *political* issue for more than fifty years. So in general we will be assuming the availability of safe abortion more or less on request until the twenty-fourth week of gestation, without stigma or shame. That is not to deny that a particular woman might find moral difficulties with terminating her pregnancy, and we accept that possibility in our discussions of various scenarios. (We will have more to say about IVF, but again we are assuming that it is morally unproblematic.) Finally, we take it as obvious that a woman can decide not to have children, and there is nothing 'unnatural' or 'selfish' about this. We reject the thought that a woman can be fulfilled *only* by having children (even if some women are). A marriage or intimate partnership can be perfectly good without children. We do not consider child-raising to be any kind of sacred calling, but one calling among many others; different women will choose different careers and hobbies and that is entirely their prerogative.[1] Despite the above – and perhaps more so, because of it – we still hope that social conservatives, and indeed readers across the political spectrum, can find things of interest in this book.

In the light of the scope of our book, we focus on families in the most widely understood sense of the word, and we do not go 'beyond' the family to discuss the commune or kibbutz; nor do we discuss the political idea of family abolition (see Lewis 2022). When people speak of 'the family', what will often spring to mind is the heteronormative nuclear family. Indeed, some of the themes discussed in this book will be concerned explicitly with the nuclear family (for example, when we examine the legal protection of 'traditional' family autonomy through non-interventionism, or when we discuss the gendered social structures and expectations that reproduce unequal distributions of within-family care work), and some will also attend more particularly to patriarchal family dynamics (for example, when we discuss domestic abuse between heterosexual intimate partners). However, it is worth emphasizing here that most of the themes discussed in this book – such as love, duty, responsibility and care – are present and important across all family forms, including families of choice, LGBTQ+ families, and intimate partnerships beyond the 'paradigmatic' monogamous pair. The ideas discussed here apply regardless of gender or number in a family. At the same time, heteronormative and patriarchal pressures continue to represent complications and barriers to family life for some, and we must recognise the more particular challenges faced by these families as a result.

Finally, a few words about the cover photo: In searching for an appropriate image, we were keen to avoid many of the cliches of family life, especially when they represented objectionable assumptions about class, gender and heteronormativity. We also wanted, frankly, to avoid something too cheerful, since our book delves into a number of darker themes that are nonetheless part and parcel of the institution and practices we discuss. In the end we were struck by the *Gypsy Funeral* of Czech-French photographer Josef Koudelka. The centrepiece is the body of a young woman in an open casket, surrounded by members of her family and village. Our thought, in choosing this photograph, was that a funeral reveals a good deal about the meaning of a person's family, for better or for worse: each member will be forced to think about their relationship to the deceased, but also about their new relationships to the other members, in the shadow of this death. In some ways a family will change and evolve, in other ways it will stay the same, and in extreme cases a death can lead to its disintegration. The deceased might be the person who was responsible for the care of vulnerable family members, in which case their death might be a matter not only of sorrow but of urgent need; when a child dies, their loss can bring parents closer together, but will just as often tear their relationship apart; when a family begins to squabble over inheritance, pernickety disputes can be blown up into bitter feuds.

Outline of the book

In **Chapter 1, 'Family autonomy and its limits',** we start with the central liberal assumption that a family should be allowed as much autonomy as possible, subject to a double-barrelled harm principle: the state is justified in intervening to prevent harm to people and groups *outside* the family, as well as to prevent harm to individuals *inside* the family. We look in detail at Brighouse and Swift's argument for intervention in family autonomy by prohibiting elite private schools and inherited wealth on the grounds that these reproduce family inequality from generation to generation, without being justified by 'family relationships goods'. We also look at family autonomy in the medical context, and the state's willingness to override parental refusals when justified by a child's best interests. Finally, we consider the ultimate intrusion on family autonomy: Hugh Lafollette's proposal to license parents in the same way that we license drivers and doctors. This may sound draconian, but LaFollette is plausibly motivated by two facts: first, that the state currently fails to prevent a lot of child abuse and neglect; and second, that we already have a kind of parenting licence in place for those seeking to adopt.

Chapter 2, 'Parents, love and duty', presents a concise overview of one of the moral concerns with which philosophy of parenthood is chiefly occupied: the scope and nature of parents' duties to their children. We first consider the debate over the grounds of parental duty, and further discuss the difference between special obligations (to friends and family members) and general obligations to strangers. The rest of the chapter focuses on one specific question: whether there can be a duty to love one's children. We analyse the concept of love as a combination of perception, deliberation, feeling and action, and examine various interpretations of unconditional love: (i) to love whatever comes out of the womb; (ii) to love whatever my child turns into; (iii) to be available for one's child whenever she needs me. Finally, we examine the relationship between love and duty as motivators for our treatment of family members. Is action out of duty 'one thought too many', or is duty an appropriate stopgap when love fails us?

In **Chapter 3, 'Dilemmas of care',** we begin with a discussion of how care is distributed. We look at the role of gender stereotypes, care-supporting social policies, the costs of childcare and modern expectations of 'full-time' employment in mediating decisions about child- and elder-care. We ask to what extent childcare is a moral and economic burden to be shared across society or carried by parents alone. We then move on to considering the status and rights of care workers, and we discuss the 'global care chain': the economic pressures that induce women in poorer countries to leave their own children in the care of others, in order to take paid care of children in wealthier countries.

If employed through an informal arrangement, care workers are not protected either by employment law or by family law. In the case of nannies for small children, the nanny can be fired from one day to the next, without reason, and without future visiting rights, and at significant emotional risk to both the children and the nanny. Such labour is thus not only economically but also emotionally precarious. To what extent is it legitimate to outsource emotional investment? Finally, we turn to children who care for their family members: we consider the 'parentification' of older siblings, and we examine the difficult moral dilemmas that arise when children and young teenagers themselves become parents.

Chapter 4, 'Identity, the past and the future', starts with the child who has many possible futures: which futures become 'real' depends on decisions made by parents and by the state. Joel Feinberg argues that children's upbringing should be designed to maximally 'open' their future, primarily by giving them the skills and knowledge necessary to be good citizens, but also to find and commit to identity-conferring projects. He thereby argues against the American Supreme Court judgement of *Yoder* (1971). *Yoder* permitted the traditional Christian Amish community to remove their children from compulsory state schooling at fourteen (two years early), in order to teach them Amish skills. The Amish elders predicted (correctly) that this policy would produce eighteen-year-olds who were physically and legally free to leave the community, but who in fact would choose to stay.

We then move on to two recent controversies over parental choice in the matter of their children's identity and their future: first, we look at deliberate conception of a Deaf child by members of the Deaf community. Is this a matter of reproductive autonomy, parental obligation, and/or the child's right to an open future? Second, we discuss saviour siblings. These are children produced specifically for the purpose of providing life-saving donor tissue for an existing, sick sibling. Concerns about the creation of saviour siblings tend to tap into one or both of two worries: that the parents are producing a child for impermissible reasons, and that the child will be harmed by her parents' treatment of her.

In **Chapter 5, 'The meaning of biology',** we start with David Velleman's question about adopted children. Sooner or later, about half of them look for their biological mother or parents. But what exactly are they looking for? According to Velleman, they are often looking for themselves. We examine the notion that knowledge of one's biological ancestry is important to identity-formation, and Velleman's corresponding thesis that it is immoral to deliberately create children who will not know their biological gamete donors. We discuss various criticisms appealing to the idea of parenthood as essentially a social bond created over time, rather than a biological relationship. We then consider these social and biological relationships through a very specific lens: the choice of surnames. Women taking their husband's name, and children being given their father's name, are both still popular trends, despite women rejecting patriarchal practices in most other contexts. Here, we link into the earlier discussion of biology and argue that the child-naming practice 'goes against' biology: in the brute sense of the child coming out of the mother, then the child is of the mother's flesh, and should therefore take her surname. Against this, we discuss a pragmatic concern: that fathers need the reassurance of sharing their surname in order to support their growing social bond with the child.

Chapter 6, 'Adoption, surrogacy and assisted reproduction', continues to investigate some of the themes of biology and family identity explored in Chapter 5. We first consider the adoption screening process: who should be allocated a baby? On what basis? Given the number of orphans in the world, is there a moral duty to adopt rather than to create a new child? We consider the relationship between parental duty and the reasons for which children are given up for adoption, and the role of the state in mediating adoption decisions. This leads us to an examination of the state's regulation of assisted reproduction. Should fertility treatment be subsidised by the state (as it is in the UK), and if so, in which forms and under what conditions? We then look in particular at the case of technologies that allow people to 'choose' their children, and the debate over how much selection should be allowed. Finally, this chapter investigates the concept of surrogacy, and the debates that continue to rage over this means of becoming a parent: regarding commodification, exploitation and the rights of children.

Chapter 7, 'Family history and fertility fraud: A case study', looks in detail at the now-infamous case of fertility doctor Donald Cline in Indianapolis, USA, who covertly used his own sperm to inseminate at least ninety-four women between 1979 and 1986. We examine the testimony of the (now-adult) children fathered by Dr Cline and consider the nature of the harm caused by his actions. We discuss the harms caused to the children he fathered – referred to in a Netflix documentary as 'the Siblings' – and focus in particular on the apparent conflict arising from their claims to have been harmed by Cline's actions, despite those actions being necessary for their existence. We then examine the harms caused to the parents of the Siblings through Cline's deception. This case study shines a practical light on many of the themes of the foregoing chapters, including the formation of individual and family identity, and the place of biology in our understandings of these ideas. In closing, as we consider whether one can regret one's child's birth (or one's own birth) even if one's life is worth living, we examine wrongful life lawsuits. A doctor is sued by a severely disabled child for failing to diagnose the child's condition *in utero*, and thus preventing the parents from choosing abortion. Are these suits coherent?

Chapter 8, **'Marriage and commitment',** starts by asking: what's the *point* of the traditional state recognition of marriage? From the viewpoint of the individual pair, why is it not enough to privately commit to each other? After all, marriage is risky – why not just 'see how things go'? One response has to do with the nature of a commitment. We then consider two strategies for reducing the risk: pre-nuptial contracts and 'marriage contracts'. The former already exists in some countries, and normally concerns a prior agreement about the division of assets upon divorce. But such 'insurance' might again seem incompatible with genuine commitment. The 'marriage contract', on the other hand, would involve a detailed written agreement about the future structure of the marriage: who's going to do the housework, how the finances will be split, whether to try to have children, who's going to look after the children, etc. The final section of the chapter is about the marital vow: most versions contain some indefinite temporal commitment like 'as long as we both shall live'. We ask, first, whether such a vow can make sense when so much of the future is simply unknowable. Then we ask whether someone can make that vow a *second* time.

Chapter 9, 'Domestic abuse', begins by discussing the distinctions between *domestic* violence between intimates and *public* violence between strangers: the location in the safety of the home, in the safety of the family, by a person whom one has hitherto deeply trusted. We examine the role of patriarchal norms and expectations in shaping a climate of permissibility of domestic abuse, the factors motivating domestic violence, and disparity in the prosecution of domestic violence compared with other forms of violence. In considering the constraints that might inhibit state intervention in domestic abuse, we critically examine the concept of 'family privacy' and the status of the family home as a place in which family autonomy (as discussed in Chapter 1) is protected – sometimes at the cost of the safety of individuals within that family. In discussing the choices faced by abuse victims – some of whom feel unable to leave and unable to complain – we come to consider the situation of abused wives who kill their husbands, with a focus on the famous English case of *R v Ahluwalia* 1992. Should such women be able to defend themselves legally by citing self-defence, provocation, or diminished responsibility? Finally, we discuss the relationship between parental rights and partner abuse. It is uncontroversial that a parent who harms their child should lose their rights to custody and control; but what about the parent who 'merely' harms their partner?

1 Family autonomy and its limits

A natural place for a book about family ethics to start is with family *autonomy*. Most people have a powerful intuition that 'in our family, we do it our way', and would resist outside efforts to monitor, criticise and intervene: 'If we need help as a family, we'll ask for it. If there are problems within our family, we'll sort them out.'

In this respect, family autonomy is no more than an extension of individual autonomy within liberalism. As an individual, I should be able to do whatever I like within the constraints of the 'harm principle': the state is only entitled to intervene if I harm or risk harming someone else. So the state is only entitled to intervene in my family if we risk harming our neighbours (or someone else). In parallel to this thought, there is also an extension of an individual's private *space* to the family's private space; within each space, the individual or family is allowed to do what they want. The inviolability of the family home is protected by long-standing laws that prevent police intrusion without consent or a search warrant.

The obvious problem of directly extending autonomy from individual to family is that the family is made up of individuals, and it might well be that one individual is harming or risks harming another one within the family – and on liberal grounds, that would already justify intervention by the state. Notoriously, however, the state has traditionally been reluctant to monitor, investigate and intervene in cases of suspected domestic abuse *unless* the victim leaves the family space and comes to ask for help.

Domestic abuse (and suspected abuse) of children, spouses, elders and handicapped family members is a huge and complicated problem, and we're going to leave our main discussion to Chapter 9. So this chapter is about dealing with certain kinds of indirect harm to individuals' interests – harm falling short of abuse – either outside or inside the family. But it also sets up a framework for discussing and justifying any restrictions on family autonomy, since we will be returning to this problem throughout the book.

Before we start, two obvious 'bigger picture' points. First, any measure that restricts individual autonomy (such as the taxation system, the criminal law, human rights, quarantine rules, international travel restrictions) will already clearly restrict family autonomy. We won't be discussing any of these directly. Second, there's a direct intervention in family autonomy that is not very controversial in principle, although there are plenty of controversies in the detail: compulsory schooling. We're not going to go too far into the huge questions of educational theory and policy. Suffice to spell out the three-fold justification: first, education benefits children by better preparing them for adult life and by somewhat compensating for (potential) bad parenting and social deprivation; second, full-time compulsory education allows parents to go back to work and contribute to the economy; third, education benefits all of society by increasing the number of skilled, disciplined, law-abiding future adults. This latter point is usually taken as justification for taxing childless people to help pay for the state education system (though we note some of the arguments *against* this view in Chapter 3).

This chapter comprises four sections, each involving a different kind of restriction on family autonomy. The first looks at the larger picture of social injustice, which is exacerbated by wealthy families buying further advantages for their children; we look at two policy restrictions that would make things a bit fairer. The second section looks at the special context of the medical world, where doctors and parents might disagree about the best interests of the child. The third section is the most radical: it considers a proposal by Hugh Lafollette to license parents, in the same way that we licence car drivers, and for the same reason. Parenting and driving have the capacity to harm others, and this harm can be reduced by making sure that actors have the requisite knowledge, skills and dispositions to avoid causing the harm. Whilst the first three sections are all directly or indirectly about protecting young children, we want to keep in mind that families are not only about young children – the children age to adulthood, and the parents age to become frail and elderly. The fourth section therefore asks whether the autonomy of those adult children should be curtailed by imposing on them a legal duty to care for their frail and elderly parents.

Family autonomy and social injustice

To what degree does family autonomy contribute to the reproduction of social injustice from one generation to the next? And how might such reproduction be reduced? This is one of the questions asked by Harry Brighouse and Adam Swift (henceforth B&S) in an important book-length philosophical discussion of the family, *Family Values* (2014).[1] The problem is obvious: upper- and middle-class families tend to pass on a lot of their wealth to their children, as well as buying them many social advantages, such as those developed within elite private schooling. B&S are struck by the unfair life-long consequences of growing up in a poor family and want to explore various kinds of restrictions on better-off families.

Before we look more closely at B&S's argument, we have to again lay out the surrounding philosophical terrain, for any mention of social injustice immediately brings to mind some of the central debates in political philosophy. Suffice to say that the major figures in these debates, on both the left wing and the right wing, have typically been interested in a society as little more than a collection of *individuals*, without much explicit attention to the family. For example, should high-income individuals be taxed more or less? What conditions should be placed on individuals to claim unemployment benefits? When the family is mentioned, it is usually supported under a broad liberal freedom of association, just like any other voluntary grouping.

Traditional political philosophy debates do not say much about *children* either, and this raises a problem for the more right-wing political philosophers. Consider the following simplified 'meritocratic' argument in favour of lower taxation, for example: an adult wage-earner should be allowed to keep more of her income precisely because she should be rewarded for her choice to work harder, and to develop and apply her talents. Perhaps that argument works for some adults, but it's important that it does not work for younger children. For younger children by definition lack the competence to choose, just as they have not started working and earning – and therefore there is an important sense that all younger children are *morally equal* and merit the same access to the resources of society. It's not a child's fault if the right-wing political philosopher would condemn her parents as lazy.

And yet the glaring truth is that the prospects of certain children are much better than those of others precisely because of the families that they happened to be born into. A child born into a middle- or upper-class family can look forward to the advantages bought by money, not only in terms of the quality of their education and the variety of their extracurricular activity, but also in terms of intangibles such as social skills, confidence and connections. Those advantages will allow them a much more advanced starting point when they become an adult at eighteen and start to make choices about how hard they want to work. (Not to mention the on-going parental financial support they will often enjoy after eighteen in the form of university tuition and accommodation subsidies.)

In this book we're less interested in the left-right debate over the relations among *adults* in a society and more in the left-right debate over the relations among *children* (i.e. how much should we tax high-income individuals in order to compensate poor families with children who are undeservedly worse off). Now there are a number of family-friendly policies in different countries (Scandinavia seems to be the vanguard in many ways) partly designed to address childhood inequality: more, cheaper and better-quality childcare, better state schools with smaller class sizes, improved school meals programmes, more means-tested bursaries for universities, all funded by high taxes. We will not discuss these programmes in detail; in line with the overall socially egalitarian orientation we spelled out in the Introduction, we are broadly supportive of such measures and do not have much to contribute of *philosophical* value; most of the programmes simply require funding, as well as a fine-tuned regulatory framework informed by on-going empirical research. They are *offers* rather than *restrictions;* our focus is on autonomy and restrictions to autonomy.

Back to Brighouse and Swift, and their concern for social inequality. They would clearly support greater taxation and redistribution. But they also explore other ways to restrict the autonomy of wealthier families, in ways that would not harm the important things of family life. How do they distinguish more from less important things? They introduce a central concept of *family relationship goods* – goods of intrinsic value, valuable for both parent and child,[2] value generated by the long-term intimate interaction. Parents can autonomously choose to cultivate such relationship goods through their choice of activities. Now some of these activities – regular reading of bedtime stories, help with homework, regular conversations about the news over dinner, and trips to museums and galleries – happen to confer significant social advantages on the children. Egalitarians have difficulty admitting, say B&S (pp. 125–6), that it is mainly the middle classes who read to their children. There is enough empirical work to show that children who undertake these activities with their parents develop more knowledge, confidence, thinking and speaking skills, and this will lead to greater success at primary and secondary school, a greater likelihood to go to a good university and eventually to get a well-paying job.[3] The parents' upper- or middle-class status is thus reproduced in the next generation, and those children without as much parental involvement during childhood are thus relatively disadvantaged in their future educational and job prospects. Because of the intrinsic value of these family relationship goods, they should be immune to any state efforts to restrict them as part of an otherwise laudable effort to improve the chances of children from deprived families. This would seem to align with the right wing. However, B&S propose two left-wing exceptions, two restrictions on family autonomy that *can* be justified for the sake of equality: they proposel to restrict elite private schools and inheritance. We will briefly consider the argument against private schools, and then spend the longer subsequent section discussing inheritance.

Elite private schools are generally accessible only to the middle-to-upper classes (although some schools will have more or less generous scholarship schemes for applicants from deprived backgrounds). Equally obviously, such schools provide the child with enormous social advantages, if one is to judge by the proportion of private school graduates attending Oxbridge[4] and then going into high-prestige professions such as law and medicine.[5]

For B&S, however, these schools do *not* contribute to family relationship goods since the parent is not involved; therefore, they cannot be defended from state restrictions aimed at boosting the chances of other children. There is a separate question of how to do this. Perhaps private schools could be simply converted into ordinary state schools.[6] Perhaps they could become semi-private by being forced to accept state money to cover staff salaries, thereby reducing their tuition fees and making them more accessible.[7] B&S's thesis is interesting and plausible. But between those two poles – bedtime reading and private schools – there would be a number of more difficult choices. Three examples.

(i) What if the parents have an expensive passion for horse-riding or sailing, and want to share their passion with their daughter? Perhaps that would land on the family relationship goods side of the equation, because neither equestrian nor sailing skills would seem to provide *that much* generic social advantage.

(ii) What if myself and my partner value education and academic knowledge, not in terms of future social advantages but as an intrinsic good, and so we want to send our academically able daughter to a private school with an excellent academic reputation (much better than the local state schools)? This will allow us to have much deeper dinner conversations as she ages, thereby bringing us closer.

(iii) What if I live in a country without good, free pre-school childcare, such as Britain and Ireland (exceptional in Europe in this respect)? If I and my partner have middle-class incomes, and the only way we can both continue working in fulfilling jobs (jobs we like to talk about at home, thereby contributing to our family relationship goods) is to enrol our youngster in a private crèche (which we can afford), would B&S allow that?

Moreover, we have to recognise how politically controversial it would be to interfere with the freedom of association and freedom of contract that are the principles behind private schools. After all, what is a private school? It is a group of teachers who agree with a group of parents to teach their kids in exchange for money – but there is no deception or coercion on either side, and importantly, there is not *direct* harm to third parties. It is the (unintended) indirect harm that is the problem.[8]

Family autonomy and inheritance

Whilst bedtime stories and private schools may confer important advantages on middle-class children, the biggest advantages usually come in the form of money: gifts and inheritance. Every country has to decide how such transfers should be taxed, and what exceptions to make. B&S are clear in their priorities: since inheritance does not itself contribute to family relationship goods, and since even fiscal conservatives would not describe family wealth as 'earned' by younger children, then high taxes on inheritance can easily be justified.

Note that inheritance taxation is but one form of state taxation. Different taxes have different economic effects that might be more or less welcome or unwelcome, depending on one's political and moral priorities. Even a left-wing government, for example, might prefer to increase income taxes whilst decreasing inheritance taxes, depending on their calculations of total revenue under different hypotheticals, as well as on the political battles they choose to fight. So we're asking about the principle of raising or lowering inheritance taxes. The best way to understand the principle is by looking at two extreme paradigms.

First, the *gift paradigm*. If I legally own an object X, then part of what ownership *means* is that I can sell it to whomever is willing to pay my price, or I can give it to whomever is willing to accept it. The only moral and legal restrictions involve deceit or coercion of others, or harm during the selling or giving process. So one position on inheritance tax would be to say that a dying person's last will is just an extension of the gift paradigm: whether I give my property to my children before or after death should make no difference. In neither case should it be subject to taxation, because it is my free private transaction with the beneficiary.

Second, the opposite extreme: the *'dead people can't own things' paradigm*. If the living Margaret legally owns an X, then once Margaret *dies* (before giving the X away) then the X can no longer be owned by Margaret.[9] So if X suddenly becomes unowned, it would seem to be appropriate for the *state* to take ownership (i.e. an inheritance tax of 100 per cent), *regardless* of Margaret's ante-mortem wishes one way or another. Fine, if Margaret wanted Britney Spears played at her funeral, we can arrange that because it's cheap and easy. But if she had expensive wishes (a €50,000 mahogany coffin), or wished to leave the €50,000 to her daughter, then such wishes expire along with her.[10] (One immediate problem is that any sensible person on their deathbed in a country with a high inheritance tax will give her property away before she dies. That's why inheritance tax usually has to include any large gifts made within a certain time period before death – or else the tax regime can impose a straightforward gift tax above a certain amount.) High inheritance taxes and explicitly linked redistribution could symbolically and factually promote the egalitarian ideal of each child starting out with similar resources, corresponding to the equal moral status of each child. One corollary (important for a left-winger) of this 'dead people can't own things' paradigm is that the largest familial wealth would never be passed on, and this would greatly reduce the inter-generational accumulation of wealth that exacerbates social inequality so much more than disparities in earned income.

Most countries have policies somewhere in the middle, closer to one or the other extreme. British inheritance tax is relatively high, and the procedure runs as follows:[11] Two spouses have to be married or in civil partnership. One dies. The remaining spouse automatically inherits everything from dead spouse: no inheritance tax is paid.

If a single remaining parent dies, then all of her property is gathered together (and valued) in the 'estate'. The first task is to use the estate to pay off any of that parent's outstanding debts. The net value of the estate is then offered to the surviving children as follows:

(i) The first £325,000 is tax-free. This is a bit more than the average price of a house in the UK, and this recognises that the house can have important symbolic value for adult children who grew up in it, and might indeed have been owned by the family for several generations.[12]

(ii) Anything above that threshold is taxed at rate of 40 per cent, unless donated to charity.

We may note another peculiarity of British and Irish inheritance law: a single living parent can write a will leaving the bulk of her fortune to anyone and anything she wants. Children have a right to have their 'needs met', but this is notoriously vague, and in practice does not amount to much. In contrast, in France (as in other countries in continental Europe), if a single living parent dies, leaving behind two children, then each child has a legal right to 33 per cent of the estate. So that means that in

Ireland/Britain, an adult child who was dutiful and caring to his/her millionaire parents for many years might end up with little more than a few grand, whilst in France an adult child who has been completely estranged from his/her millionaire parents for decades might end up with a third of a million.

In what follows we're not going to follow B&S directly, but another (2020) article by Pedersen & Bøyum (henceforth P&B), which deploys the same concept of *family relationship goods* as B&S. P&B start by supporting a high inheritance tax, but they organise their article as a set of responses to five arguments *against* a high IT (i.e. *in favour* of a low IT). The first of these claims a 'right' to benefit one's children, and P&B deploy B&S's argument about family relationship goods against it. The more interesting arguments are the third and the fourth, which we combine and paraphrase as follows:

> Children have a right to their parents' belongings, because of *common ownership*. The idea is that a single family breadwinner might see herself as earning money not for herself but for her family. As such, all the family property already belongs to all members of the family. When the parents die, the children retain the ownership they already had, and so there is no need to transfer anything. In addition, a parent will typically think of their children as part of her *identity*: in the sense that the parent will say things like 'when my child is happy, I am happy; when my child suffers, I suffer'. Within such a spirit it is easy for a parent share, give and bequeath to a 'part of themselves'.

There are, of course, some problems with P&B's appeal to the idea that a breadwinner earns money not for herself, but for her family. First, we run directly into an idea that was used for many decades to deny equal pay to women: that a family breadwinner should be paid more than an unmarried or childless employee for the same work, because they (and usually *he*) were supporting a family. This is clearly an argument most would reject now. A second problem is that whilst breadwinner A may indeed see herself as earning money *for* her family, this is far from a universal attitude; we are all familiar with the stereotype of breadwinner B, who tells his offspring 'As long as you live under *my* roof, and *I* pay for the food on your plate, you follow *my* rules.' (Another problem has to do with modern 'fractured' families – marriages and remarriages, step-children and step-parents – it is hard to make precise sense of joint ownership across all these fault lines.) However, P&B follow British law in acknowledging the special importance of the family home, which is genuinely shared by all family members, and this would be an exception to their overall argument for raising inheritance tax. In addition, they acknowledge the importance of a *family farm* (or family business), where the teenage (or older) children have already worked for several years, i.e. have mixed their labour with it (John Locke's justification for private property), and therefore earned the right to share ownership of it. Other than those two exceptions, P&B see no reason why the children should have a *complete* (i.e. untaxed) right to the money that someone else, i.e. their parents, made during their lifetimes.

Family autonomy in the medical context

We will now look at a very different context for intervention in family autonomy (or more specifically, intervention in family medical decision-making autonomy). Again, in clear cases of harm or a threat of harm, as in the case of child abuse or neglect, the liberal state is entitled to intervene, although the onus will be on the state to prove abuse or neglect. Teachers and doctors are trained to look for signs of abuse or neglect, and in the event of suspicion to call in social workers to investigate more closely.

We first need to say something about the medical context in the case of competent adults and doctors. There is a long-standing (ethical *and* legal) principle of patient autonomy: as long as the patient is informed of the consequences, then she can refuse any medical treatment, even urgent life-saving treatment. Competence is to be presumed; in borderline cases, the patient will be judged competent if she can use, understand and communicate the information necessary for a decision. The corollary of this is that when the patient is *in*competent (e.g. because they're a child, or senile, or because of intellectual disabilities), then a legal guardian will have to make decisions on the patient's behalf, and without a legal guardian a doctor will make the decisions, guided by the patient's best interests.

The complications begin when we consider the sheer extent of family autonomy, and the amount of discretion that parents have in looking after their children, not only in terms of practical day-to-day needs, and not only in terms of shaping the child's beliefs and values, but also in terms of her health. It's the parents who are the main people to feed the child, for example, even if the school will also instruct the children about nutrition. It's the parents who spend the most time with the child, and therefore it is mostly up to them to make their living space safe; to notice and respond to signs of illness or injury; and to administer first aid and/or take the child to see a doctor.

Now the vast majority of parents want the best for their child, and will happily defer to the doctor when it is clearly in the child's best interest. Technically, the doctor has to ask a parent for her consent (whether or not the other parent disagrees) before treating any child under sixteen, and of course the parent or parents will nearly always consent.[13] But there will be some tricky borderline cases of family autonomy where a parent thinks they know better, or where a particular treatment has a special status.

The classic example of a serious conflict between parent and doctor is the Jehovah's Witness (JW), who is religiously prohibited from 'consuming' another human's blood, including a life-saving transfusion. Blood is a spiritual pollutant, and will hinder their chances of going to heaven. From the JW perspective, mere biological death followed by heaven is infinitely preferable to a bit more biological life and the loss of heaven. In the case of a competent adult, this raises no special legal problem, since she can refuse any treatment, including life-saving treatment. The more controversial case is when a JW parent wants to refuse a life-saving transfusion for their minor child, despite the warning that their child will die without it. English law has consistently overridden the parent in such cases.[14] When the medical treatment is safe and reliable, then the law considers it in the minor's clear best interests to receive the treatment and thereby to maximise her chances of a normal biological life span. The implication is that whilst the law is happy to assume that parents will normally promote the child's best interests, on this occasion their request for reliable medical treatment to be withheld effectively constitutes neglect and justifies the courts' authorization of medical treatment.

There are two ugly consequences of this. If the transfusion is safe and reliable, and if the underlying condition was no more than the loss of blood through trauma, then there is a high chance that the child will make a good recovery. However, in her parents' eyes, the child will be irrevocably polluted by the experience. It's all very well the hospital administering the transfusion and saving the child's biological life, but eventually the hospital discharges the child, and the child has to spend the rest of her childhood with her parents. The second ugly consequence is that the child might well come to see *herself* as irrevocably polluted, and this will undermine the normal development of self-respect and self-confidence. There will inevitably be a question of whether certain forms of religious practice and upbringing generate consequences serious enough to constitute a form of psychological abuse meriting more robust state intervention – especially when such religions carefully exclude alternative points of view from the maturing teenager. We will return to this question when we discuss the American Supreme Court case of *Yoder* 1972 in Chapter 4.

In cases of a serious threat to best interests, the law is willing to override family autonomy in offering reliable medical treatment to the minor. In less serious cases, the law is willing to defer to the parents' views. The classic example here is ordinary childhood immunization. There is a strange fudge here, for the medical establishment is agreed that vaccinations are in the best long-term interests of the individual child *and* of other children. However, because of the word 'long-term', and the role of probability, this means that the risks to the child's interests are not sufficiently *imminent* or likely to justify overriding the family autonomy of so-called 'anti-vaxxers'. At most, a GP can strongly recommend to the parents that (i) the risks to the child arising from missing vaccinations are significant, even if not immediate or high; (ii) the risks to the child after receiving the vaccinations are clearly negligible (given extensive evidence from other children); (iii) the fact that *all* children benefit from 'herd immunity' requiring a minimum proportion (about 80 per cent) of vaccinations within a given population, and so the anti-vaxxers are not only free-riders but also actively endanger others. Nevertheless, this can only remain a strong recommendation and not a command, out of respect for family autonomy. However, when dealing with the parents of a young child, often the GP will speak matter-of-factly that 'of course' the child be vaccinated – a kind of paternalistic nudge. That is, unlike other treatments, she won't highlight the element of choice, she won't emphasise the patient's right to refuse, and she will leave it to the determined anti-vaxxer parents to make the conversation awkward.

The British situation with non-obligatory child vaccinations generally works in nudging enough parents to consent and thereby achieve herd immunity. Most countries in Europe involve more explicit threats: in France the child will not be admitted to a state preschool or school without evidence of the right vaccinations. This is still not compulsion, of course, but it is fairly strong pressure. There is a question of how the French can make school attendance compulsory whilst denying entrance to the unvaccinated. The answer would presumably be that the anti-vaxx parents would then have the right and obligation to home-educate their child, with all the costs and efforts associated with that – and such parents might be suspicious enough of the malign intentions of the state to prefer home education anyway. Nevertheless, whilst every parent has the right to home-educate, the state still has to oversee such education and remedy any deficiencies.

Licensing parents

Consideration of family autonomy and regulation need not begin from the family itself, but even earlier: at the point of asking who can start a family, and how. Hugh Lafollette asked this question in a famous piece from 1980. Lafollette's starting point was simple: he quoted the child abuse statistics in America. Under the current legislative framework and social work principles, he argued, the removal of a demonstrably abused or neglected child comes *too late*: the child has been permanently damaged, and the rest of his life will be affected for the worse. Indeed, there is evidence that many abuse victims go on to abuse others. So his licensing proposal is no more than a scheme to identify and prevent some of the potential abusers from being parents.[15]

The numbers are truly disturbing in Britain too. According to a survey by the Office of National Statistics, 9 per cent of adults aged sixteen to fifty-nine had experienced psychological abuse, 7 per cent physical abuse, 7 per cent sexual assault and 8 per cent witnessed domestic violence or abuse in the home.[16] And these figures are self-reported; the real figures are probably far higher.[17] Lafollette says that we need to be more proactive in trying to distinguish the 'good enough' potential parents from the 'clearly bad' potential parents, or at the very least we need to implement some compulsory educational measure designed to improve the parenting of all potential parents. After all, it should not be forgotten just how ignorant most couples are about the full, complex practicalities of parenting, unless they are primary school teachers or paediatricians, or have direct experience with raising younger siblings.

A licence would only be issued to those who passed a parenting test. The analogy would be with other skilled and potentially harmful activities where applicants have to pass a test: Lafollette mentions medicine and driving. Medicine is not the best analogy, since only a small minority of people even apply to become doctors, and of those, only a minority are successful; in contrast, presumably the great majority of driving licence applicants eventually become drivers, even if they have to repeat the test two or three times. The thought is that anybody with sufficient motivation will eventually learn the theoretical portion and practice the skills portion to pass the test. Henceforth they will be good enough, and they will probably improve with further driving. And with driving tests, we suggest that most people (drivers and non-drivers) are happy with the principles of 'however long it takes', combined with 'if you're still failing after the third attempt, you probably shouldn't be a driver'. Nobody should see themselves as having an absolute right to drive, given the risk of harm to other road users and pedestrians. Of course, the driving licence regime cannot guarantee that an individual driver will drive safely on a particular occasion, but a universal licence requirement must *generally* increase safety.

Lafollette does not need to describe in detail how the parenting test would work, since he can leave the details to a testing authority comprising (e.g.) social workers, paediatricians and family therapists. But some of the devil in the detail can be spelled out here. First, would the couple take the test before or after conception? If they fail the test before conception, then the state's response would amount to a hypothetical threat: '*If* you get pregnant, we will take the child away at birth.' If they fail the test after conception, it will no longer be a hypothetical: 'We *will* take the child away at birth.' Either way, one has to appreciate how drastic an intervention this is. Yes, it's carried out in the best interest of the child, but one can imagine so many ways that the test might get it wrong, just as one can imagine a couple who desperately want at least the opportunity to *try* to be good parents.

In practice, the state already does take a very small number of babies away at birth, once the mother has already conclusively demonstrated (with a past child who has since been removed) that she lacks even the basic ability or interest to be mother (usually because of severe drug addiction or severe mental health issues). To address a more common problem, we already have restraining orders to keep violent or otherwise abusive parents away from their partner and child if there is sufficient evidence of a threat.[18] So Lafollette could bite the bullet, point again to the abuse statistics, and say that this category of 'advance child removals' should be expanded.

A more plausible way for Lafollette to respond would be to say that the parenting test does not need to be *punitive*. It can serve merely to identify those parents who need *extra* support and monitoring after the birth; and the monitoring need not be looking for signs of failure, but rather for signs of changing needs.[19] In addition, we do not even have to make such a parenting test compulsory; we could simply attach financial incentives to take it, with further financial rewards for passing it. It should also be noted that plenty of sources of information and skills already exist: antenatal classes, parenting support groups, parenting manuals. It is plausible to claim that there is some basic information that every would-be parent should know about nutrition, clothing, equipment, finances, first aid, schooling, state support structures, etc. So perhaps the *most basic* parenting test would merely be a test on this basic information, with lots of support for those re-taking the test. In some cases too, the sufficiently detailed information might be enough to *deter* those who were already half-hearted about parenthood, or it might give extra intellectual and volitional strength to half-hearted women to resist being pressured into motherhood by the rest of their family.[20] Again, merely testing basic information would not guarantee anything, especially in those (perhaps many) cases of abuse that do *not* result from ignorance, but rather some kind of emotional or volitional failure. Sometimes more support will reduce the stress of child-rearing and therefore reduce the likelihood of abuse. But perhaps the parenting test could also be designed to reveal certain personality types who might be persuaded to address their issues before parenthood (e.g. by taking an anger management course) and/or who might merit closer monitoring after parenthood begins.[21]

Of course none of these modifications would guarantee an end to abuse and neglect, especially when so many would-be parents inevitably have such a poor idea of what their *particular* child will be like, the particular way it will develop in response to events and environmental stimuli, and how the potential parents will cope as actual parents at each stage of childhood, given unpredictable events in the rest of their own lives. But it is surely not implausible to claim that some kind of testing or licensing regime would reliably lower the general incidence of child abuse and neglect, as Lafollette claims. There is another important precedent for a parental licensing scheme, and that is the *screening* process we already use for adoption applicants. The applicant(s) have to prove that they are ready for a child by submitting to a detailed and intrusive screening prior to approval: they have no right to parent, let alone to parent a particular child.[22] The screening is both formative and summative: not only do the social workers learn whether the applicant(s) have the necessary skills, knowledge, dispositions and resources to be good enough parents, but the very screening process allows the applicants to learn about the realities of parenting and about their suitability for it, and they have the option to back out.[23] (We discuss adoption in Chapter 6.)

For the moment, the question is whether 'natural' reproduction is sufficiently different from adoption to disqualify adoption screening as a model for parenting licensing. At the present time, natural reproduction generates a strong legal presumption in favour of the child belonging to its parents (or at least its mother) at birth, until such parents can be shown to be a threat to the child. Lafollette would argue against this presumption, and would point to the general success and public acceptability of the adoption screening as a reason to extend it to natural reproducers. However, this proposed extension does not do justice to the sheer power of the phenomenon that the legal presumption reflects: the mother's experience of giving birth. The powerful sense of '*this is my child*' is much more deep, private and fierce than any socio-legal rulings that would purport to establish new care obligations. In contrast, adoption has a very different *starting point*, namely the existence of a child who has been abandoned or removed, and needs a home – and the adoption process is a rational way of placing the child in the best home.

One thing is striking about Lafollette's proposal: that it has not been adopted, and indeed not come close to being adopted, by *any* national legislatures (at least not under the label of 'licence' or 'test'). However strong his concern for child abuse, and however intuitively plausible the analogy with a driving licence and with adoption screening, the proposal would create instant resistance as an excessive state intervention. This widespread reluctance reveals something crucial about the place of children and families in our societies.[24] Lafollette responds to this failure by making a good point about the nature of *property*. He believes that too many parents tend to see their children as their property, alongside their houses and cars and clothes, to do with what they please, within the ordinary liberal constraints of the harm principle. Instead, says Lafollette, we as a society should recognise that we owe these children protection as extremely vulnerable fellow citizens with basic rights to welfare, and that parents should not be seen as *owners* but as *trustees* of the child on behalf of society and/or on behalf of the child's future self. Normally a parent is well placed and well motivated to look after the child, but the parents' wishes should ultimately be subordinate to the child's best interests. Such subordination is well expressed in Section 1 of the UK *Children Act* 1989: 'When a court determines any question with respect to (a) the upbringing of a child; or (b) the administration of a child's property or the application of any income arising from it, the child's welfare shall be the court's paramount consideration.'

Lafollette's idea of an inappropriate understanding of parenthood as liberally constrained property ownership perhaps explains some of the resistance to parenting licences, but surely not all. Another way to look at the situation is through the concept of *belonging*. The expression, 'That table belongs *to* me' certainly invokes the norms of property and ownership; but 'I belong *in* England' does not. The second sense of belonging has to do with emotional attachment to a place or an institution, and with the importance of that place or institution in providing a meaningful background scaffolding for my life. So the phrase 'a child belongs with its parents' can be read both ways. Lafollette thinks that those who resist his licencing scheme do so because they inappropriately read 'belong' in the sense of property. But it will be *more* appropriate to resist the licencing scheme by reading 'belong' in the meaningful scaffolding sense. Part of a child's identity is tied up with its biological and social family relations, in a way that is much more intimate than either the property relation *or* even the trusteeship relation would suggest.

This sense of belonging is at play in many child custody decisions which would otherwise seem incomprehensible. A mother and a father divorce, the mother is granted custody of their ten-year-old child, but the father is granted visitation rights *even if* the father is an angry, insecure individual who has never seemed to be very interested in the child, and *even if* the child has no great wish to see the father. The thought is that it is good for the child to maintain contact with him, a good that is not defined solely in terms of pleasure of or usefulness to either party, but also in terms of identity and meaning for the child's developing understanding of the world and of her place in that world. At some deeper level, these visitation requirements are based on the presupposition that the child still needs the father in order to develop an optimally healthy future adult identity, *even if* the child later (as an adult) decides to cut off all contact with the father.

Filial duty

The restrictions on family autonomy covered so far might all be justified by reference to the young child's interests and wellbeing. In this section, we want to remember that intra-familial issues are not just about small children but also about relations between financially independent adult children and vulnerable elderly parents. Is there an objective moral duty to look after them? And if so, should we therefore impose a legal duty that would constitute an intervention into family autonomy? This section will therefore serve as a link between this chapter (about family autonomy) and the next (about family duties).

Of course, if the adult child still loves her parents, and as an expression of that love feels a duty to care for them, then there will be no issue. Such a child will feel spontaneous, friendly concern for her parents' lives and interests, will visit regularly, will help them with their practical difficulties and eventually with their physical needs, perhaps with the assistance of paid carers. Similarly, maybe the parents have enough money and organizational skills to hire caregivers to meet their increasing needs, and maybe they have neither affection for nor interest in their estranged adult children. But outside those two ideals, can we make sense of a filial duty on adult children already insufficiently conscientious or interested in attending their parents' real needs?

Let us start with the sceptical position: adult children have *no* filial duty. Whatever duties the child had, e.g. to obey her parents, expire at eighteen. Any talk of duty applies only from the parents to the child (obviously up to eighteen, and to a lesser extent beyond eighteen as well) in proportion to their ability. This parental duty is clearly based on the parental decision to bring the child into existence. Any 'duties' of the adult child to the parent only emerge from the contingencies of friendship between them. An adult child might have good reasons to abjure friendship with her parents, especially if they have been abusive or neglectful, or if they evince little interest or affection in her. But even when the parents are not blameworthy in such a way, they and the child might drift apart in the same way that friends drift apart, and this can lead to a legitimate attenuation of any remaining sense of duty on the child's part. As with dying friendships, the child *might* feel some lingering duty 'for old time's sake', but she might not. This outcome might be sad for the parents, or just generally sad, but we cannot blame the child for it. Indeed, we could support this position by speaking of the ideal of pure parental love: a love that expects *nothing* in return. Anything short of this would be a kind of investment, based on enlightened self-interest, something that would contaminate the love.

British law follows this sceptical position, and treats the adult child and the parent as two legally discrete individuals. The elderly parent only has a right to health or social assistance from the state. Some countries, such as Singapore, do impose a legal duty on adult children to at least contribute financially, in proportion of their income, to the cost of institutional care for their frail elderly parents.[25] (We return to such care arrangements, and the dilemmas they generate, in Chapter 3.)

Many of us would accept that we have *some* filial duty. If we found out that a millionaire daughter refused to pay anything at all to her destitute parents, we would think that she is remiss – or we would think she at least owed us some kind of strong reasons. But what grounds such a duty? Simon Keller (2006) asks whether it makes sense to speak of a long-term *moral debt* in this context. The thought is not only that the parents gave the child the 'gift' of existence, but that they also looked after the child for the first eighteen years, probably at considerable cost to themselves. Even if the parents did not see this care as an investment, and even if the parents do not expect anything in return, there can still be a debt.

Keller rejects the idea of a debt, however. He compares the notion of a debt to one's parents with a paradigm of long-term debt: a mortgage. There are important dis-analogies. First, the mortgage debt is incurred *voluntarily*. The client chooses to walk into the bank, to negotiate the contract, and to sign it. She did not have to do any of these things. As chosen, there is a clear sense in which we can speak of *her* debt. In addition, she could sell the house at any time in order to pay off the debt, but she continuously chooses not to. Second, a mortgage debt can be precisely quantified (and explicitly renegotiated), so that it is clear what exactly the client owes and when exactly she can pay it off – after which she owes the bank nothing. Third, she can rent the house out to tenants, and get them to pay the debt off directly. None of this applies to the putative filial debt. It is not incurred voluntarily, it is not quantifiable, and there is no end date earlier than the parents' death,[26] and – insofar as filial duty comprises some element of companionship – nobody else can carry it out for me. When my mother is sick and has to go into hospital, she is obviously grateful for the professional care from strangers, but what she also wants is *my* presence, even if I have no technical skills to offer.[27]

There might be a different kind of debt, which we call 'absolute'. Or rather, *two* debts: one from parent to child, the other from child to parent, and both based on the fact that the parents brought the child into existence. On the one hand, the parent has an absolute debt to offer the child a reasonably comfortable life proportionate to their resources (and not just up to the age of eighteen), precisely because the parents are the cause of that life. The debt is absolute in that the parents are *never* entitled to renounce or disown their child, no matter what the child does or becomes – that's part of what unconditional love means. On the other hand, the child has an absolute debt to her parents precisely because her very existence necessarily depends on the parents' decision to bring her into the world. For our purposes, we're looking at the second as possibly grounding filial duty. At least such an absolute debt need not be quantifiable or voluntary, and so it can deal with those objections founded on Keller's analogy with the mortgage.

Now it might be that the parental absolute debt 'wipes out' the filial absolute debt, and we are back at the sceptical position. But an alternative would be to see the two debts as incommensurable. Even so, we have to be careful with the idea of the filial absolute debt. After all, my parents did not choose to create *me*, they chose to create *a child* – and they might indeed have preferred a very different child. That would at least reduce my debt. They certainly didn't choose to create me *for my benefit*; when we ask parents why they chose to have children, the answer usually starts with 'We wanted … ' That would reduce my debt still further. And indeed, they might not have *chosen* to have a child at all; it may be that the pregnancy was unplanned, and the mother could not bring herself to have an abortion or give the child up for adoption. In such a case would it make sense to speak of debt at all, or rather of fate acting through the parents?

Even if a child were absolutely indebted to her parents for her mere existence, there are further problems. Consider another analogy: if Agnes saves the life of Bertram (they're both adults, and strangers), then it makes sense to praise Agnes, and for Bertram to be grateful. Bertram would not be alive if it weren't for Agnes, and we're presuming Bertram is *glad* to have been saved. Indeed, Bertram can intelligibly see himself as indebted to her for the rest of his life. But surely parents do not deserve praise (or not the same kind of praise) just for creating life; and surely it would be a kind of bullying for a parent to keep reminding a child that she 'should be grateful' for her existence (not to mention for 'everything we've done for you').[28] However, there might be a minimal way in which an absolute filial debt could ground a sense of awe and humility, that might lead to a sincere, engaged concern for one's elderly parents even when spontaneous friendly affection was lacking. This weak conclusion is a way of making sense of *some* adult children who claim to act on a sense of filial duty; it is not a description of an objective reality that would bind all adult children. In addition, there remains a strong argument against this 'absolute debt' conception of filial duty, and that has to do with abusive or neglectful parents. The Singapore legislation mentioned above has the following provision in Section 5:

(4) If the Tribunal is satisfied upon due proof that the applicant abandoned, abused or neglected the respondent, it may dismiss the application or may reduce the quantum of maintenance ordered by an amount determined by the Tribunal to be just.
(5) The onus of proving abandonment, abuse or neglect is on the respondent alleging it.

Any conception of filial 'absolute debt' based on metaphysical necessity would make the parents' post-birth behaviour irrelevant, and this would be problematic. One way around this would be to distinguish between *having* an absolute debt and *acting* on the absolute debt. The parents' post-birth behaviour could justify the adult child's inaction, even if it would not change the fact that her existence still depends on the previous actions of those two people. This would indeed create an awkward tension, but we suggest that such a tension might be an essential part of the experience of abuse survivors.

There remains the question of whether the state should restrict family autonomy and impose some kind of filial duty on adult children to look after – even if only financially – their frail and elderly parents, as in the case of Singapore. Clearly such a policy would benefit the parents. However, trying to impose a legal duty on one autonomous legal individual to look after another autonomous legal individual requires a more robust discussion of family duties more generally. We turn to that discussion in the next chapter.

2 Parents, love and duty

Whilst many people become parents after thinking about the prospect for a long time, others stumble into parenthood without thinking much about the 'job description'. Whichever the case may be, those people recognised by the state as parents (or guardians) have certain rights and responsibilities towards their children as a matter of law. On top of that, however, philosophers often posit *moral* parental rights and responsibilities. These may parallel their legal counterparts, but (depending on whose account of moral parenthood we agree with) they may exceed or fall short of those. In the case that legal and moral rights and responsibilities don't match up, this is sometimes taken as a sign that legal parenthood should be reformed in some way. There is, however, a reluctance to let the law regulate too much of the private sphere, which is a theme that we already introduced in the last chapter, on family autonomy.

Special obligations

There are some obligations that we, as rational moral agents and citizens, have to every other person, in virtue of intrinsic shared characteristics such as their humanity, dignity and so on. These general obligations can be distinguished from 'special' obligations, owed only to certain people, and in virtue of something other than their intrinsic nature. These obligations might instead be held in virtue of one's role (e.g. as a person's doctor, teacher or legal advisor), one's relationship with that person, or the specific act of undertaking an obligation by making an implicit promise to that person (Jeske 1998).

This all sounds rather abstract so far, so let's put it into context: I'm a parent. I have a certain amount of time, energy and money. In theory, I could spend all of that on my own child, or I could divide it between my child and my neighbour's child. (If the neighbour's child is deprived, it's plausible that she would benefit from a share of my resources a lot more than my own child.) But most parents would barely give their neighbour's child a tenth of what they give their own; nor would they think of their special obligation to their child as an *obligation* most of the time. They will simply see it as obvious and natural to spend the bulk of their money and efforts on 'their own'. However, as we saw in the last chapter, inequalities between families give rise to sticky philosophical questions. Are we really required – or even allowed – to do so much more for our children?

Special obligations to somebody might come from some characteristic of the relationship we have with that person – for example, that it is a loving relationship – or they might arise from the entry conditions of that relationship. Alternatively, our special obligations may simply be the result of our taking on those obligations explicitly. On some accounts, I might have an obligation to keep your secrets because of the nature of our friendship as intimate and deeply trusting; alternatively, I might have an obligation to keep your secret because I explicitly promised that I would do so. The obligation to keep a promise to someone, Jeske suggests, 'appears to many to be an unproblematic type of special obligation' because it is acquired deliberately, freely and explicitly (1998: 532). Special obligations we have to our friends in virtue of the close, trusting relationships we have voluntarily built with them may thus appear reasonably plausible for the same reasons. Most familial relationships, on the other hand, are unchosen: we do not choose our parents, grandparents, siblings or further relations.[1] These relationships simply 'happen to us'. Whilst a couple choose each other, as parents they don't choose the particular children they produce, or that are allocated to them through adoption.[2] We can choose to *become* parents, however, whether this is the choice to adopt, the choice to stop using contraceptives, the choice to try *in vitro* fertilization (IVF) or the choice to carry an accidental pregnancy to term. Even without the choice of a relationship with a specific person, we can put a lot of moral significance on the choice to procreate, given the meaning of biological parenthood, informed by cultural norms and expectations (see Chapters 5 and 6). Below, we look at the role of that choice in explaining our duties to children.

Volunteers

'Voluntarists' regarding parental obligation, like Elizabeth Brake, argue that parental obligations are so morally burdensome (we expect parents to do a huge amount for their children – certainly much more than the bare minimum of keeping them safe and healthy) that they can only be properly acquired when someone deliberately takes on the parental role and so accepts the associated duties (Brake 2010; 2005). Just as someone doesn't have duties to teach children or care for sick patients unless they take on the role of teacher or nurse, we don't have parental duties unless we take on the role of *parent*.

What does it mean to take on this role? One need not sign a public declaration or take out advertising space. For Brake, 'once someone has chosen not to abort, undergone pre-natal medical care, bought some baby clothes, and taken an infant home, the role of parent has been tacitly accepted' (2010: 171). She does note, however, that this presupposes that abortion is an option. The woman or girl who finds herself involuntarily pregnant (and is unable to access safe termination) is still not free to simply abandon it. That, according to Brake, would violate a general duty of rescue (which all of us, regardless of our relationship to the baby, would have in a situation where its life depended on us). However, as we observed above, parental obligations go far beyond general obligations, and so whilst the involuntary mother can't just abandon her baby, she is also not obliged (by the voluntarist account) to take on a parental role; she can give it up for adoption or foster care.[3]

However, on many other accounts of parental obligation, the special obligations that biological parents have to their offspring arise from the particular causal role that they played in bringing those children into existence.[4] Here, causal responsibility gives rise to moral responsibility: we have created a vulnerable being who would not otherwise exist, a being in need of care, and we are therefore obliged to provide that care (or at least, to ensure that someone provides that care). Whilst most prospective parents have a vague idea of what children need, and some will have taken parenting classes and cleared out the 'toddler taming' section of their local library, very few indeed fully grasp the responsibility involved in parenting until they take it on. Parenting is a deeply complicated project, with very high stakes. Should those who get involved – regardless of how or why – consider themselves, and be considered, morally responsible for how the child turns out?

Causes

There are different ways in which 'causal theorists' justify the step from causal responsibility to moral responsibility. They may suggest that (even if it's not a harmful situation) existence is a situation in which parents have unilaterally chosen to place a child, and which they are now obliged to help her navigate. This is the existential version of 'You signed me up for the marathon, you have to help me train for it'. Alternatively, causal theorists sometimes argue that existence presents a risk of harm that procreators are obliged to mitigate or protect their offspring from as best they can. ('You pushed me in the lake: you have to jump in after me if an alligator appears.')

The extreme neediness of young children leads Rivka Weinberg (for example) to argue that engaging in 'risky' activities such as sexual intercourse (where there is a danger that our gametes may join and result in conception, despite reasonable precautions) means assuming the foreseen costs of those risky activities. People with functioning eggs and sperm are 'comparable to owners of pet lions or enriched uranium' (2008: 170).[5] My decision to behave in a risky manner by taking my lion for a walk makes me responsible for compensating anyone the lion attacks, even if I have taken all precautions that could reasonably be expected of me. That's called 'strict liability'. Similarly, according to Weinberg, 'it is the risks we choose to take with our gametes that make us parentally responsible for what happens to them, should they develop into beings with moral status' (2008: 171). In this analogy, my potential offspring is compared to whomever the lion attacks. If I bring a baby into the world – whether accidentally or deliberately – she will be at risk of harm, because babies are quite simply very vulnerable, and the world's quite a dangerous place for them without someone to look after them. Just like I have a duty to watch out for hapless members of the public when I'm walking my lion, I'll have a duty to take care of that baby if I put it in a dangerous situation. (Of course, a slightly different analogy can also be made: just as with the lion, I have responsibility for whomever my young child bites!)

We might look at an account like this and think that it's ridiculous to compare casual sex to owning a pet lion or handling radioactive isotopes. The implication seems to be that we have to avoid even well-protected sex entirely if we want to avoid having parental responsibilities – and for some people, that will be a cost high enough to make the entire account implausible.

However, again assuming that abortion is available, the cost of avoiding a risk of parental responsibilities is (for men) simply to abstain from penetrative sex with women who are not willing to terminate any pregnancy that might occur.[6] For women who want to avoid the risk of parental responsibility entirely, the cost is either to commit to termination or to avoid penetrative sex with men. Alternatively, we simply accept that sex is risky business, and take appropriate precautions: when handling uranium, the hazmat suit, and when getting busy at home, contraceptives. An insistence on casual sex without contraception can, after all, be criticised as carelessness both with regard to potential offspring and with regard to our sexual partner, to whom many would think that we have a special duty of care.

Conventions

We might go a little further than the causal theorist and argue that causation isn't the only important factor in determining parental obligations. After all, there are plenty of people who play a causal role in bringing a child into the world, but whom we don't consider duty-bound to raise those children. Classic examples might be egg or sperm donors and IVF clinicians. The *social conventions* associated with these causal roles, the way in which they are performed, and the extent to which we could reasonably be expected to be aware of those conventions are also relevant. Joseph Millum suggests that this explains the difference between our moral expectations of the father whose child is conceived as a result of sex, and the father whose child is conceived after he donates sperm to an infertile couple (2008: 81).

This account combines some elements of the causal approach and some of the voluntarist approach, suggesting that we sometimes acquire moral obligations through actions we voluntarily perform (such as procreating) but that this is at least partly a result of the meaning with which our moral community imbues that action. In our society, people who conceive children through sex are generally expected to take care of those children, and this is sufficiently well-known that the father in this case cannot escape moral responsibility by claiming ignorance or unwillingness.[7] But imagine that my friend takes me to a meeting of his secret society and offers me a plate of biscuits, without telling me that by taking a biscuit I give my consent to participate in their performance of *Othello*. Yes, I am voluntarily taking a biscuit – but I cannot be held morally responsible for memorizing lines, acquiring a costume, and appearing on stage at the right moment. The secret society is not my moral community and there is no reason I should have known that *in that society*, taking a biscuit is understood to constitute the taking on of that duty.

Two things to note here: first, the link between sex and parenthood (of any resulting child) is widely understood in our society, certainly more than the link between biscuits and Shakespeare for my friend's secret society. But second, this is a link that can potentially be renegotiated. The man who wants to engage in casual sex without contraceptives can do so without the risk of moral parental responsibilities if he only does so 'with women who commit to aborting or otherwise absolving them of responsibilities for any children that result (that is, with women with whom they negotiate a different significance for the sexual act)' (Millum 2008: 90). Of course, here we can see a gap between moral parental responsibilities and legal/social responsibilities: a man can engage in casual sex without much risk of the latter if he simply 'disappears' afterwards without leaving contact details or identifying information.

All of the above accounts presuppose a certain characterization of what parental duties involve. Proponents of voluntarist, causal and other views generally take for granted that both options require that someone develops a particular kind of relationship with the child. Rivka Weinberg and Elizabeth Brake, whose accounts we explored above, have directly opposed ideas about where our parental responsibilities come from, but both assume that parents owe their children specific kinds of care and a specific kind of relationship. Brake, for example, presupposes that parents owe their children a 'rich, intimate, daily personal relationship' (2010, n. 2). We can find similar descriptions of moral parenthood in many other accounts. Where we *do* find debates over which specific duties we owe our children, those debates have mostly been restricted to the more abstract questions of whether we owe children 'the best' or 'enough' of what we are capable of providing, and how parents are to balance their own interests and needs against those of their children.

Over the next few sections, we examine a specific kind of duty: the duty to love. Do children have a right to be loved, and what is the nature of parental love? For those parents who can admit that they do not *feel* love for their child – for whatever reason that is – do they nevertheless have a duty to act lovingly towards the child?

Is there a duty to love?

To non-philosophers, this will seem like a strange question. It's uncontroversial that the majority of parents *do* love their children and find it relatively easy to want to care for them, and some philosophers take it for granted that parents will love their children even in particularly difficult circumstances. J. David Velleman, for example, in discussing the hypothetical scenario of a girl who has a child at the age of fourteen, states that she 'may wish that she hadn't had a baby, may believe that she shouldn't have had one. But of course she still loves the baby and is thankful that it was born' (2008b: 268). He also speaks later, in somewhat pessimistic terms, of parents who are 'doomed to love' a severely disabled child, suggesting that this love is not only out of their control but something that might be regretted (2008b: 272). Velleman does not characterise parental love as either a duty or a rational response to parenthood but as a simple inevitability. Luara Ferracioli, who likewise assumes that most parents love their children, argues that people who intentionally bring a child into the world have a 'weighty pro tanto reason for loving the child deeply and robustly' (2018: 87).

But there are quite clearly some cases in which parents don't love their children, even though – as Sara Protasi (2018) notes – studying the statistical frequency of parents who are willing to declare that they do not love their children is likely to be incredibly difficult, particularly in the case of mothers (see below for a discussion of gendered normative expectations of parental love). As Protasi observes, women who state that they regret having children are stigmatised even when this is accompanied by a statement that they love the children that they have; furthermore, women who do not love their children may struggle to accept this truth themselves. There is a broader and more complex discussion to be had about regret and parenthood. Unlike marriage or house-buying (which can be 'un-done' if not entirely reversed by divorce and re-sale) parenthood is an entirely irreversible decision. It is also difficult to understand whether, and how, one might regret the choice to become a parent if one loves one's existing child.

More generally, there is a broad taboo in discussing *regrets* about having had children. One of the minimal components of the 'good mother' norm has to do with regularly reaffirming gratitude for the existence of the children: however much of a burden they have been, however much of a sacrifice one has made, at least the result justifies it all. But what happens when the unanticipated costs greatly outweigh the disappointing benefits? Not just the costs of parenthood, but the costs of *me* being a parent to *this child*? What if I end up simply not liking the child very much, or not admiring the child, or just losing interest in the child, and in childish things in general ... ? In every other major decision of our lives, we can express our regret – I married the wrong person, I chose the wrong career, I chose the wrong place to live – so can I not regret becoming a parent?[8]

The question is whether such parents are failing to fulfil a moral duty. Does proper parental care require affection? Love? *Unconditional* love? And what is it to love a child? There are important differences between positing a duty of parental love on the one hand, and a duty to ensure decent nutrition, playtime and education on the other. For one thing, whom we love is generally assumed to be something that we have little control over. (Indeed, this is key to the plot of countless works of literature and art.) To posit a parental duty to love one's child may therefore be as unreasonable (from the perspective of human psychology) as positing a duty to continue loving one's spouse forever. Even those who consider marital vows to impose life-long duties to one's spouse rarely include in this a duty to *love* a spouse with whom one has fallen out of love, or with whom (e.g. in an arranged marriage) one never fell *in* love.[9] If we cannot control whom we love, it seems unreasonable to claim that loving anyone in particular is a duty. Conversely, it is generally reasonable to assume that parents have control over the contents of other classic parental duties of care, such as what they feed their children, whether they give them suitable rest and medicine when they are sick, and whether they ensure their school attendance.

The importance of love

An impersonal upbringing, in which the children are provided with food, clothing, shelter, entertainment, education, play and discipline, may allow children to grow safely to maturity. However, good *parenting* requires more than merely good domestic care. Rather, we characterise this as an intimate relationship involving trust, nurture, a sense of belonging and *love*. The unloved child may become an adult capable of gainful employment and independent living, but it is no coincidence that one of society's classic tropes is to 'blame the parents' for the character and emotional defects of the adult.[10] The absence of love in childhood is often something that must be actively overcome in adulthood if one is to be able to give and receive love oneself in healthy relationships. Brighouse and Swift, whose work we discussed in the last chapter, note that some defenders of parental rights 'point out (rightly) that autonomy can only be learned and practiced by children who have the emotional security provided by loving and caring parents' (2006: 84). We might think that this is a strong claim – intuitively, we'd think that any child can develop autonomy if they are looked after 24/7 in a good creche, offering emotional security. But Brighouse and Swift argue that if attention to a child is shared between too many adults, or one adult's attention between too many children, it cannot have these desired effects:

> In order to learn self-control, empathy, deferred gratification and other modes of self-regulation – all of which are important to autonomy – the child needs to observe these traits modelled in her immediate environment, and in people with whom she identifies. For children, identification comes through love and admiration, which are themselves responses to loving warmth in the carer. (Brighouse and Swift 2014: 73)

Love can thus be uncontroversially identified as key to a good childhood, and to a good life thereafter. Whilst of course love can come from other sources than one's parents – e.g. grandparents, friends, siblings, teachers – the fact that parents usually have a hefty monopoly over a child's time and care means that the absence of parental love will have greater effects. This might, of course, be compensated by a particularly affectionate aunt, uncle, sibling, grandparent, or family friend, but it will not be compensated *much* unless those relatives/friends also get a significant time-share of the child's care. Furthermore, parents will usually be those who have control over the kind of care a child has and the time they spend with others; they will have the last word if any of these other friends or relations disagree with their childrearing policies, for example.

In the light of this, it might be suggested that parental love should fall under the same umbrella as healthcare, nutrition, education and play – that is, that we should take it as one of the key ingredients to a good upbringing, and therefore as one of the fundamental rights children can claim against those who parent them. If parents have a duty to ensure a child's *physical* wellbeing (now and in future) by taking them to the doctor and by providing a suitably varied diet, opportunities for exercise and appropriate time to rest, then why not say that parents likewise have a duty to ensure the child's *psychological* wellbeing (now and in future)? A parent who impedes the development of their child's emotional and psychological capacities by failing to love their child would then fail in their parental duties. This is the argument made by Norvin Richards, whose account of the duty of parental love is not grounded in the parent-child relationship itself, but in the child's needs during development. In particular, he argues that parents have a duty to love their children 'in part because that love has so much to do with the children's being happy as children and in part because it is crucial to helping them become persons of their own' (2010: 211).

For this instrumental reason, Richards suggests, we have a duty only to love our young children, but we have no equivalent duty to love the same children once they are adults. This might at first seem like quite a jarring claim – surely this clashes with our usual beliefs about parental love (non-instrumental, non-time-bound). We explore those beliefs more deeply below. However, we can also understand Richards' claim as relating not to the nature of love, but the origins of the duty to love one's child *qua* young child. When our children have grown up, we no longer have a responsibility to help them to become 'future pursuers of acceptable projects'; they have taken over the responsibility for both their projects and their future selves.

That doesn't mean we no longer have any duties – of love or otherwise – towards those adult children. Richards does suggest that many parents will have a responsibility to help their adult children to be happy, but that such obligations will stem from the contingent relationship that happens to develop between this parent and this child, rather than from the mere fact of parenthood (2010: 213). This may still seem a little bleak – does it suggest that, if the adult child loses interest in her parent's life and drifts away, then the parent owes her nothing?

Love as affect, state or behaviour?

At one point, Richards contrasts the parent who loves their child with the parent who expresses 'unrelenting venom' towards that child (2010: 204). But this seems a bit quick. A distinction might be drawn here between love as an emotional state directed towards a specific object (a person, an animal, a city and so on) and love as a set of behaviours. We can and do describe behaviours as loving, independently of the presence or absence of this affective state. The emotional security, trust and intimate connections enabled by parent-child love can be equally enabled by loving behaviours.[11] In a spirit of 'action speaks louder than words', we should judge the parent not on how much they *say* they love Junior, but on what – and in what manner – she *does* for Junior. A parent who acts *as though* they love their child may provide these core benefits even if they do not, in their heart of hearts, genuinely love the child.[12] There's also a chance they'll grow into that role, developing love over time in a way akin to spouses in some arranged marriages.

Of course, how (and whether) this happens may depend on the reasons for which a parent doesn't love their child, and some of those reasons may require some work to overcome (e.g. with a family therapist). The process of learning to love the child might, in these situations, need to begin with acceptance and respect. But we might wonder if the parent who has *no* expectations at all and expects nothing from their child is displaying the opposite vice. The parent who 'merely' acts as though they love their child might also stoically think that their lack of 'deep down' emotional love is irrelevant. Coming back to the question of whether there's a parental duty to love one's child: this is more plausible if we understand it as a duty to *be loving* – to act in a way that is caring, patient, empathetic, forgiving, sacrificial and so on – regardless of one's emotional state. This is the difference Kant draws between 'love out of inclination', and 'kindness done from duty', the latter of which he calls 'practical love'. This second kind of love 'lies in the will and not in the propensity of feeling, in principles of action and not in melting sympathy; and it alone can be commanded' (1996: 55). This is the only kind of love it makes sense to speak of in the context of duty, according to Kant, precisely because 'others cannot put one under obligation to have feelings' (Kant 2017: 214).

However, the Kantian trajectory might bring one not only to the conclusion that parents have duties to behave lovingly, but even to try and cultivate loving feelings. Examining the biblical injunction to 'love God and thy neighbour', Kant argues that 'to love one's neighbour means to practice all duties toward him gladly. But the command that makes this a rule cannot command us to have this disposition in dutiful actions but only to strive for it' (Kant 2015: 69). This would suggest that the duty of practical love is not only to act in a certain way, but to *strive* to make one's character such that you would act that way gladly and not just out of (perhaps grudging) duty. If parents have duties of practical love to their children, the Kantian might therefore see them as having a duty both to act lovingly *and* to try and cultivate a loving disposition.

That said, insofar as an account of parental responsibility justifies this duty by appeal to the child's present and future interests (rather than the fact of the parent-child relationship) it seems that the most that can be demanded is the *appearance* of love, or appropriately loving behaviour. That's not to say that the bar is low – we already observed that parenting is a hell of a task, and so mustering up that kind of loving behaviour on a daily basis may still be laudable. As noted at the beginning of this section, however, it is also clear that many parents *do* love their children. In the next section, we consider the nature of parental love, digging into one characteristic often ascribed to it: *unconditionality.*

Unconditional love

There are a few different ways in which we can understand the idea of unconditional parental love, and we will spend the rest of this chapter discussing these ways. These include

(a) loving 'whatever comes out of the womb';

(b) loving 'whatever my child becomes';

(c) 'being there' for my child regardless of the circumstances.

The first of these interpretations, (a), is central to the debates concerning the morality of abortion and of embryo selection during IVF. The thought is that a pregnant woman can ascertain certain characteristics of the foetus *in utero*, and can decide whether to abort the foetus on the basis of these characteristics. Similarly, a couple can undergo IVF, resulting in a half-dozen fertilised embryos, which can then be tested (through pre-implantation genetic diagnosis (PGD))[13] and compared on the basis of certain characteristics before choosing the one to implant first. In either case, the would-be parents are laying down conditions, and this usually means discriminating against 'undesirable' characteristics having to do with future impairments. The question then is whether such 'fussiness' is somehow incompatible with the love the parents later feel towards their children, once born.

Interpretation (b) is about parental disappointment. Clearly it makes no sense for parents to be disappointed in physical traits (such as height) that neither child nor parent can alter. But there is a question of whether the parent should allow herself to be disappointed in more malleable properties – intelligence, resilience, aesthetic sensitivity and more generally character – and should help the child improve. Here the ideal of unconditional love seems to conflict with the whole point of upbringing and education. One compromise would see the parent as unconditionally accepting something like the child's 'inner being' whilst helping the child improve in those more superficial traits she wants help with. But once the child reaches adulthood, does this mean that the good parent should love the child under interpretation (c) as well, regardless of character, ambitions, actions, opinions? Does this love look like a blanket acceptance of my child's qualities, or would a really loving parent push their child towards further success? Once children become adults themselves, they may still need their parents in certain ways, and here questions arise as to whether unconditional parental love comes with an expiry date, or whether love simply requires different things of us when our children have grown up.

For many of those who hold that parents do have a duty to love their children, it would seem that this is a duty to love their children *no matter what*. This seems to follow straightforwardly from the view that this is a duty arising in virtue of the child's need for love (indeed, it does not seem too much of a stretch to speak of a child's *right* to be loved), as opposed to arising in virtue of a contingently good relationship with one's child, or one's child being particularly delightful. If we only had to love loveable children, there wouldn't be any need to frame this as a duty. However, regardless of whether parents are morally obliged to love their children or not, the broader social expectation of parental love seems to be that it is unconditional: parents are supposed to love their child *because s/he is their child*, rather than because of any specific properties about them. Many people would be shocked by a parent openly admitting that they do not love their screaming five-year-old, or (as we saw above) their disabled child. We may greatly sympathise with a parent's description of the fatigue and emotional toll extracted by 24/7 care for a child with special needs, a toddler throwing constant tantrums or a teenager who picks fights on a daily basis; and we probably wouldn't be shocked to hear them say that they are finding it 'difficult to love' this child. However, social norms constrain this sympathy, and most people would expect these complaints to be tempered by some statement to the tune of 'but of course, at the end of the day, I love my child'. (Here, we can make a distinction the underlying *orientation* of deep unconditional love, and the shallower practical reality of wavering love in dealing with the difficult bits.) And as hurtful it may be to hear 'I don't love you any more' from a romantic partner, most would agree that this hurt would pale in comparison to hearing the same thing from one's parent.

Mothers and fathers

Parental love is generally expected to withstand serious challenges.[14] As Sara Ruddick suggests: 'Although economic and social conditions, such as the poverty that is widespread and the isolation that is typical in America, may make that love frantic, they do not kill the love' (1980: 344). However, as the title of Ruddick's work suggests, she is mainly interested in *maternal* love. Alongside other early care ethicists, Ruddick took maternal love and the practice of mothering (regardless of whether this was done by men or women) as the paradigmatic caring relationship. The needs of the child, together with the social context in which one raises a child, impose certain demands; to be a mother is, for Ruddick, 'to be committed to meeting these demands by works of preservative love, nurturance, and training' (1989: 17). Parental love is often characterised as unconditional, and *paternal* love is likewise sometimes explicitly described in this way. However, literature that distinguishes the normative expectations associated with motherhood and fatherhood elucidates the far more common assumption that only *maternal* love is expected to be unconditional – consider the insulting idiom 'a face only a mother could love'. As Protasi puts it: 'Entire libraries could be filled with the stories, songs and lullabies that instil this ideal into our minds' (2018: 35). Dominant cultural ideologies 'represent mother love as unproblematically selfless, unconditional, and a source of continuous joy' (Takševa 2017: 152). Paternal unconditional love, if it exists, is not seen as the *real deal,* and seems to go beyond the normative requirements stereotypically bestowed on fathers by society.

This discrepancy in our normative stereotypes of parental love might be partly due to the different opportunities for bonding with one's child available to mothers and fathers; gestational mothers often develop strong attachments to the foetus *in utero* as a result of both the biological and social aspects of pregnancy and childbirth. Even in gay and lesbian co-parenting arrangements, gestational mothers are expected to have a deeper bond with the child and greater primacy in care (as compared with both the genetic father and the biological parents' respective romantic partners). As Herbrand observes, 'the biological mother was indeed perceived as playing an essential role in the child's life, not only because of her perceived "natural" ability to take care of the child but also because of the special physical bond she had created with the child through pregnancy and breastfeeding' (2018: 322). This, she goes on, 'reflects a common tension in participants' accounts: most co-parents were simultaneously in favour of gender equality, while essentialising abilities and roles when it comes to parenting' (ibid).[15]

However, this love-stereotype gap can largely be placed at the feet of the more general discrepancy between our normative expectations of motherhood and fatherhood. The stereotypical 'good mother' is expected to sacrifice herself continuously for the wellbeing of her children, and to prioritise them over career, friendships and personal interests, as an expression of 'legitimate' unconditional love. These oppressive norms are often internalised at a young age.[16] In contrast, the 'good father' is defined at least in part *by* further career, friendships and personal interests. Ideals of fatherhood are frequently characterised by reference to one's capacities as a breadwinner, as a good *partner* to the child's mother (whose own parenting is defined exclusively by reference to her care for the child), and as a role model and guide in work, sports and other aspects of life outside the family (Baron 2023: 76–82).

Finally, we may note the likely influence of widespread gender stereotypes – regardless of parenthood – painting men as simply less emotionally capable than women. If men are believed to have less emotional response all-round, why would society expect the well of paternal love to be as deep as that of maternal love? It is important, however, to distinguish between social stereotypes of parental behaviour, and the actual parental experience. Sociological and psychological research into paternal attitudes towards their children frequently reveals themes of unconditional love. For example, Bucher's (2014) investigation into masculinity and homophobia in the relationships between fathers and gay sons (and between sons and gay fathers) revealed that a majority (88 per cent) of fathers expressed enduring love 'despite' their struggles with their sons' sexual identity:

> I don't get it, I don't like it, I won't like it. But I still love him and will always back him in whatever he wants to do.
>
> He's not what I thought of when he was born and the doc said "it's a boy", but he's still *my* boy. I don't agree with who he likes, but I'll support him just the same.

Does unconditional love require acceptance? Or does it require more engagement, something like endorsement? Must we love all facets of a person's identity and qualities in order to say that we love them? In general, it would seem not. Many people would be happy to say something along the lines of 'I can't stand cigarettes, but of course I love my wife despite her smoking'. Of course, refusing to accept something as close to a child's identity as their sexual orientation and choice of life partner seems closer to a refusal to accept them as a unique individual than does a rejection of a hobby or habit.[17] Claims of love seem to be straightforwardly inconsistent with a rejection of the former, unless parental love is so divorced from a child's attributes as to be entirely morally arbitrary. That option may itself be disconcerting!

Kinds of (un)conditionality

Simo Vehmas argues that parenthood is itself 'essentially an unconditional project' (2002: 475). In deliberately undertaking a parental project, parents commit themselves not just to care for a child they like, but *whichever* child they end up with:

> A conscious decision to procreate should bring about conscious assent to assuming obligations as a parent. That is, conscious assent to parenthood means committing oneself to acting and evaluating one's actions and decisions in the light of the project of parenthood. One dimension of parenthood is committing oneself to caring for any kind of child. (Vehmas 2002: 475–6)

The context of this claim is Vehmas's argument against the moral permissibility of selective abortion. The idea of parenthood as an unconditional project emphasises the importance of resolve: committing to whatever it takes to care for one's child. However, we have to acknowledge the limits of knowledge, including self-knowledge: 'I really don't know how difficult it's going to be, and I don't know how well I'm going to cope.'[18]

However, we may draw a distinction between (a) parental responsibility for a child's care and wellbeing, and (b) the more specific obligation to *love* this child. Rivka Weinberg, whose 'Hazmat' theory we looked at earlier, suggests that obligations to care for – and indeed, to love – one's own offspring are acquired by virtue of causing the child's existence, and cannot be delegated to others:

> When you incur parental responsibility, and thereby the responsibility to love your child, it may be your love that is required since it is those parentally responsible for the child, and not just anybody, who must love the child (2008: 174).

But others, like David Archard (2010) and Lindsey Porter (2014), argue that original parental responsibility for one's offspring doesn't entail the obligation to raise or love them personally, but only to ensure that *someone* does this. This could be fulfilled by transferring the child's care to other willing parents, for example via the state adoption process. To describe parenthood as an 'unconditional project' might therefore be understood according to sense (a): regardless of the child's characteristics, parents are ultimately responsible for their care and wellbeing. Even if they have transferred duties of care to others, the buck stops with them, morally speaking.

However, Vehmas clearly means this claim in sense (b), arguing that 'after the decision to procreate [parents] have to accept any kind of child, and they have the duty to try to cultivate an unconditional love for their child' (2002: 481). There is a question of what 'cultivation' means in this context. It goes further than the Kantian idea we explored above, wherein parental duties of love might also include the duty to try and cultivate the disposition to carry out one's existing duties gladly. Kant, after all, states clearly that 'it is not within the power of any human being to love someone merely on command' (2015: 69).

Unconditional welcome and PGD

Similar to Vehmas' idea of parenthood as an unconditional project, Asch and Wasserman (A&W) regard 'the commitment to welcome and nurture any child the parents have … as the moral foundation of the family' (2005: 203). The principles to which A&W appeal are sympathetic insofar as they are consistent with the characterization of parental love described above. But many would disagree with the conclusions they draw from these principles, one of which is that PGD is not morally permissible. PGD is the screening of embryos produced during IVF to identify single-gene disorders or defects, like those that cause Tay-Sachs disease, Huntington's or cystic fibrosis.

Currently, PGD is allowed in the UK only in order to let parents avoid passing on disease-carrying genes by 'selecting against' the embryos that present with these genes, and implanting only healthy embryos.[19] The Human Fertilisation and Embryology Act 2008 prohibits 'any practice designed to secure that any resulting child will be of one sex rather than the other' *except* 'where there is a particular risk that a woman will give birth to a child who will have or develop (a) a gender-related serious physical or mental disability, (b) a gender-related serious illness, or (c) any other gender-related serious medical condition'.[20] So, screening one's embryos and choosing only female embryos would be allowed if the father had a Y-chromosome-linked disease they wanted to avoid passing down, but would not allowed if the parents were simply motivated by their preference for a girl. Julian Savulescu (2001) has argued against this restriction, proposing a principle of 'procreative beneficence': once we are already in a position to screen and select embryos (because a couple has undergone IVF), we are morally required to select the embryo(s) that we expect to have the 'best' life, based on all available genetic information. That is, not just disease-linked genetic information, but also anything from physical size to IQ. Savulescu understands the 'best life chances' of the future child(ren) in terms of wellbeing – that is, the best life is the life with the most wellbeing.

But Savulescu defends the principle of procreative beneficence alongside a principle of procreative autonomy, and accepts that we might sometimes find 'irresolvable conflict' between these commitments. Parents whose strong personal preference is for a child with some characteristic *x* (where *x* would not maximise the child's chances of the best life in comparison to other gene-linked traits) should be free, he argues, to exercise their autonomy.[21]

A&W argue specifically against the use of PGD to avoid bringing into existence children with diseases or disabilities – much as Vehmas argues against the use of selective abortion of disabled foetuses – on the grounds that this conflicts with the ideal of unconditional welcome that should characterise the parenting project. We can imagine, then, that they'd be even more strongly opposed to eugenic PGD selection on the basis of non-disease traits. Here we can go back to our different interpretations of 'unconditional love', some of which do seem to be an unconditional commitment to 'whatever child we conceive' and some of which are more reasonably seen as a response to the relationship with *this specific* child we have ended up having. Vehmas compares parents who selectively abort a disabled foetus with those who reject an existing child who becomes disabled as the result of an accident, arguing that prospective parents 'should take a similar, unconditional attitude towards their prospective children as parents should take towards their actual children' (2002: 476). Some parents do develop a strong emotional attachment to the foetus *in utero* (and some gestationalist accounts of parental rights characterise this attachment as the beginning of a morally significant relationship). Nonetheless, most of us would still consider love for, and obligations to, one's existing child to be grounded in very different phenomena than love for and obligations to one's hypothetical child (one of a number of possible embryos in a petri dish, or a foetus that one has not yet decided to carry to term). In other words, Vehmas's comparison doesn't work precisely because we already have a relationship with our actual children. Common to both Vehmas' and A&W's arguments is that they consider unconditional parental commitment to one's child to begin prior to the child's birth; this may simply not reflect the lived experience of many parents.[22]

Loving my child 'no matter what'

Following on from parental love as an aspect of an existing parent-child relationship, let us now consider the second possible interpretation of unconditional parental love: that I love my child 'whatever s/he becomes'. It is a near-universal aspect of parenthood to experience, numerous times, the feeling that whilst you love your child, you really don't *like* them right now.[23] Some parents will suffer more extreme tests of their affection for their children, for example if those children become school bullies, petty criminals, or simply spiteful, selfish, or vapid. Some parents describe the heart-breaking internal conflict they experience when faced with a child who they love deeply in the 'I would give my life for you' sense, but whose personality they despise in the 'I can't stand to be around you' sense, or whose interests they may find it very difficult to sympathise with.[24] The uncertainty of whether love can or should endure at this moment is made clear by media fascination with the parents (and particularly, the mothers) of mass murderers, terrorists and serial rapists brought to trial. We mentioned earlier that social expectations of parental love will give rise to shock in response to the parent who says that they no longer love their tantrumming toddler or their pilfering teenager; however, this expectation seems to fade when an individual has done something we consider heinous. At this point, enduring parental love may not be morally required – as Protasi suggests, 'While we admire a mother who is capable of loving her son and at the same time condemning his actions, we do not think that ceasing to love a moral monster is inappropriate' (2018: 40).

Even this admiration may fade in the face of despicable wrongdoing, and we are more likely to feel pity or even disgust for the parents who staunchly continue to declare their love for an adult child found guilty of certain kinds of crimes, without explicitly rejecting those crimes (and even more so if they attempt to prevent justice being served by e.g. hiding the adult child). Pity for the murderer's mother is a trope sometimes depicted in media, and seems to reflect the belief that parental love is unconditional because it is in some way instinctive and beyond conscious control. For example, in the *West Wing* episode 'Take This Sabbath Day', White House press secretary C.J Cregg expresses her political ambivalence regarding the death penalty; however, her disquiet over the execution of a serial killer appears after she reads the file containing his biographical information, including the name of his mother. She tells a colleague, 'I have to go in and tell the President that Simon Cruz is dead and we're the ones who killed him. So … I just wish I didn't know his mother's name was Sophia, is all I'm saying.'

Prompting empathy for strangers by appeal to 'the mother' has a long history, whether in the form of war propaganda (depicting weeping women holding the bodies of soldiers in an echo of Michelangelo's Pietà), or in the form of early care ethicist appeals to the idea that 'every person is some mother's child'. This notion was promoted by Eva Kittay as not only an organizing principle for political thought, but as its centrepoint (1999: 24). A 'more perfect' society requires us to cultivate not only a sense of justice but the moral sentiment of care, and to bring these together. But the notion that 'every person is some mother's child' as an impetus to show care for others could be interpreted in two ways: either to care for that person as a reflection of maternal love, stepping into maternal shoes (so to speak), or to care for that person out of care and respect for the unconditional love of some mother, somewhere. In the context of war, the declaration that every enemy soldier is 'some mother's child' is more often understood through the latter: to shoot is to break someone's heart, somewhere further afield. Taking this interpretation, to stay the execution of Simon Cruz is not to show care for him, but for Sophia.

Do we need conditions on love? Suki Finn argues that unconditional love is love 'that will not change according to any information, as it was not built on the basis of information in the first place'.[25] This is certainly the ideal of parental love discussed above: a love for one's child that is not based on any facts or characteristics (beyond the fact that they are *your* child). As she observes, when love is not based on any reasons, then 'it can persist through changes and will not be shaken (nor stirred) by opposing reason, evidence or information'. However, if love for someone is not based on or responsive to reasons, then it cannot be within our control; as Finn points out, the only way unconditional love can be lost is *also* 'for no reason'. Genuinely unconditional parental love would therefore appear to be both morally arbitrary and irrational. This seems consistent with the widespread view that love isn't something over which we have conscious control; it would also seem consistent with the different possible responses to grievous wrongdoing by one's child. The parent who ceases to love their child after learning that they have committed a heinous crime is understandable: their love, whilst it may have been strong, was not entirely unconditional. The parent who continues (perhaps with regret) to love that same child is also understandable: their love is not responsive to reason, and as such it would be inappropriate to say that they *ought* to either stop or continue loving their child.

This conclusion does, however, present a further challenge to Vehmas' claim (mentioned above) that prospective parents 'have the duty to try to cultivate an unconditional love for their child'. Saying that we have a duty to do *x* nearly always implies that *x* is actually possible. Genuinely unconditional love, as something based on no reasons and responsive to no reasons, can no more be cultivated than it can be consciously cut back. It makes little sense to *try* and cultivate it, or to say we have a duty to do just that.[26] The most we might reasonably require of parents is to actively cultivate the 'practical love' we discussed earlier in this chapter. It might be that (through this behaviour) a deep love for their child does end up developing, but whether it does or not may be beyond the parent's control.

Love or duty?

As we've seen, many people assume that there are moral obligations parents have to their children (though some of those people disagree pretty strongly on how and why we get those obligations). These are formalised in our *legal* parental responsibilities. But whilst it's common for parents to talk about being 'responsible *for*' their children, we don't usually like to talk about care being motivated by moral responsibility or duty – we'd rather think of the family as being about love. The concept of 'duty' in this context sounds stuffy, reluctant and Victorian.[27] The classic answer to this is to say: love is all well and good, but it is unreliable, unstable and contingent. Duty has to be there to pick up the slack when love fails. After all, even the most spontaneously loving of relationships between friends will have moments of friction, and both parties will usually be grateful for remaining together – even if not physically together for a while – until the affection returns. And some family relationships can be valuable and important even if they are unloving, and indeed exhausting; caring for the very old is the classic example. And not only is love uneven in itself, but its position relative to a person's other affections to other people outside the family, to their jobs, and to projects will also change. In asking about one's duty, one is not asking about the primary motivation, but about the backup motivation, necessary to keep the show going at all. When parents are *not* sufficiently motivated by duty, that's when the real problems start.

We might say the same about familial duties and love more broadly. Imagine the following conversation between a husband and wife. Wife declares: 'I still can't get over what my sister did last year. That was unforgivable. I haven't spoken with her since, and I'm never going to.' Husband responds: 'But she's your sister. You can't just cut her off like that.' To which the wife replies: 'So what? That's just an accident of biology.' There might be an *academic* question about whether the 'accident of biology' grounds duties beyond basic liberal non-intervention, and if so which duties exactly; but we think most people *outside* the academy would agree that biology counts for something between adults in most societies. There's still a lot to say about the duties in question: we merely want to suggest with this invented conversation that there might be something wrong with a family member rejecting *any* sense of family duty.

We've discussed the ideal of unconditional love at length in this chapter, but there is also a discussion to be had about *conditional* love and its relationship with duty. Parent-child relationships – at least those involving young children – will involve asymmetric duties, and it doesn't seem right to say that a parent's responsibility for their child, or their love for that child, should be conditional on the child fulfilling duties of any kind. But older family members may well have duties to each other that temper how we can or should care for them. In daily life, love for one's spouse, siblings and parents is generally more conditional than our love for our children (though as we discuss in the next chapter, there may be some 'debts' we have to our parents that come without conditions). One of the conditions may well be the fulfilment of family duties. Imagine again the example above, of Wife and Husband arguing about Sister(-in-Law). If Sister violated a family duty, for example by endangering Wife & Husband's children by driving drunk with them in the car, then not only would we sympathise with Wife's adamant refusal to forgive, but many would be surprised that Husband is putting 'blood' over duty.

However, maybe the above dichotomy between love and duty is simplistic because it construes love as a mere feeling. Of course, feelings come and go, without any control over them, and are therefore unreliable. But as we saw above, love has to be described as so much more than a feeling. Whilst the discussion in this chapter points towards the conclusion that there isn't a duty to love one's child 'deep down', there may well be a duty to *be loving* to them. In the grand scheme of things – given what it is that children need – a parenting relationship motivated by this duty may still be deeply important to a child even if it isn't a loving one in the affective sense. And a failure to acknowledge duties to our children may undermine 'proper' love for them. Where we have both love and duty, and so care for one's child is overdetermined, this is not necessarily a problem – it just means that our backups are installed and ready, *just in case*.

3 Dilemmas of care

Care is one of life's constants, and will come to most of us at multiple times in our lives. As babies and small children, we needed round-the-clock care. If we ever become seriously ill, we may be cared for by nursing professionals, or by our spouse or other relatives. And for many of us, the preamble to one great certainty (death) will also involve care by others, as our bodies and minds get tired and less able to carry us from place to place and from thought to thought. Care can be a practice, but it can also be an affective state, a personal relationship and an emotional bond (especially when people take care of their own family and friends). That means that roles can become blurred, ethical and legal complications can arise, and we face dilemmas about how to deal with care.

Who cares?

The very short answer to this question is 'mostly women'. This is still the case today whether we're talking about care as an abstract concept or affect (still stereotypically associated with women, and especially mothers) or we're talking about caretaking practices like childrearing, elder care, disability aid or nursing. In institutional settings, women dominate the caring professions. In 2019, the World Health Organization found that women make up about 67 per cent of the health workforce across 104 countries, though they are far from evenly distributed across that workforce; for example, women are around half of physicians in European countries, but well over 80 per cent of nurses (Boniol et al. 2019: 2).

In the family home, things are no different, with women carrying out the majority of care for children, elderly parents and other relatives. Spouses (or long-term partners) are usually the first port of call when someone becomes ill, but even within these relationships we find stark gender differences in care. For example, a study of married couples following the diagnosis of serious disease in one partner found that 11.6 per cent of these marriages ended after the diagnosis; but in 88 per cent of *these* cases, the affected partner was female (Glantz et al. 2009). In other words, men are more than six times more likely to leave their sick wife than women are to leave their sick husband. When considering the reasons behind this statistic, the authors note that:

> Some studies have in fact suggested that men are less able to undertake a caregiving role and assume the burdens of home and family maintenance compared with women. Thus, a woman becomes willing sooner in the marriage to commit to the burdens of having a sick spouse. (Glantz et al. 2009: 5241)

But of course, there is a difference between ability and willingness. We know that men are able to care for children, for parents and for sick relatives. The critical factor that determines whether they *do* so seems to be about the options available for passing this care along: 'Typically, men who are primary care providers [for parents] are either without siblings, without sisters, or the only geographically available child' (Campbell and Martin-Matthews 2003: 350). Men provide relatively less care for elderly parents if they have sisters than if they have brothers – and as we might therefore expect, women provide relatively more care if they have brothers than if they have sisters (Grigoryeva 2017; Luppi and Nazio 2019). Gender stereotypes that might lurk in the background of decision-making are sometimes made explicit, as by one adult son talking about his caretaking role: 'telling a person that you are caring for your mother ... they look at you as if to say "that's not a job for a man"' (McDonnell and Ryan 2014: 794).

These stereotypes even have an influence on normative expectations regarding childcare and housework in same-sex parenting households. Doan and Quadlin studied the relationship between such expectations and the gender expression of partners in a (same-sex or different-sex) relationship, using hobbies with strongly gendered associations as a proxy for gender expression; they found that 'feminine and masculine same-sex partners were consistently expected to perform divergent chores and child-care tasks' (Doan and Quadlin 2019: 157). Participants were more likely to allocate certain childcare tasks – taking care of the child's physical needs, and listening to children's problems – to the partner described as enjoying shopping and romantic comedies, than the partner described as enjoying basketball and action movies (154).

It has been well-established, through research on heterosexual two-parent households, that children in middle childhood and early adolescence rely on their parents for different needs. As Carone explains, 'mothers are used more for safe haven needs and fathers are used more for secure exploration' (2020: 271). Safe havens provide comfort in times of stress, whilst secure bases provide space for exploration in the absence of threats. However, studies of childcare divisions and children's attachment in same-sex parenting families suggest that attachment style is determined not by parental gender but by distributions of care (although as this chapter shows, parental gender has a significant role to play in this distribution). Among same-sex parenting couples, caregiver role (primary or secondary) determined which parent was relied on as a safe haven or as a secure base (281–2). Whether a parent is more suited to care for a child's physical and emotional needs clearly has little to do with their proclivity for romantic comedies or basketball, regardless of persistent gender stereotypes.[1]

It is of course important to distinguish between normative beliefs about the distribution of such tasks for same-sex couples, and the actual distribution of such tasks. As Biblarz and Savci (2010) observe, a number of studies have found significantly more egalitarian arrangements of childcare and household labour in same-sex parenting couples than in heterosexual parenting couples. It is still worth noting, however, that in both heterosexual and same-sex parenting households, the arrival of children tends to disrupt generally egalitarian distributions or widen existing gaps, with one partner inevitably carrying out more childcare and housework than the other. Inequality in the distribution of caring labour in a two-parent household is not only a matter of gender, but arises from the way in which we organise paid labour.

Who works?

In post-war Western societies, the 'traditional' urban or suburban middle-class household divided care work (mostly childrearing and domestic labour) from paid work (undertaken outside the home), effectively erasing the economic value of the former.[2] This division fell strictly along gender lines. As Barbara Katz Rothman wryly observes, 'I would regard full-time, live-in homemaking help as a luxury too decadent to even consider, not even if I won the lottery. That luxury used to be the birthright of every middle-class man. It was called a wife' (1989: 137). The breadwinner's absence from the home for most of the day, and the fact that what he earned through gainful employment he (or the family) could keep, were both enabled by the fact that someone else (the housewife) was carrying out all manner of domestic and caring work for free. When middle-class women entered the labour market in large numbers alongside men, one of these two things had to change: either working parents couldn't be absent from the home for most of the day, or they couldn't keep all their earnings. The 'standard' working pattern has stayed the same: a full-time working week is forty hours, and for most people this is eight hours per day, Monday to Friday. What is the cost of this social shift?

Childcare now represents a hefty deduction from the paycheck of the average working parent. Precisely how hefty that deduction is will depend on geographic location, number of children, and whether parents engage formal or informal childcare. The debate is very different in Sweden compared to Poland, in the United States compared to the UK – different states provide different levels of parental leave, financial support and so on. In 2015, the average weekly cost of full-time (fifty hours per week) nursery for a child under two in Britain was £212.09 (Rutter and Stocker 2015: 9). By 2022, this had already risen by 25 per cent to £269.86 (Coleman, Shorto, and Ben-Galim 2022: 12).[3] To put these numbers into perspective: in 2022, the British minimum wage for a person aged twenty-three and over was £9.50; someone working forty hours a week would therefore get £380 before tax. There are a variety of governmental support schemes offering assistance for parents, but these do not come close to covering childcare costs. It will therefore often be the case that the costs of childcare go beyond one partner's salary.[4]

Some families might be in a position to take this kind of financial hit to protect the lower-earning parent's career development during the years when their child or children need pre-school care. Some families are also fortunate enough to be exempt from this kind of calculation, for example because they have one or both sets of grandparents (or other extended family) living nearby enough to take on part- or full-time childcare. However, more often, the financial burden of childcare is sufficient to push one parent to drop out of the paid labour force and undertake this caring work for free. In the majority of (heterosexual) cases, this is still the mother for a number of reasons, including the force of gender stereotypes, the gender wage gap (which continues to ensure that the lower-earning partner in a family is more likely to be female) and physiological considerations such as breast-feeding.

Who pays?

When individuals carry out all the domestic chores needed to keep their own home running, and when they take care of their own family members, we tend not to see it as work in the ordinary sense. A crucial reason for this is the artificial division we noted at the beginning of this chapter: between paid employment (work) and domestic labour (duty, love, care). But as we saw above, the productive nature of this work, and its necessity for economic activity, becomes visible when we begin to outsource it. Nannies, maids, cooks and cleaners all have to be paid for their work at quantifiable market rates, at which point it is easier to see that it really *is* work, and indeed hard work.

Of course, informal carers still need something to live on, even if they are not paid for their caring labour directly. The Care Allowance is currently £70 per week in the UK, less than one-fifth of the national minimum wage – in other words, a pittance. (And of course, a carer might end up working a lot more than forty hours a week for that.) We can compare this to the situation in Sweden:

> The other benefit is carers allowance (anhöriganställning), which is actually not an allowance: the municipality employs a family member to do the care work. Carers allowance is taxed, and gives the same salary and similar social security as for home-help workers in the municipality's own services.[5]

Feminist arguments have been made both for and against wages for care. On the one hand, a generous care allowance is seen as a just reward for work that will be carried out anyway by those motivated by love or a sense of filial duty. Feminist campaigns like Wages Against Housework used the rhetoric of demands for payment to draw attention to the nature of women's domestic labour as real labour, arguing that their work in the home would not be respected unless it was seen as equivalent to work outside the home. This was tied directly to women's ongoing inequality, in society and in private relationships. In Silvia Federici's words:

> [T]he unwaged condition of housework has been the most powerful weapon in reinforcing the common assumption that housework is not work, thus preventing women from struggling against it, except in the privatized kitchen-bedroom quarrel that all society agrees to ridicule, thereby further reducing the protagonist of a struggle. (Federici 1975: 2–3)

On the other hand, a care allowance that parallels 'real' wages has been seen as an incentive for women to leave the workplace, reinforcing gender stereotypes and therefore reproducing discrimination against women in the labour market. In other words, it seems to have anti-feminist consequences. Similar criticisms have been made of generous parental leave allowances, such as those offered in Sweden and the Czech Republic (both providing up to three years maternity/parental leave) on the grounds that this, too, incentivises women to drop out of the labour market for extended periods, and *disincentivizes* employers from hiring or promoting women.[6] Anca Gheaus notes that such policies might well benefit some women, but at a cost to other women, by further engraining workplace gender biases: 'A policy that enables women to avoid the labour market therefore will also, indirectly, cause other women to pay for these choices with a more limited set of opportunities for positions in which employee turnover is costly' (Gheaus 2020: 12). Nonetheless, she argues further that this kind of concern is insufficient to stand against care-supporting policies, in the light of a broader background of widespread social injustice. Whilst care allowances and similar measures might reinforce stereotypes that hold some (better-off) women back in the labour market, they would also provide valuable remuneration and a safety net for less privileged women: 'denying care-supporting policies (assuming they are otherwise desirable in terms of justice) to disadvantaged women, in order to give other women more equal opportunities to the top positions is one of the worst ways to attempt to undermine gender norms' (17).

The continued omission of unpaid care work (and other kinds of unpaid domestic work) from gross domestic product calculations has been criticised for reinforcing the invisibility of this labour, and (as observed above) social attitudes regarding its nature as labour at all. As well as economic benefits, caring – and especially childrearing – makes other vital contributions to the ongoing function of society, providing the law-abiding citizens, workers, taxpayers and of course *caregivers* of the future (the latter being a particular concern for ageing populations). Seen this way, some are inclined to say that those who provide childcare, especially when unpaid, are providing a huge net contribution to society. Children, and the adults they become, can be seen as a collective good – should childcare therefore be a collective responsibility?

All Western societies already recognise the value of free state schooling, paid by taxpayers, including childless taxpayers. This is partly a matter of social justice; it is partly about the potential need to compensate for bad parenting to better prepare future citizens. However, it is also about allowing both parents into the workplace. We may well therefore ask why the same logic does not lead to state funding of afterschool and pre-school childcare. Serena Olsaretti points out that welfare states do currently take collective (economic) responsibility for some of the costs of children, through tax-payer-funded policies like parental leave, public/subsidised childcare, and child benefits or tax credits (2022: 413).

However, we could also imagine a different way of setting up our social institutions. Under an alternative imagined arrangement, which Olsaretti calls the *Parents Pay Unified Welfare* system, parents would have full financial liability (perhaps managed through a collective fund) for their children's needs throughout their lives:

> In this regime, parents would pay fully for the costs of taking parental leave, of child-care provision and of school while their children are growing up. Parents' liability would, moreover, extend through their children's adulthood; they would have to contribute a special parent tax to ensure that they pay for their adult children's welfare benefits. (Olsaretti 2022: 413)

Far from a serious proposal, *Parents Pay* is imagined as a way to draw out the intuition that fairness to parents requires the standard welfare-state status quo, in which many of the costs of childrearing are distributed across society, and thus partly absorbed by non-parents. On the one hand, Olsaretti observes, liberal egalitarians are generally committed to the idea that we are responsible for our choices. As long as parents choose to have children, we can justifiably hold parents responsible for the costs of having children – and not just the costs associated with what *those* parents think their children should have, but the costs of giving children what they should have as a matter of justice. On the other hand, children can be seen as public goods: 'Parents, by having and rearing children, produce positive externalities for everyone, and nonparents would be unfairly free riding on parents if they accepted the benefits but did not share the costs' (Olsaretti 2013: 229). If the benefits of children are socialised, then the costs should be likewise. Not everyone agrees, however; Sabine Hohl argues that individuals contribute and receive benefits to and from society at different stages of their lives. Children (as the service providers of tomorrow) may contribute to society, but children (as the consumers of tomorrow) will also receive benefits. We might just as well argue that the addition of any given person has a 'net zero' impact on these benefits (Hohl 2021: 17).

Intimacy, employment and rights

Crucial though caregiving is to the function and survival of society, it remains undervalued, poorly remunerated, and – especially when carried out by unpaid family members – often simply invisible. One reason for this is the relationship between the two kinds of care mentioned above: care-as-affect, and care-as-practice, or caring *about* others, and undertaking the practical tasks involved in providing care. Often, characterizations of practical caregiving suggest that caring *for* the subject in an emotional sense (e.g. by empathizing and developing a relationship with them) is necessary for good caregiving. Nannies to small children are expected to develop a bond with those children rather than simply attending to their physiological needs in a state of emotional detachment; full-time aides to elderly people would be seen as shirking their duties if they didn't at least feign interest in their charges' personal and emotional lives. And feigning interest often leads to genuine interest and concern.

On the flip side, the widespread failure to appropriately value or remunerate care work can be partly explained by the expectation that caregivers will be primarily (or even exclusively) motivated by care-as-affect. That is, we expect nannies, nurses, child-minders and home aides to *want* to look after their charges because they are personally, emotionally invested in their wellbeing – and not just for a paycheck – just as we expect parents and filial caregivers to be motivated by familial love alone, and forego any demands for greater financial support from the state.[7] As Nancy Folbre notes, 'the importance of intrinsic motivation is often turned against care providers with arguments that they do a better job when they work for love, rather than for money' (2008: 376). Going back to the previous section, and the normative expectations surrounding unpaid domestic work in the family home, we find that domestic employers (e.g. middle-class couples) may be less willing to give domestic care workers adequate respect or remuneration, and may even think less of them for being motivated by wages rather than by affection for their charges: 'Insofar as domestic servants are conceived as a substitute for the wife in a traditional household, they are expected to conform to an account of their work that is only partly real "work"' (Tronto 2002: 37). These normative expectations are therefore gendered, reflecting and reinforcing the stereotypes we talked about above. Even where a family hires domestic helpers or nannies to help with caring, fathers more often see their responsibility in the arrangement as entirely transactional – limited to signing contracts and paychecks – leaving mothers to direct, supervise and communicate with helpers on a daily basis (Groves and Lui 2012). The mother's 'natural' share of domestic work and childcare has been 'bought out' by hiring help, and so she is the one expected to take responsibility for delegating it, and to pick up the slack if the arrangement falls through.

Quite often, care-as-practice and care-as-affect do overlap and intertwine deeply. Those who look after the needs of sick or vulnerable people often do invest emotionally in their welfare and develop personal relationships with them. But that leaves caregivers in a vulnerable position themselves when it comes to advocating for their labour to be recognised and remunerated: their bargaining position is weakened by the difficulty they face in *withdrawing* their labour. Unlike the factory worker or train driver who can lay down her uniform, tools and badge to demand better working conditions and recognition only at the expense of company profits (and inconvenience caused to service users) the nurse or pre-school teacher can't go on strike without harming someone whose wellbeing she often cares about deeply: the sick patient or young child (Tronto 2002: 39). Caring labour isn't just economically precarious, but emotionally precarious. In the light of that, to what extent is it legitimate to outsource emotional labour?

Outsourcing love

Given that The Problem we described above is generally a strict numbers game ('can we find childcare for less than one partner's salary?'), the outsourcing of care generally follows class and wealth lines: from upper- and middle-class to working class, from Global North to Global South. Parents who work outside the home have to be able to find childcare for less than their own salary – and usually quite significantly less, unless their partner makes enough to comfortably support the entire family. As a result, childcare (like other forms of care work) has been identified as both high-demand and under-valued, leading to domestic recruitment difficulties and an increasingly high proportion of migrant uptake, including informal arrangements with migrants without a work permit and therefore even more vulnerable to exploitation.

There are two levels on which we can talk about the outsourcing of childcare. First, we can look at individual families who bring in outside help (often to address The Problem and allow both parents to work). Here, important questions arise about the *location* and *institutionalization* of this help. Our first question is whether outsourced care should take place inside or outside the home; the second question is, if outside the home, whether parents should choose an informal child-minder or a formal crèche (and a contract). The default market view would be that location and institutionalization make no difference: it's all about payment for services. However, the institution (e.g. a nursery or crèche) provides workers *qua* formal employees with greater protection (and allows the mediation of complaints in either direction).[8] A location outside the house allows the minder or the creche employees to set their own terms and adopt their own creative 'parenting style'. This is not only good for the caregiver – allowing them greater freedom to develop the caring relationships central to their work without external constraint or control – but it is also arguably good for the child. Anca Gheaus argues that the monopoly of care and control that parents currently have over children (by law, and according to Western social norms more generally) is undesirable, making children exclusively dependent on their parents and therefore overly vulnerable to abuse, neglect and exploitation. However, children may also benefit significantly from being cared for by multiple independent adults. These can expose them to different ideas and interests, helping them to develop their beliefs and capacities, and also potentially make up for one another's shortfalls:

> Not only can [children] draw on richer caring resources but, plausibly, exposure to different caregivers can help correct the effects of more minor failings of care and increases the chances that all children have at least one competent caring adult in their lives. (Gheaus 2018a: 64)

When outsourced care is provided inside the family home, on the other hand (e.g. by a live-in *au pair*) the parental monopoly of care and control is left intact. As Tronto notes, the control an employer is able to exert is far greater in such a context, and the domestic worker or caregiver will be expected to act according to their wishes and values, and to comply with their parenting principles. This relationship may in turn affect the child's own view of the world: 'as feminists have asked about male domination in the household, what kind of moral education does one learn from being in a household in which one adult is so clearly subordinate to others?' (Tronto 2002: 40).[9]

The second way in which we can look at the outsourcing of care is at a national level, examining the global movement of care: as a country, the UK outsources (or rather, imports) a huge amount of caring labour, with growing reliance on migrant workers in health and social care systems, including in the retirement homes we just mentioned (Yeates 2009; Cangiano and Shutes 2010). Many migrant care workers have their own children back home, and their absence as they work as a nurse or nanny reproduces The Problem.[10] The result, when repeated across borders, is what Arlie Hochschild calls a 'global care chain'. A typical global care chain 'might work something like this: An older daughter from a poor family in a third world country cares for her siblings (the first link in the chain) whilst her mother works as a nanny caring for the children of a nanny migrating to a first world country (the second link), who, in turn, cares for the child of a family in a rich country (the final link)' (Hochschild 2006: 357).

Rhacel Parreñas (2000) uses the term 'international transfer of caretaking' to describe this phenomenon in the context of her research in the Philippines. The technical terminology might obscure the intimate, emotional aspects of this phenomenon, but it seems that precisely these aspects that stand out as requiring attention: 'Being in the middle of the international division of reproductive labor entails geographical distance in families and consequently emotional strains for "lonely" mothers and "miserable" children in the Philippines' (2000: 576). Whilst unable to give love directly to their own families, their work demands that the former care intimately for their employer's children. As we saw above, this isn't just about seeing to a child's practical needs, but also to their emotional and psychological needs. As Rothman notes, it may be almost impossible for a caregiver to respond to these needs whilst staying emotionally detached themselves:

> To soothe a child, it must feel cared for, nurtured, loved. To make the child feel that way, the caregiver must act like she indeed loves the child. To act so convincingly – and children are a tough audience – requires calling forth her own feelings of love, of tenderness. (Rothman 1989: 142–3)

Children need loving, nurturing care, and this is not something that can be separated from the person providing care – love isn't something we can pass from one person to another in the abstract, such that the *employer's* love comes to their own child *via* their nanny's embrace. If someone is providing intimate care (feeding, dressing, soothing, chiding, encouraging, reassuring), emotional intimacy is almost unavoidably created between provider and recipient.

When care-as-affect and care-and-practice can be so closely intertwined, this leaves Hochschild wondering: 'is there – in the realm of love – an analogue to what Marx calls "surplus value," something skimmed off from the poor for the benefit of the rich?' (Hochschild 2006: 358). Certainly those children left behind by migrating care workers (and cared for by either older siblings, extended family or local paid nannies) describe a sense of loss, or of inadequate nurture by mothers who have migrated for work. Parreñas notes, however, that this discontent 'is notably aggravated by the stronghold of the ideological belief that mothers are the proper nurturers of the family and the view that mothers should nurture their children from up close' (2005: 333). The problem of outsourcing love, and whether this is something we can legitimately do, is therefore actually a tangle of other, interconnected problems: our social and economic structures are built on expectations about maternal and paternal care that we have yet to shake off, even when both mothers and fathers work for pay; one person's pay cannot comfortably outweigh the cost of childcare unless childcare is cheap; if childcare is cheap, the childcare worker's salary is unlikely to be enough to support their own family, leaving a(nother) care gap that has to be filled.

So far, we've focused mostly on the outsourcing of care for existing children, but parents can also outsource the process of bringing those children into existence. Is surrogacy a means of outsourcing love? (We discuss surrogacy further in Chapter 6.) There are certainly overlaps between attitudes towards paid caregivers and surrogate mothers. Like the nanny expected to be motivated primarily by concern for the children she looks after, the commercial surrogate mother who explicitly describes her motivations as financial would shatter normative stereotypes. Kajsa Ekis Ekman highlights the way in which – despite the fact that few women are willing to become surrogate mothers without financial compensation – surrogate mothers describe their motivation as anything *but* financial, referring to generosity, love, altruism, of wanting to help others create a family or experience the joy of parenthood (2013: 177). This kind of attitude 'is encouraged by agencies that urge women to "give the gift of life" and advertise: "It's not about the money, it's about the experience"' (181). Likewise, both the nanny and the surrogate mother are expected to engage in the emotional labour of caring genuinely about their charges, whether born or unborn, but *without* getting 'too attached'. The nanny is simultaneously expected to care 'genuinely' for her employer's children, and not be motivated just by her paycheck; and yet ironically, she may be at risk of losing her job for doing so, as 'the mother might think of the worker as competition for the affection of the children' (Tronto 2002: 39). The commercial surrogate mother is similarly expected to juggle contradictory expectations: to treat surrogacy as a job and not to become attached to the child, but also to nurture the foetus with characteristically maternal care (Pande 2010).

The rights of caregivers

What happens when caring work comes to an end? We've seen that this kind of work isn't exhausted by detached, practical duties; it also involves, almost by necessity, the creation of caring relationships. But it's also the nature of employment that it ends at some point: a contract may be fixed-term, the position may become redundant, an employee may go into retirement, or they may simply be fired, for good or bad reasons. Terminating a contract and terminating a relationship are two very different things (and we treat them very differently in social and legal terms) but in this sphere, they usually go hand in hand. This can be deeply emotionally difficult for those at the receiving end of both terminations.

> What happens to the discarded, outgrown caregiver? Some move from job to job, home to home, child to child. One friend told me about firing the babysitter her child had outgrown. A responsible employer, she found another job for the woman, in a household with a baby, and for more money. The child took it well, the mother told me – didn't seem more than passingly sad that the babysitter was leaving. But the babysitter – she cried. (Rothman 1989: 142)

Parents often speak with bittersweet sentiment about the moments they realise that they're no longer needed by their children; a child no longer needs to be dressed by her parents, can strap herself into the car alone, no longer needs to be carried. There will come, inevitably, a moment when a parent puts down their child and never picks them up again. But we don't cut parents or other relatives off from children's lives when the child has outgrown this kind of care. Why do we think we can do so with the people to whom we delegate childcare? If employed through an informal arrangement, care workers are not protected either by employment law or by family law. In the case of nannies for small children, the nanny can be fired from one day to the next, without reason, and without future visiting rights, and at significant emotional cost to both the children and the nanny.

Elizabeth Brake notes that certain kinds of relationship are granted legal protections such as special immigration eligibility, evidentiary privilege, in-state residence, hospital or prison visiting rights, eligibility for spousal relocation policies, bereavement or caretaking leave, or inheritance tax provisions for a family home (2018: 77). Not all relationships are seen as deserving of this protection. Caring relationships are widely considered valuable in themselves, justifying state discrimination between caring and uncaring relationships; the former 'have a close, irreplaceable connection to mental health goods such as self-respect, goods normally needed in the pursuit of life plans and not simply good within contested moral or religious doctrines' (83). But is it legitimate to exclude caring relationships from this protection when they are mediated by an employment contract? Insofar as a nanny or a carer for an elderly or disabled person becomes 'part of the family', should they acquire some family law rights, such as visitation rights?

The relationships protected by the state – primarily through marriage, which is Brake's focus, but also through legally recognised parent-child relationships – are, in theory, intimate, loving and committed. And yet there are plenty of legal family relationships that are detached and impersonal, if not downright hostile, whereas informal but deeply caring relationships between caregiver and care-receiver are not recognised at all. More ironic still is the legal focus on sexually consummated marriage as the most intimate of voluntary relationships; and yet surely it is the voluntary *care* between two individuals that the law should promote and protect, with or without the sex. A principle of equal treatment demands that the state provide the same benefits and protections for people in such close and committed relationships regardless of whether they are heterosexual or, in fact, sexual at all.

Brake argues that the personal relationships developing between paid caregivers and their clients (e.g. between a home aide and an elderly person) are no less valuable or worthy of state protection just because they exist alongside (and are enabled by) a contract. Such relationships have the same morally important features, such as non-fungibility: unlike in a merely professional relationship, where the employee could be replaced with someone else equally competent to do the job, caring relationships have relationship with *that specific person* as part of their object (2018: 85). This is not to say, however, that paid care relationships should be treated identically with marriage or other legally protected relationships:

> … given the special features of such relationships – physical dependency on one hand, economic dependency on the other – different provisions may be appropriate to protect these relationships. These might include, for example, protections against the employee's arbitrary reassignment, visitation rights, a role for the care worker in end-of-life decision making, and a symbolic or expressive shift in the law's regard for such workers as family members. (Brake 2018: 86)

It is not that recognition of one's status as 'one of the family' should come at the cost of labour protections, or that being protected as an employee requires disregard for the significance of interpersonal relationships and emotional ties. Rather, care workers should be entitled to *both* sets of protections.

Brake's vision relies on competence to give mutual consent to register for the relevant legal protections, and therefore cannot easily be extended to cover close relationships that form between childcare workers and their charges. However, intimate caring relationships between non-parents and children have still been defended as morally important. As discussed earlier in this chapter, philosophers like Anca Gheaus have argued that parents should not have unfettered control over their children's relationships with others, and that rights to maintain such relationships can be claimed by anyone for whom it would be in the child's interests that they have that right. In other words, if it's in the child's best interests to keep seeing Nanny on a regular basis, parents don't have the moral right to arbitrarily fire her and/or cut contact between her and the child.

When children become carers

We've discussed at some length The Problem faced by dual-earner couples with children, many of whom struggle to balance work outside the home with the care demands of childrearing. The Problem is amplified for those who have been described as 'the sandwich generation', caring for the needs of both their children and their own ageing parents, at the same time or one after another. The appearance on the horizon of a new caregiving burden when childrearing seems to be nearly 'finished' can be a source of fatigue and resentment – in the words of one woman, 'I think I've waited on people so much of my life and I wonder why I still have to do it' (Robinson and Thurnher 1979: 591). Care for parents by adult children gives rise to various dilemmas, some practical (like the time bind and economic costs faced by the 'sandwich generation') and some ethical (like considerations of how much personal care is owed to one's parents).

What are the costs of care? A study of unpaid caregiving in the United States found that 'informal care of any type has a negative and significant effect on hours worked for working women, decreasing work by about 3 hours per week on average, or 150 hours per year' (Van Houtven, Coe, and Skira 2013: 249). As might be expected, caregiving is also associated with a wage penalty for working women (although according to the same study, informal care provision had little effect on men's working time or wages). A similar participation gap (and associated wage gap) for carers has been demonstrated in the UK, with similar gender disparities (Heitmueller and Inglis 2007: 826). But the costs of caregiving for elderly parents – and especially for those with degenerative disorders such as Alzheimer's disease – go far beyond mere time and money. Personal impacts can include physiological fatigue, stress, depression, caregiver burnout and the loss of time for maintaining other relationships. The nature of caring for elderly people with dementia, for those with complex medical needs, or for those whose health is deteriorating, means that many of these effects are invariant across formal and informal care. However, in the case of adult children caring for their parents, 'an inevitable change occurs in the contours of their lives', as they look after their parents' practical needs whilst also grieving 'the loss of the relationship as it has been known' (Parks and Pilisuk 1991: 502).[11]

In China, 60 per cent of people with dementia are cared for by adult children, including children-in-law. One of the most important drivers of this is reported as 'a strong sense of filial piety' or *xiao* (Yu et al. 2016: 1845). Do children owe their parents a debt of care or gratitude, for bringing them into existence or for raising them to adulthood? The idea of 'reciprocal filial piety' may reflect both concepts of obligation; it 'demands children to show gratitude toward their parents in multiple ways because their life is attributable solely to their parents' (1846). The idea of filial piety has been identified by some as a specifically Asian cultural value that can have an important role in influencing models of caregiving, and caregiver experiences, including for those living in the Asian-American diaspora (Yu et al. 2016; Sun, Ong, and Burnette 2012). This view might be reinforced by a look at filial-support laws in Asian countries. As we noted in Chapter 1, a number of countries encourage adult children to provide their elderly parents with maintenance funds and/or to ensure that their healthcare and social needs are met, using the threat of criminal penalties, or by allowing elderly parents to sue their children, to ensure compliance (Serrano, Saltman, and Yeh 2017).

But Asian cultures do not have a monopoly on this view of filial duty – France likewise passed a law in 2004 mandating that adult children provide their elderly parents with an allowance, provide them with a home and stay in frequent communication with them (although it's unclear how this could be enforced).[12] Themes of gratitude and obligation often appear across socio-cultural contexts when we study motivations for, and attitudes towards, caregiving for parents by adult children. For example, a study of adult sons providing care to parents with dementia in rural Ireland found that these sons 'had a strong sense of duty and derived satisfaction from their caring role in the belief that they were "doing the best" and giving something back to their parents' (McDonnell and Ryan 2014: 792). Expressions of love, reciprocity, devotion and duty frequently intertwined in these interviews; one son stated, 'Mother was always there for us … we were her life and she done everything for us and now we are going to do everything we can for her … it's payback time' (792).

Regardless of the metaphysical and moral dilemmas we've been exploring throughout this book, these attitudes are clearly widespread: according to Stuifbergen and Van Delden, the idea that adult children owe their parents care in return for being nurtured and provided for as children 'can be viewed as a commonsense moral belief' (2011: 64). Social values and state institutions nonetheless play an important mediating role in how adult children understand their duties to their ageing parents, and whether care is provided informally out of love or as a matter of necessity. Comparing (for example) institutional care availability and cultural norms in Poland and Sweden highlights the relationship between care structures and beliefs regarding family duty. In Poland, the social care system presupposes '"private maternalism", where family members, in particular women, are responsible for arranging help for close relatives' (Radziwinowiczówna, Rosińska, and Kloc-Nowak 2018: 4). The lack of public spending on elder care depends on, and reinforces, a cultural status quo in which the families of dependent adults are held responsible for their care. Unpaid family caregivers are idealised but provided with little-to-no support. In Sweden, by comparison, until recently 'the support needs of frail older people in Sweden have been met primarily by the state, with there being little expectation that the family would provide care' (Sandberg, Lundh, and Nolan 2002: 353). It is therefore unsurprising that adult children of ageing parents envision their obligations differently in this context: they describe the importance of 'keeping in touch' and 'making it special', but – whilst feeling a need to 'keep an eye' on their parents' wellbeing in a general sense – were 'usually quite happy to delegate [instrumental care] to the staff' (358).

Parentification of children

Parentification is a kind of role reversal between parents and children. Unlike the situations described in the last section (in which adult children take on a caregiving role for parents who have become frail and dependent), 'parentification' describes situations in which children who are still *underage* come to look after, support or protect their parents and/or younger siblings. Some risk factors for this kind of age-inappropriate caregiving include 'a chronic disease of a family member (parent or siblings), a parent being addicted to a psychoactive substance, divorce, and family migration' (Chojnacka and Iwański 2022: 2911). For example, siblings of young children with chronic illnesses or disabilities may find themselves either pressed into the role of 'extra' caregiver for that sibling or may assume these responsibilities themselves as a way of adapting to, and accommodating, greater family stress.

In other cases, parentification takes the form of emotional management, whereby children take on the role of confidante or counsellor for their parent, mediate arguments in the family, or try to soothe, distract, console or entertain a parent who is angry or upset:

> Much like your favourite therapist does for you, these children developed a way of intuiting how to support their parents and others. This was necessary for their own psychological survival. Not caring for their parents was not an option. The consequences could range from the parents withholding love from the children

to outright violence between the parents themselves, and the child would then blame herself.[13]

Not all children within a family will necessarily be parentified the same way. An obvious case is that of the family in which one child is parentified as a result of their parents' inappropriate handling of another child's illness. But there are other factors that affect the distribution of family pressure on children. One of these is birth order, and another – as might be expected, having observed the effects of gender stereotypes on care distribution in adults – is gender. As Połomski et al. explain, 'The child that is most sensitive to the expectation of help from a parent is often the firstborn, and the oldest daughters are also included in a special risk group' (2021: 11456).

Parentification gives rise to a number of dilemmas. The first is in understanding parents' obligations in addressing the problem if a child starts to take on responsibility for other family members without being asked to do so. It is one thing to say that parents shouldn't place caregiving burdens on their children explicitly, but it is likely to be more challenging for parents to recognise and address parentification if it originates in the child's own response to family tensions. This is especially the case when the signs of parentification blend into gendered expectations of 'good behaviour' – consider the daughter who takes extra time to care for her younger siblings, or listens patiently to her parents grumbling. Those parents might not notice this behaviour as unusual at all, or may simply think it praiseworthy sensitivity and thoughtfulness.

The second dilemma is in recognizing the line between appropriate sharing of care and responsibility within a family, and age-inappropriate care by a child leading to role reversal. Nancy Chase notes that siblings in such cases might have 'positive opportunities to handle added responsibility, develop greater nurturing skills, and experience healthy identity formation with a heightened sense of self-esteem' (1999: 76). However, if caregiving demands consistently exceed the child's capacities and maturity levels, their development and identity formation may be negatively impacted, with damaging short- and long-term consequences:

> The extreme helpfulness, hyper-responsibility, and pseudo-maturity exhibited by some siblings may be accompanied by a flip-side clinical picture of depression, shame, excessive guilt, unrelenting worry, social isolation, psychosomatic problems, and conduct disturbances that characterize the parentified child. (Chase 1999: 76)

Is parentification only a problem because it leads to these consequences? Role reversal between children and parents could be seen as morally problematic even if it did not have negative psychological effects on the child. Our family norms and social structures have shifted dramatically in the last century, from a state of affairs where (at least in working-class families) it wasn't just normal but *necessary* for older children to contribute to the family's survival by working outside the home or taking care of younger siblings. Today, in contrast, both philosophical accounts of parental duty (as discussed in Chapter 2) and widespread 'common-sense' views of parenthood comprise heavily asymmetric normative expectations: parents are supposed to look after children, and not the other way round. Even if a child is capable of providing practical caregiving or emotional support to a parent, it would clearly seem to contradict these expectations for a parent to seek or accept that kind of care from their young child.

Children who become parents

Pregnancy and childbirth in young adolescents are (thankfully) rare but are nonetheless possible, and still occur. A girl may be physically capable of pregnancy and childbirth, albeit at significant risk to her own health, whilst still at the age we would ordinarily consider her a child: according to current records, the youngest girl to give birth was not yet five when she became pregnant. The question is whether a young girl can, or should, parent her child.[14] As noted at various points above, children can and do provide care to other family members, whether this is the child who cares for her younger siblings as part of a global care chain, or whether this is the parentified child who takes on responsibility for her parent's emotional needs. But our ordinary characterizations of parenthood – and especially of parental duties – seem to be clearly at odds with parenthood by a child who doesn't yet have responsibility for her own wellbeing. Even if a child is biologically capable of reproduction, 'as long as we presume that she does not have full liberty rights regarding her own education, living and travel arrangements, and healthcare, it would seem strange to suppose that she has the right to parent her own child, where we take this to include making similar decisions for that child' (Baron 2020: 242).

Our understanding of the rights and responsibilities of parents is generally shaped by our view of children's own needs and rights (for example, parents have rights and responsibilities to provide or otherwise ensure their child's education and medical treatment *because* that child has a right to education and appropriate healthcare). A young child is incapable of independently meeting the needs of her infant. Logically, she therefore cannot have all the rights we usually characterise as parental rights. However, as argued elsewhere in more detail, that does not entail that she has *no* rights regarding her own offspring, and that the newborn can be whisked away for adoption. That solution might seem, to many people, to be clearly in the best interests of the baby – and indeed, may be best for both children if the young mother expresses no desire to keep her child with her and would likely recover better from the experience in its absence. However, there are two children here whose best interests must be considered, and if the young mother would be distressed by the loss of her baby, her rights must be carefully weighed.

Having gone through the morally significant processes of pregnancy and childbirth, and being at risk of serious harm if separated from her newborn against her will, it may be argued that she has at least certain minimal parental rights, such as a right against that forcible separation (Baron 2020: 243–6). But this gives rise to a particularly complex dilemma of care: how can both children's rights be protected, and their needs met? The child-mother's parents/guardians already have a duty of care to her – but does that mean they 'inherit' responsibilities to her infant? In practical and logistical terms, the teenage mother's parents will probably be in a better place to look after a child than the teenager herself is, and they will probably be keen for her to finish her schooling. But they may not have enough energy or money to start parenting an infant all over again. It is deeply implausible 'that one could thus enter a regress and acquire a series of new parenting obligations to which one has not consented' (249). However, it may be that those with a duty of care to the child-mother will have a duty to arrange things in a way that allows her relationship with her infant to be maintained for as long as this is in her best interests. This might be more complicated, but practical complexity isn't enough to speak against moral obligations.

4 Identity, the past and the future

Identity is a huge and complicated topic, not only for philosophers, but also for psychologists and sociologists. For our purposes, it is enough to start by defining identity as the sorts of things you would say about yourself when you meet a stranger. For many people, their family origin and present family membership are fairly sizeable components of their identity.

At the heart of identity is a paradox. Most healthy adults have a sense of *who they are*, which we can understand in the broadest terms possible: I know where I'm from and where I belong, I am a member of a particular nationality and culture, perhaps a member of an organised religious community, I have a certain mother tongue, I have a certain job and career; more abstractly, I have certain values and political opinions, certain tastes, preferences, etc. From the inside, many of these memberships and commitments seem very important to who I am; without some of them, I would not be *me*. At the same time, I can accept that almost all these memberships and commitments are a huge accident. I might have been born somewhere else, grown up in a different culture, developed different values under the influence of other experiences or other people, been offered different study and work opportunities. That means that my identity is at once radically necessary and radically contingent: I am me, and yet I could so easily have been lots of things other than 'me'.

The paradox of identity becomes particularly acute when dealing with children, precisely because they are so malleable; they have so many possible futures ahead of them. To take an easy example: if a Hindu marries a Muslim, they might choose to bring their child up as a Hindu, or as a Muslim, or as both, or neither. They might bring her up with more or less religious commitment, in one or another religious community, attending one or another religious or non-religious school, in one language or another (or several). Although there is no guarantee that a child will acquire the identity her parents want her to acquire, the parents still have a lot of influence. In our example, if they bring up their child as a devout Muslim, there is a good chance that she will become a Muslim adult. This is not determinism, of course, since she may reject Islam as an adult, for any number of reasons and under any number of influences.

Because of this malleability, many people have strong opinions about how much the parents *should* shape and steer, not to mention how much teachers, social workers and priests should shape and steer. Later, when the child is an adult with a (more) determinate identity, some elements of this identity may annoy her: 'if only my parents had not done X, I would be a much better person by now.' This element of counterfactual comparison is central to identity; and given the influence of our families on us, it is essential to the conversations we have with our parents – either explicitly or merely in our heads – throughout our lives.

The 'open future' argument

Joel Feinberg (1992) asked which areas of the child's life a parent can legitimately direct, and what areas she cannot. Ultimately the distinction had to be justified by the child's interest in having a maximally 'open' future; that means, for the child, once she turns eighteen, to have the largest number of viable identity-conferring options to choose from and thereby to shape her own life. Obviously this does not mean letting the child do what it wants, but any restriction on the child's present autonomy has to be justified by its likely contribution to opening the future.

Certain restrictions are easy to justify: the needs of nutrition, health, hygiene, etc. More abstractly, a child has to be taught careful behaviour so as to avoid harming herself, and has to be taught basic pro-social behaviour so as to benefit from co-operation. She has to learn to control her emotions and how to organise her time. And she needs to be educated about her community and her place in it. All of this can be done by parents in loose co-operation with compulsory education. The six-year-old child does not want to go to school now, but both the parents and the state compel her in order for her to learn how to read and write and count – precisely because this will greatly increase the number of her future options, and therefore will 'open her future'. Making education, or at least literacy and numeracy training compulsory is confidently paternalistic: there is no doubt about the benefits to future autonomy. In theory, we *might* have designed a school system with more choice for children early on; literacy classes would be optional, and children would have to discover the advantages of literacy for themselves and then choose to attend. But there's a real risk that some children would not attend at all, and some would start attending very late, and therefore benefit much less in terms of opening the future (especially given the difficulty of learning about other fields without fundamentals in literacy). So we make it compulsory from a young age.

Feinberg's main focus was in religious education. Right away, we have to distinguish two kinds of religious educating: informing and inculcating. When I inform the child *about* a religion, this is an academic subject just like geography or history; when I inculcate a child *into* a religion, this involves bringing the child into seeing the world (and herself) from within the religion.[1] Feinberg has no objection to informing about religion. But he does feel that inculcating closes off certain options in the future. Of course, the religiously inculcated child will still grow into an autonomous adult, and that adult will be free to reject her childhood religion and choose another. However, it seems to be a safe assumption that a child inculcated into a religion will be more likely to remain in that religion through adulthood, and therefore less likely, once an adult, to contemplate other religions as viable options. She is not prevented from joining another religion, but she is unlikely to be attracted enough to another religion to try membership. In that way the inculcated religion narrows her future.

In comparison, says Feinberg, a child who has not been thus inculcated will reach adulthood with many more religions open to her to try out, and more curiosity about what membership might offer her. (Feinberg is careful not to encourage parents to inculcate a militant atheism in their children, for this would be just as mind-closing and future-closing as religious inculcation.)

Recall our discussion of Brighouse and Swift (B&S) in Chapter 1. B&S share Feinberg's basic commitment to liberal upbringing and are also worried about religious inculcation and closing futures. Because of their emphasis on 'family relationship goods', B&S are willing to allow some degree of shared religious activities between parent and child. However, they still lean more towards informing than inculcating, and would discourage the children from getting too directly involved in the activities. Presumably, this means that the Catholic parents can bring the child along to the Catholic mass to observe, but not to recite the communal prayers. Instead of telling the child 'God loves you', they should say '*Catholics believe* that there is a God and he loves them.'[2] Certainly, some religious parents might seek to inform rather than inculcate their child. But would we really blame religious parents who genuinely believe that the child would *benefit* from being inculcated? And even if it narrowed the child's future, would they not see it as important to *share* this essential part of them with their child? Surely the 'family relationship good' that is so central to B&S's account would support the child's full participation alongside the parents, that they might all become full members together of the religious community.

Consider an analogy with language. The population of Estonia is 1.3 million. That means that the Estonian language is *tiny*. It is also not closely related to many other languages except another small language, Finnish (population 5.5 million). And yet we would not blame Estonian parents for bringing up their child with a mother tongue of Estonian, even if this closes down many future options for them. Why? Because it's *their* language and *their* country, and they want to share both with their children. With the language comes all the national literature, the national politics, the national history. In this sense, language is not just a tool but is also full of cultural meanings, similar to those contained within a religion. It's true that many Estonian children also learn English or Russian, and these will be useful. But the open future argument would suggest that 'inculcating' Estonian as a mother tongue (with all that time and effort, both at home and at school) can never be justified.

There are limits to the analogy with language. The first is that a religious believer normally identifies closely with the religion and the religious community, with a set of sacred texts and rituals and ceremonies. The religion also provides a source of comfort and meaning at difficult times. Whereas there are presumably many Estonians who are ambivalent about their country. Second, many adults choose to learn a second language because they judge, autonomously, that it will be useful for them. Their mother tongue does not prevent this, even if it is much more difficult to achieve fluency as an adult. Perhaps the same could be said about religion: one's inculcated religion does not prevent anyone from switching as an adult. But an adult will probably not judge a religion to be useful in the same way as a language, and so will normally have to wait on some kind of 'religious experience' to join the new religion. As a matter of brute fact, it seems that choosing a new religion in adulthood is just not very common.

Yoder

Feinberg introduces a striking example of inculcating a religion *and* a culture: the American Supreme Court case of *Yoder v Wisconsin* from 1972. Yoder was an elder of the Amish community in Wisconsin. The community is isolated from mainstream society and is characterised by a devout Christianity and a very traditionalist lifestyle (strict gender roles, for example, and a reluctance to use any kind of technology, even in house construction or farming). According to Wisconsin state law, every child has to attend school and follow the state curriculum through to the age of sixteen. The curriculum is, in theory, what the legislators and the State board of education had worked out as the optimum balance between restricting the child's autonomy and opening the child's future. However, Yoder and other elders asked permission to remove Amish children from the state curriculum after fourteen, in order to focus on Amish skills taught by Amish teachers: basic agriculture and construction skills for boys and basic cooking and household management skills for girls.

Yoder's argument for exemption was about the survival of the Amish community. As a matter of empirical fact, the age of fifteen and sixteen was a time when the Amish children were seriously distracted by the future options presented in the state curriculum. Once those children reached eighteen, they tended to leave the community. In contrast, if the fifteen-year-olds could be compelled to learn the Amish skills for two years, they tended to identify with the community, and then remain after turning eighteen – even though, as adults, they were of course physically and legally free to leave.

The Supreme Court accepted the request, with the result that the Amish are thriving today. It is important to stress the point about choice: every liberal would want to protect the eighteen-year-old Amish adult's right to come and go, just as they would respect their informed choice to remain. The Amish cannot be called ignorant about the outside world: there is plenty in the state curriculum up to fourteen years, there are relations with nearby businesses and doctors, and the community also encourages outside sojourns called 'rumspringa' (between the ages of fifteen and twenty).

Feinberg objects to the *Yoder* exemption, because it results in a situation where the eighteen-year-old Amish adult is not in a position to consider the outside world as a locus of *viable* options. Perhaps there is some fear, perhaps some prejudice, there is certainly some ignorance; but above all there is little parental support or advice or money. Feinberg concludes that their future is less open than it could have been, and that they are less autonomous than they might have been. Whilst this is no doubt good for the Amish community, it is not good for the Amish children-turned-adults.[3]

This notion of counterfactual comparison is important: Feinberg is not suggesting that the Amish children or adults are badly off, in objective terms. Nor is he suggesting that they are significantly worse off than their non-Amish fellows. If anything, the Amish seem to be better off than other low-income social groups precisely because of the physical and emotional support from belonging to a tight-knit community. There is also a lot to be said for being free of manipulated yearnings for the objects of capitalism: the adult Amish are not distracted by the fashion and beauty industry, by cars and electronic goods, by foreign travel. But for Feinberg, the inaccessibility of viable 'outside' options constitutes an illegitimate deprivation.

Re G [2012]

Yoder pitted an isolated but unified community against the secular majority. The English case *Re G* involves a similar dispute about education, identity and community, but between two separated parents.[4] The man and the woman, both members of the ultra-orthodox Jewish Chareidi community, had married in 2000, and by the time the marriage broke down in 2010, had five children. Throughout this period, the children had been educated in the single-sex Chareidi schools, with the curricular content dominated by the information and skills required to be future members of the Chareidi community: boys had a lot of Talmudic instruction, and the girls were explicitly steered towards becoming home-makers and mothers. Once the parents had separated, the mother was granted custody of the children, and the father was satisfied with extensive visiting rights. Where they disagreed concerned the children's further education. After the separation, the mother had rejected the ultra-orthodox lifestyle, although she still considered herself orthodox; she now wished to move the five children to Modern Orthodox, co-educational schools, on the grounds that such schools would provide the children with better educational opportunities and future career prospects. The father deeply opposed the change of schools, arguing that it would disrupt the children's relationships with the father's wider family, with the children's Chareidi friends, and with the Chareidi community. Clearly both parties were interested in the welfare of the children, but it was not clear which set of values should be used for the assessment of that welfare. Munby LJ, giving the leading judgement in favour of the mother, declared that 'reasonable men and women' would uphold the following values (thereby recognizing legal rights): equality of opportunity, the encouragement and fostering of aspiration, and 'to maximise the child's opportunities in every sphere of life as they enter adulthood'. So here we have the opposite outcome from *Yoder*.[5]

It is worth saying something here about rights. The US Supreme Court case recognised Yoder's First Amendment right to freedom of religion. The judgement was framed within the modern discourse of human rights launched by the 1689 English Bill of Rights and the 1789 American Constitution, and anchored in most Western legal systems today. This discourse led naturally to the formulation of the United Nations Convention on the Rights of the Child, which came into force in 1990.[6]

In his article, Feinberg spoke of the child's 'right' to an open future; in so doing he was adducing a moral right rather than discovering a legal right; and Feinberg was arguing that the child's right should be understood as outweighing the community's legal right to freedom of religion (and the child's parents' right to inculcate their religion in their child). Presumably Feinberg would have agreed with the outcome of *Re G*.

As should be clear by this stage in the book, we have not relied on the discourse of legal rights to express our philosophical points. Indeed, we also resist Feinberg's use of moral rights, and prefer to argue in terms of what is or is not best for the child. Rights discourse certainly has its central place in modern political and legal discussions, but for philosophical purposes it suffers from two defects: (i) it is often too *stipulative*, with each party in a dispute claiming authoritatively to have 'discovered' a right; (ii) the discourse also relies too much on stipulation when it comes to *weighing* one right against another. *Yoder* went one way, *Re G* went the other, without any deeper attempts to justify the selection of the winning rights paradigm in either case.[7] With that in mind, we will gladly allow the rights discourse to proceed in parallel to our own discussions.

Aside: Hot-housing

The *Yoder* example is extreme. Most parental decisions to bring up their children in a particular religion do not close their futures quite so drastically. If a child grows up as a Catholic, she may resent the time 'wasted' in prayer or at church, she may feel embarrassed at the sexist training for the first communion, but by the age of eighteen her knowledge, skills and preferences will not really be adversely affected, and she can just reduce or drop her Catholicism if she wants to.[8] But Feinberg's argument can be applied to a different area of parental choice, and that concerns the hot-housing of young talent, which can be analogous to religious belief in the depth of commitment, and the importance of a community of practice. If the parents are themselves passionate about music or mathematics or sport, then the hot-housing can also be part of a special relationship good as described by Brighouse & Swift (see Chapter 1).

Wealthy parents discover that their eight-year-old is exceptionally talented in tennis. They remove her from conventional school and hire a trainer for six hours a day. She agrees at first, without being sure what she is agreeing to. She enjoys the game, and she enjoys doing well at tournaments, but she occasionally needs more pressure from the coach or the parents. When she is twelve, they move to a country with a better climate so that she can practise year-round. Throughout, she is subject to a strict diet and sleep monitoring, with limited social contact or academic instruction. The important point about hot-housing is that the child's body and brain are malleable enough for her to adapt to this intensive regime and eventually to win Wimbledon. Although the hot-housing is not a sufficient condition, it seems to be a necessary one, particularly for certain kinds of sports and certain musical instruments. The stakes are high, since even among those with the best of prospects, the chances of reaching the very top are still minimal. For those who fail, there might be little to compensate for a lost childhood, and they might well come to hate their sport or instrument, just as their relationship with their parents might be compromised. On the other hand, for those who succeed, perhaps there is nothing so sweet as victory, and this can justify all the effort and eliminate all regret.[9] In the same way that Feinberg would advocate a non-committal anthropological sampling of religions over Amish immersion, presumably he would also support a sampling of different sports and musical instruments in order to expand the options available for later autonomous choice as an adult. If a certain sport or instrument 'clicks' with the child, then the child should be encouraged to develop competence in it, as long as it remains pleasurable and does not occlude other valuable childhood activities. Once she is an adult, she can continue to decide how much time and energy to devote to the sport or instrument. But of course such a child will never win Wimbledon.

Mills' response to Feinberg

Claudia Mills (2003) offers a spirited response to Feinberg.[10] Mills interprets Feinberg as suggesting that the child should be encouraged to sample various religions as part of an anthropological education. But whilst the child might learn lots of important things from such a 'smorgasbord', says Mills, the approach virtually guarantees that she will never become a full member of a particular religion. The child might flirt with membership, might 'try it on' for size, but full membership – and genuine faith – requires some sort of single-minded commitment and immersion, without self-conscious embarrassment or sceptical reflection or detached comparison. Immersion is much easier if the child is inculcated into the religion right from the start, and then grows into the structure of meaning and sees herself naturally as a member of a religious family and religious community. Feinberg is worried about future options, says Mills, but he thereby greatly reduces the viability of any future option of full religious membership. A religion is not something like a choir or a political party, which one can choose to try out.

Feinberg had argued that in the *Yoder* case, the interests of the fourteen-year-olds were being sacrificed for the survival of the community, and Feinberg thought this was too much to ask, regardless of the objective benefits of Amish membership. This brings us to Mills' second argument: parents should act to promote the best interests of their children in a way that does not impinge on any third party, true. Parents should also promote their children's autonomy so that they can find their own way in adulthood, true. But both of those goals are compatible with parents legitimately choosing to promote certain *values* (including religious values) over others in their children. Parents are not impersonal guardians assigned by the state to look after children arbitrarily assigned to them; rather, the children belong to them (in the identity sense, not in the property sense). This does not give the parents licence to do with the children whatever they please – some notion of the child's best interests should still guide parenting decisions. But typically, parents want to bring up their children not only as full members of 'our family' and 'our community', but also see their children as benefitting from such membership.

In response, Feinberg might be worried about parents inculcating not only a religion, but also religious *intolerance*. If the child believes that 'Thou shalt have no other gods before Me', then it would seem a short step to the idea that other children, who believe in other gods (or no god), must somehow be mistaken. Religious parents concerned with avoiding intolerance would have to teach their children a specific kind of double-mindedness: on the one hand, full commitment to their own religion as if it were the Single and Obvious Truth; on the other hand, full respect for other people and their mysterious beliefs, as if there were multiple truths in the world, or as if their own 'truth' were not obvious enough to demand wider acceptance. On the one hand, the child is to be fully absorbed by the religious practice, and to organise her life in accord with its meanings; on the other hand, she is to downplay it as a mere private hobby when she discusses it with her school friends. There is room for confusion and disorientation here.

Some religious parents and children manage this balancing act better than others. Even if religious intolerance doesn't lead to overt conflict, it can still lead to interpersonal distance. Among the future options that Feinberg is interested in, he presumably includes the options of meeting and befriending others, and becoming close to them regardless of any divergent religious beliefs. Even when the adult religious believer manages to overcome this distance by marrying someone from a different religion, she might meet with deep disapproval from her own family or her spouse's family. Mills might respond to this concern by an analogy with the distinction between patriotic pride and insecure jingoism. The former is compatible not only with a respect for other countries and cultures, and not only with a delight in discovering the variety of cultural practices; most importantly, patriotic pride is compatible with a spirit of respectful criticism and discussion about one's country and its politics. And of course patriotic pride is perfectly compatible with international marriage. In the same vein, religious parents can bring their children up in a spirit of critical engagement with priests and theologians within their church. It has to be said, however, that states are a little more flexible than churches in responding to such criticism: one thinks of the way that women have been gradually allowed greater parity with men over the past 200 years, through the right to own property, vote, run for public office, etc. In contrast, it is hard to imagine a young Catholic girl getting a satisfactory answer from a priest about why women are still not allowed to become priests.

Will that particular prohibition be enough to put her off remaining a Catholic? Or will it force her to fashion her 'own' kind of Catholicism, in the way that many Catholics use contraception and celebrate their friends' same-sex marriages? As such, Catholic church membership could be flexible enough at the personal level to allow cherry-picking alongside all the other ways in which children drift into their specific identities as they become adults. In this latter case, Mills would presumably conclude that religious inculcation is not necessarily incompatible with the child's 'open future'.

Disability and community membership

Hot-housing, choice of mother tongue and political/religious inculcation are far from the only ways in which parents may aim to shape their child's future characteristics, community memberships and identity. Consider the controversial choice made by a Deaf lesbian couple in 2002: to use a Deaf sperm donor to increase the likelihood of their children being born congenitally Deaf.[11] Central to the debate around this case was the status of Deafness – is it a handicap or is it a culture? The two lesbians in the case considered themselves to be part of a Deaf community; the resulting child was indeed born Deaf, and the parents were delighted. Arguments in support of the parents' aim have, as well as appealing to parents' reproductive freedom, emphasised the value to the child of belonging fully to the Deaf community, in a similar way that a Catholic child can belong to her parents' community. Many in this community see Deafness not as a disability, but 'as a passport to enter into a rich, shared culture. They see being deaf as defining their cultural identity and sign language as a sophisticated, unique form of communication' (Camporesi 2010: 88–9). Some philosophers (not to mention many theorists in the field of Disability Studies) have also objected to the treatment of disabilities as inherently undesirable/harmful, and indeed criticise the very terms such as 'disability' and 'impairment' as stigmatizing. Of course, we acknowledge that many people whose physiological conditions might be described using these terms would instead view them as mere variations, or even enhancements. Elizabeth Barnes observes that whilst many things in life make it harder, 'they can also enhance and enrich it. Disability is just one of many such features – the sorts of things that create difficulty and hardship, but which make the world a more interesting and vibrant place in the process' (2009: 352).

The arguments above combine an argument that the arrangement was for the good (the 'culture' argument) and an argument that the arrangement is *not for the bad*. Those born Deaf never know what they are missing. They learn that most people have a fifth sense that they do not, but there is no reason why they should think that this fact, and the knowledge of this fact, harms them. Any of us might have been born with any number of advantageous genetics-based properties, but few of us dwell on it. The more tragic cases are not the children genetically determined to be less than averagely X (a particular property), but rather those children born healthy who then suffer a misfortune resulting in the *loss* of their average X.

Here and elsewhere in the coming discussion, we have to draw attention to the importance of the temporal perspective on an event. For many kinds of events, the view *ex ante* (beforehand) only differs from the view *ex post* (afterwards) in terms of epistemic access. Before the 2022 Women's Euro, nobody knew who would win, and a lot of people were hopeful for England. After the final, everyone knew that England had won. But the meaning of the event did not depend on the perspective: the English players *imagined* what it would be like to win, and then they *discovered* what it was like, and those experiences weren't so far apart. In contrast, the view *ex ante* of a child's birth is very different from the view *ex post*. If one hears that a Deaf lesbian couple are *planning* to have a child with a congenitally Deaf sperm donor, one might protest to them that deliberately creating a disabled child was immoral. Once one hears that the lesbian couple have now produced a child who is in fact Deaf, this is now a 'fact on the ground', and a fact worth celebrating, just like the arrival of any child. For the sake of the child, it would no longer be appropriate to protest to them, just like it would be inappropriate to pity the child. This distinction between temporal perspectives is part of a larger issue, the non-identity problem, to which we return below.

Reasons against

Some of those criticizing the choice appeal to ideas such as those underpinning the principle of 'procreative beneficence' we discussed in Chapter 2. That is, they argue that when bringing children into existence, we should choose to create the children with the greatest chance of a good life. Tim Murphy, for example, argues that parents should not deliberately try to conceive children with impairments of major life functions (sight, hearing, mobility, etc.) but rather that they 'should work to protect the intrinsic values to be found in human capacities' (2009: 49). Others appeal to the child's own autonomy and their future options; the problem with deliberately trying to conceive a Deaf child (or selecting one using embryo screening) 'is that it violates the child's own autonomy and narrows the scope of her choices when she grows up; in other words, it violates her right to an "open future"' (Davis 1997: 8).[12]

We noted above that some people reject labels such as 'disability' in the case of Deafness and other conditions. However, Camporesi dismisses concerns over terminology as irrelevant to the *ethical* question of whether parents are permitted to 'carry on a cultural bloodline' by choosing to have a Deaf child. Whether or not Deafness is categorised as a natural variation, a disability, an impairment or something else entirely, we also have to be able to define what Deafness itself *is:*

> Is it or is it not 'not being able to hear'? If we agree on this, then we should agree that it is a limitation on the future of the child, and not a minor one, as it is a general hindrance for a vast array of plans of life (2010: 94).

Here, we might compare the parents who attempt to ensure that their child is born Deaf to those parents we mentioned above, who choose to raise their child speaking Estonian as their mother tongue. Even though both might narrow the child's future options given the predominance of other forms of communication, the child is also *enabled* to grow up immersed in a culture – importantly, their parents' culture – from which they might otherwise feel detached. Such clear immersion is foundational to identity and to an early sense of belonging. Even if, as an adult, I drift away from my parents geographically and emotionally, at least I know where I came from.

This may not be a persuasive analogy to all, however, as the Estonian child (who we might agree benefits from their rich ties to Estonian culture and their sense of community belonging) is not entirely barred from learning to speak another language and embracing another culture. The Deaf child, on the other hand, cannot autonomously learn to hear. Since a hearing child can learn sign language (and almost certainly will if they grow up surrounded by people Signing, just as a child will learn any spoken language in this way), it could be argued that the choice of a Deaf child isn't necessary to ensure community membership for them. As Levy points out, we live in a 'logocentric culture':

> Choosing deafness is, therefore, choosing a real (though not an especially severe) limitation. To that extent, deaf children have their future somewhat narrowed. Moreover, there is a sense in which this narrowing is uncompensated. For the children of the deaf, access to deaf culture is not the compensation they receive for their disability, it is their birthright. (Levy 2002: 284)

There are several different ways in which someone might pursue the goal of having a child belonging to the Deaf community, and these have inspired increasingly fervent moral condemnation. We accept that people are at liberty to choose their romantic and reproductive partners (i.e. without IVF or embryo selection), and so could not plausibly condemn someone seeking a Deaf partner in the hope that the children they had together would also be Deaf (in the same way that many Estonians seek to have children with other Estonians).

Deliberately choosing a Deaf sperm donor is just a step removed from this, and yet clearly provoked significantly greater moral outrage from some quarters. This is presumably because someone using donor sperm to conceive, unlike someone attempting to conceive with their partner, is not committed by circumstance to passing down any specific characteristics *because* they belong to their chosen reproductive partner. The anonymous donor with whom one conceives the child can be 'reduced' to their genetic traits; the conclusion drawn by many is that one should choose the best bundle of genetic traits possible.

We can then compare the selection of a Deaf sperm donor to the use of embryo screening and deliberate selection of an embryo carrying genes for Deafness. As we discussed in Chapter 2, IVF involves the production of a half-dozen embryos which can be compared, with a view to implanting the 'best' one (however defined).[13] This – perhaps only because of the greater certainty with which it lets parents shape the child's future – has been more strongly condemned than preferential selection of a Deaf sperm donor, although still fervently defended by some. But both sides of this argument can agree that the desire to raise one's child in the Deaf community would be no justification for painlessly perforating the ear-drums of a hearing newborn, i.e. one who already exists. The motivation (to fully share one's culture, language and community with one's child) and outcome (creating a Deaf child) would be exactly the same; the only difference is the source of the impairment and the identity of the impaired. The healthy newborn loses a capacity they previously had when their eardrums are irreversibly perforated, and so this action seems clearly to be a harm in the sense of reducing their future options. But harms can, in theory, be outweighed by benefits, and the above discussion shows that many in the Deaf community consider not only Deafness itself but also full immersion in their community to be a clear and genuine benefit. Whilst embryo selection – that is the choice of *which child to have* – might be defended as a form of reproductive autonomy, Häyry argues that this autonomy does not extend to the choice 'to interfere with the bodily integrity of an already existing child' (2004: 511). That choice must be justified by appeal to the best interests of the child. At this point, the onus would be on the Deaf parents to demonstrate that the child would in fact be better off as a 'full' member of the Deaf community. But of course, the congenitally Deaf child could not have existed without being Deaf, and so *this particular* child isn't necessarily made worse off by being Deaf. This is a 'non-identity' problem.

The non-identity problem

The non-identity problem, coined by Derek Parfit (1984), concerns actions that seem clearly to be harmful, and yet the putative victim turns out not to be harmed. It gives rise to two overlapping paradoxes. According to the first paradox, I cannot logically be *harmed* by the act of procreation that leads to my existence, no matter how immoral I might consider the act, and no matter how wicked I might consider the procreative actors. This is because the two definitions of harm cannot be applied to a procreative act:

- The *temporal* definition of harm: I am harmed if I am made worse off than I had been. My shirt was clean before you spilled wine on it, and now it will cost me £X to have it cleaned. But before the procreative act I did not exist, so I cannot be any worse off by existing.
- The *counterfactual* definition of harm: I am harmed if I am made worse off than I would otherwise have been. Your negligent driving broke my leg, and therefore I was not able to earn money as a footballer for three months. Without the broken leg, I would have been £X richer by now. But insofar as the procreative act created *me*, then if you had not created me, I would not be here. So my existing cannot be worse than my non-existing.

According to the second paradox, if I am basically glad to exist, then I cannot consistently condemn any act that was causally necessary for me to come into existence. For in condemning it, I am implicitly wishing that the act had not taken place; and if it had not taken place, I would not exist. I cannot, for example, both be glad that I exist and robustly condemn my mother's adulterous fling with the postman that brought about my conception and existence. If I wished that my social father had supplied the sperm instead, then I am effectively wishing that someone else would be here instead of me. Moreover, insofar as my parents love me, then they too may find it difficult to condemn the procreative act that was necessary for me to come into being.

Why is the non-identity problem a problem? Because, as Parfit points out, it brings about a clash of intuitions:

(i) The belief that an act is morally wrong only if it harms some existing or future person. In Parfit's words, the 'bad' act must be 'bad for' someone (1984: 363);

(ii) The belief that causing someone to have a flawed existence (crucially, *as long as* that existence is worth having) does not harm that person if (i) it does not reduce their wellbeing from one moment to another, or if (ii) the alternative was that they never would have existed otherwise;

(iii) The belief that existence-causing actions in some non-identity cases are wrong.

Consider, for example, the following case: Susan is taking a six-month course of medication, and her doctor warns her that if she becomes pregnant during this time, the medication will cause her foetus to develop abnormally. She decides to conceive now anyway. Nine months later, her child is born with a congenital heart defect. At first glance, we might want to blame her for knowingly harming her child by conceiving during the treatment. But Susan reasons that *this* child would never have been born if she hadn't conceived at that time, and so she hasn't harmed this child. At the same time, the child's existence is still worth having; the congenital heart defect does not stop them from enjoying many of life's pleasures, making friends in childhood, going to school or making ambitious career plans. According to (i) and (ii), then, Susan is right: she hasn't harmed anyone.

The same logic applies to the case we discussed in the last section: morally, it makes no difference how the Deaf couple choose. We rightly resist interpersonal moral comparisons of already-existing children: we cannot say that this Deaf child is somehow worth 'less' than that hearing child. But that also means that we cannot say that the Deaf child's life is worth less than the hearing child that the lesbian couple in the case above *might have had* – all we are left with is the *ex post* appreciation of this child (who happens to be Deaf, and glad to be alive).

The non-identity problem is a juggling problem: we have three intuitions and we cannot hold them all at the same time. The question for those aiming to solve the problem is which intuition to drop. An approach taken by some consequentialist philosophers is to reject the person-based intuition represented by (i), on the grounds that moral law is impersonal in nature. It's the net level of utility/wellbeing (or other unit of moral significance) resulting from my actions that makes the action morally wrong or right. An existence-causing act can be morally wrong if it causes someone to exist with a significantly lower 'level of wellbeing' than someone else who might have existed instead. So, knowingly conceiving a foetus that will suffer from developmental abnormalities results in a net loss of utility/wellbeing compared with knowingly conceiving a foetus that will develop normally, and is therefore morally wrong. If we accept this, then we can reject (i) whilst hanging on to (ii) and (iii).

But this consequentialist approach is at risk of a *reductio ad absurdum:* it puts deliberate non-conception on a moral level with not only abortion, but (on some accounts) with post-natal infanticide. Given the impersonal principle that we ought to maximise the amount of worthwhile life in the world, it can be argued that abortion has the same consequence as deliberate non-conception (assuming that the foetus terminated and the one not conceived would have had lives equally worth living). The outcome of these two situations is identical: one worthwhile life fewer than there might have been otherwise.[14] But of course, an account that cannot deny the justifiability of infanticide is going to be deeply implausible (and give consequentialism a bad name to boot).

A different way of combating the non-identity problem is to throw out intuition (iii) and say 'Well, I guess my gut is wrong: there really is no harm here, and therefore no moral wrong'. We may think that Susan behaves irresponsibly in choosing to conceive whilst on medication (for example, because her choice will contribute to a strain on medical resources, or reduce the time and energy she can give her existing children), but we cannot morally condemn her actions by pointing to some harm to the child. As Rebecca Bennett puts it, we may still have good reasons to avoid implanting an embryo with a congenital disability, but these are not moral obligations. They are 'merely preferences about what sort of children we believe we would like and what sort of a world we believe we would prefer to live in' (2009: 269).

Saviour siblings

Another debate pertaining to 'choosing' children through embryo screening is the debate around so-called saviour siblings.[15] Saviour siblings can be produced through pre-implantation tissue typing (PTT), a form of embryo testing that can be combined with IVF to allow parents to choose specific embryos to implant from a half-dozen already fertilised embryos. In the UK, PTT is allowed in cases where an existing child of the parents has one of a number of blood disorders, the best treatment for which would be a stem cell transfusion from a matched donor. If a close relative who would match the sick child isn't available, parents can use PTT to select the embryo that would be a match: a saviour sibling. The embryo can be implanted, and the resulting child will be capable of donating life-saving tissue or stem cells. In terms of the future child's identity, the parents can be genuinely indifferent about which embryo is selected here and now, since they are committed to loving unconditionally whoever comes out of the womb. Given that indifference, the doctors might as well choose the embryo with the 'correct' genotype. The parents are not necessarily thinking instrumentally: they are not creating another child *only* to save the sibling, but they want another child *anyway*.

PTT has been defended by philosophers on various grounds. Some have appealed to general consequentialist principles (e.g. saving a life outweighs possible negatives) and some have argued that it is inconsistent to allow parents to select *against* sickness through PGD, but not allow them to *treat* existing sickness through PTT (see e.g. Boyle and Savulescu 2001; Sheldon and Wilkinson 2004; Bellamy 2005). Since banning PTT or PGD for the purpose of creating a saviour sibling would preclude the only means by which a sick child's life can be saved, Sheldon and Wilkinson argue that 'the onus of proof rests clearly with the prohibitionists who must demonstrate that these children's deaths are less terrible than the consequences of allowing this particular use of PGD' (2004: 533). They note that negative responses to the idea of creating saviour siblings tend to 'run together two distinct worries: concerns about people having children for the wrong reasons, on the one hand, and concerns about the way in which the child will be treated by his or her parents, on the other' (ibid).

Let us consider the first of these worries. Is saviour-siblinghood the wrong reason to bring a child into the world? It is of course true that those who choose to have children (including those who choose to continue an unexpected pregnancy) always choose to do so *for* some reason. Some possible reasons are more justifiable than others. We might think that the choice to create a saviour sibling is a more noble motivation than the choice to have a child because parenthood is a cultural default, or so that Grandma stops nagging you about babies; or to have a second child because you're convinced that children with siblings fare better as adults than single children. However, as Christine Overall points out, this argument 'depends on the assumption that it is morally unobjectionable to create a baby for the various purposes of completing a family, giving a playmate to an existing child, delighting grandparents, saving a marriage, and so on' (2012: 83). She does not consider these instrumental uses acceptable reasons to procreate; neither does she think saviour-siblinghood is an acceptable reason to create a child.

Of course, many people's reasons for having children could be criticised in this way. Let us therefore assume that there are some reasons for wanting children that are morally acceptable, and that the parents in such a case had already decided to have another child before they knew that PTT was an option for their sick child's treatment. Again, we have the situation where they 'might as well' choose the saviour sibling. On the other hand, they chose this embryo and not the others because it might be useful, and this creates a strong implication to the child herself that if she had not been useful (or turns out not to be useful enough) that she is otherwise unwanted. (Every child has moments of natural insecurity as they grow up; the saviour sibling will be unlucky in that her moments of insecurity might well crystallise around her status as 'saviour', and this might make the insecurity worse.)

That leads us to the second worry: how the saviour sibling will be treated by their parents. It is difficult to imagine that the personal identity of a child created partly for this purpose could go un-shaped by the circumstances of their birth, and the relationship they then have with the rest of their family and especially their sibling. Will they identify more closely with the sibling they saved, or resent them? Will they feel more loved and cherished by their parents for their lifesaving power, or will they worry that their value is dependent on their utility as a medical resource? Of course, we know that our existence as the person-we-are-genetically is highly contingent (something we discuss in further detail in Chapter 7) and that there are a huge range of reasons for which we might *not* have existed. But many people would feel that there is significant difference between 'If my parents hadn't met in Bruges that summer, I wouldn't be here' and 'If my brother had been healthy, I wouldn't be here.'

The question is – is that a morally significant difference? How can we evaluate parents' choices to take the saviour sibling route? Here, it might be argued that children whose identity veers from the path imagined by their parents may experience difficulties in their family identity and relationships *regardless* of whether their parents' expectations reach as far as their genetic makeup. When the last child in a family is a daughter with six older brothers, she may be well aware that her parents kept trying until they 'finally' had a daughter, with certain expectations in mind. She might feel particularly cherished for that reason, but she may also feel unwanted if she doesn't conform to expectations, e.g. the standards of femininity dominant in the cultural context. Even more so, the younger brothers in the same family may feel unwanted for the same reason, knowing that each subsequent pregnancy after the first few boys were born had been initiated with the same goal (which their own births had then 'frustrated'). When such aims in family-making are made clear, we cannot be surprised if they affect the identity of the resulting children or the relationships between them.[16] Overall notes that tying the new child's reasons for existence to the health of their sibling comes with risks for the futures of both children. The sick child may need a stem cell transfusion from the saviour sibling's cord blood, and maybe this will work. But what will happen if, later on, the older sibling relapses?

The novel *My Sister's Keeper* (Picoult 2009) dramatised this dilemma for mainstream audiences. In this book, saviour sibling Anna is conceived through PTT for the purpose of saving older sister Kate, who was diagnosed with acute promyelocytic leukaemia as a toddler. Cord blood is taken from Anna at birth; at the age of five, donor lymphocytes are taken from her when Kate relapses; at the age of six, Anna donates granulocytes to fight Kate's infection, and then bone marrow. Since Anna is a small child during these procedures, she cannot voluntarily donate – and in fact, she has to be physically held down in order for the doctor to place the needles. Instead, her parents give their consent for her to be used as a donor for their older child. The tipping point comes when Anna, at the age of thirteen, is expected to donate a kidney to Kate; instead, she sues for medical emancipation.

We might ask: is the saviour sibling so far away from the expectations on normal siblings? If Kate were bad at maths and Anna were good at it, wouldn't the parents put moral pressure on Anna to help her? We might expect them to encourage it strongly – not just because it would be a 'generous' thing to do, but because 'we're all part of a family, we all have to help each other.' But of course, there is a difference between maths tutoring, which takes nothing away from Anna except her time and energy, and medical donation of tissues such as bone marrow or a kidney, with the much greater discomfort and health risks such procedures carry for the donor. Parents might quite justifiably encourage their children to make sacrifices for one another when it comes to choices of movies or playing with beloved toys ('sharing is caring') but it seems like a stretch from this to an expectation of sharing one's own flesh and blood.

To be identified as a match for another individual – someone sorely in need of donor tissue or organs – is taken by many people to represent a unique kind of moral responsibility. This is especially the case within families, where a sense of familial duty may increase the pressure that an individual feels to donate to their sick family member. Precisely for this reason, as Kingma observes, ‘some advocate that it should be especially difficult to donate to a family member, as there is some concern that, out of care for the ill family member, the consent may not be genuinely voluntary, and hence be morally invalid’ (2021: 459). Parents who create a saviour sibling choose to place the child in this position, with the attendant burden of moral obligation they may come to feel.[17] Of course, there is no certainty that the child would feel burdened – conversely, it may be uniquely beneficial for their sense of pride and self-worth to have the chance to save their sibling’s life. But it is implausible to think that their choice would not be influenced *at all* by the knowledge that they were selected partly for precisely this purpose. We can more reasonably compare the child who is talented at maths with the child who, entirely coincidentally, is a bone marrow match for their sick sibling; both can share a gift with their siblings. But when your gift has been carefully engineered by your parents, is it still a gift?

In the light of the arguments for and against saviour sibling-hood, a middle-ground view might make the moral permissibility of creating a saviour sibling conditional on certain limits: never reaching for any donation beyond umbilical cord blood, and never telling the saviour sibling how and why they were conceived. However, in the case that the older child were to relapse and the medical solution were not just in sight but living under the same roof, it is difficult to imagine parents being able to pass up the opportunity to save the sick child – and perhaps we would even condemn them for passing it up.[18] The moral dilemmas that would predictably arise once a saviour sibling *existed,* given the ‘facts on the ground’ at that point, might be enough to push us to avoid that situation entirely.

5 The meaning of biology

The traditional concept of a family involves appeals to blood, biology and birth. By 'biology' we mean *essentially observable* biology, rather than the mainly unobservable biology of the scientific picture. The science of genetics, for example, is mostly unobservable in its molecular detail, in the structures of the cell, in the biochemistry of life and so on – and that science has only been around for the last seventy-odd years. The basic ideas of reproduction and heredity, however, are more directly observable and have been a source of meaning for families through all of human history (as well as observable and controllable in animal breeding). One kind of observability is facial and other bodily resemblance between family members, but perhaps the most obviously observable biological connection is that demonstrated through birth: *mater semper certa est*, or 'the mother is always certain'.

Blood and biology have a long history of negative connotations: racism and sexism on the larger scale, nepotism and anti-adoptee discrimination on the smaller scale. It might be tempting to argue that the whole notion of biological belonging is dangerous and fictitious, and that a 'mature' civilization should focus instead on voluntary and revisable contractual associations and on purely social bonds.

However, family belonging is arguably much more fundamental to our sense of identity, more so even than racial belonging. Whilst Western society has reached a point where no serious politician would publicly admit to being racist (at least not using that word), almost every serious politician will speak of the importance of supporting 'family values', pose for photoshoots with their children, and continue supporting the tax advantages for families. Even though the concept of 'family' now accommodates more biologically unrelated members than before, the *paradigm* still seems to be biological. Importantly, blood still trumps behaviour in many family contexts. Even an uncaring or abusive family can still be a source of the narratives shaping one's identity, and that is what this chapter is about.

Velleman's argument

In his 'Family History' (2005),[1] David Velleman starts with the following empirical claim about adopted children: about half of adoptee adults (those who know they were adopted) attempt to seek out their birth mothers.[2] Some of them want to get to know them, some want to talk to them in depth, some just want to meet them once and never again, perhaps without much conversation. Velleman asks: what are these adoptees looking for, exactly? After all, by the time they reach adulthood, they have an established relationship with their adoptive parents and any extended family: they already know where they belong, they already know who cares for them. There is rarely a sense that they are looking for their 'real' mother. Velleman's answer is striking (2005: 368) – he claims that the adoptees hope to find *themselves*. By this he does not mean biographical information, such as birth date and location, for many of the adoptees already know that. Indeed, they also might already know about the circumstances that compelled the mother to give them up.[3] Instead, Velleman claims they are seeking in a very primitive way to meet their maker (our words, not his). The meeting is the important part, not necessarily the conversation or the creation of any subsequent relationship. It is enough for the two to look in each other's eyes, each seeing herself reflected in the face of the other. They need not say anything at all. As the philosophers say, this seems to be a fundamental case of acquiring knowledge 'by acquaintance' rather than 'by description'.

We could support Velleman's intuition about the ineliminable importance of blood and birth by considering the accidental 'baby-swap' cases.[4] In the maternity ward, two similar-looking neonates are removed from their two mothers, and put in a separate room for further observation and testing due to some minor medical concerns. The next day, the two babies are returned to the incorrect mothers and the mothers do not notice the mix-up. The babies grow; they and their new mothers bond. Several years later the mix-up is discovered, and there is a problem: each child has a social identity partly constructed by its healthy social relationships to the new mother and her other family members, but each child has a biological identity relating to the other family. What to do? One answer would be to declare that social identity, after a certain time, trumps biological identity: to re-exchange the babies now would do more harm than good. But we think a lot of people would be inclined to speak about the 'right' and the 'wrong' mother, precisely in terms of biology; that each mother would be inclined to speak of the other baby as 'hers', and would frantically try to get it back.[5] In contrast, a 'social' conception of identity would say that the child's origin is irrelevant – whether by natural parental intercourse, by the mother's infidelity, by donor conception or by adoption. All that matters is the social relationship developing and deepening over time, within which the generic baby *becomes* 'my daughter'. Such a view might have a religious inflection, whereby the child is seen as ultimately a gift of God, regardless of the contingent route by which the child arrived in my family. So this richer social conception is what Velleman wants to challenge.

The first question of identity, for all of us, is simple (but also very difficult!): *who am I?* The second question is more difficult in various ways: *where did I come from?* Importantly, the answer to both questions is not just some pieces of information, but is better described as a kind of awareness. Adopted children, once they are old enough to understand what adoption is, might have a profound sense in which their identity seems 'unmoored'. Even if their adoptive parents give them plenty of information about their mother, these are just words, abstract and imprecise, just one story among so many others; for all the adoptee knows, she might as well have just popped out of thin air. However emotionally and socially close she is to her adoptive parents, she knows that what brought her to them was radically contingent, and this can be unsettling. She was adopted by *this* family, but she might well have been adopted by *that* family, or by that one, or by that one. Her resulting social identity might have developed in countless different ways. In contrast, there is nothing contingent about your biological mother; for you simply could not have come from anyone else. And that represents a kind of mooring, a point of origin stretching back before you were born.[6] This is the meaning of biology that Velleman is interested in. This is the sort of thing that the adoptee is looking for. We have to understand this point first, since otherwise we are likely to be distracted by his more controversial conclusions.

One of his conclusions runs: deliberately creating a child from anonymous donor conception is immoral. Why? Because we are deliberately creating an unmoored child, permanently deprived of essential components of her identity.[7]

In arguing against donor-conception, Velleman seems to veer towards social conservativism, opposed to 'unnatural' family-creation practices. It is important to stress that he is not opposed to single motherhood or to lesbian adoption *as such*. He would presumably tolerate a lesbian being artificially inseminated by the sperm of a friend who is prepared to hang around as a godfather-figure in the child's life, with the child fully informed of her origins. And if a woman makes use of anonymous donor sperm, the resulting child will still be half-moored. Velleman acknowledges that some couples and women find infertility deeply distressing, and desperately long for a child to complete their lives. He is not one to trivialise such distress or such longing, but he argues that the possible relief offered by donor-assisted conception is greatly outweighed by the harm to the resulting child.[8]

One quick argument against Velleman here is to say that the donor-conceived child, as the locus of alleged harm, would normally be the main person to assert the grievance against the parents. And yet if the child's alternative was non-existence, then, following the non-identity problem described in the last chapter, we can assume that the child is grateful to be alive, despite her unmoored state. And Velleman accepts the distinction between *ex ante* and *ex post* perspectives: if a person or couple is contemplating donor-assisted procreation in the future, that option should be rejected as immoral, argues Velleman. If the couple has *already* produced the child through donor-conception, then there is an important sense in which it is too late to call its creation immoral, for the child's existence should be unambiguously celebrated like that of any other child. In the same way, Velleman is careful to refrain from arguing against adoption, anonymous or otherwise – if the child already exists, then the *ex post* question is about what to do now, not about what should or should not have happened in the past. And of course there are plenty of scenarios where adoption will clearly be the best option for a particular child. The relevant comparison is not between *children* (the adoptee vs. the children living with their biological parents) but rather between *pathways* for a single child (the child being adopted vs. living in an orphanage or with an ill-equipped foster parent).

The meaning of biology

It is not just that biology is important for the way adoptees look for their birth mothers, and the way that the baby-swap is described as getting the 'wrong' baby. Velleman argues that biological family relationships go even deeper. After all, some of the great stories of world literature would simply not make sense without a widely shared understanding of the importance of biological relationships (2005: 369). So Oedipus kills a stranger at the crossroads – it's disturbing as a story of hot-tempered murder, certainly, but it becomes a profound tragedy when it's revealed to be parricide. And yet in purely *social* terms, the old man was a stranger to Oedipus, since Oedipus had been abandoned by his parents and raised by another couple. Although we would blame Oedipus for his temper and for its fatal consequences, we would not blame him for not knowing who the person was; and yet it is clear that, first, *he blames himself*, and second, that his self-blame makes sense for the audience, both then and now. Darth Vader tells Luke Skywalker 'I am your father.' Under a social conception of parenthood, Luke could reply 'So what?' Or he could say: 'no you're not – Uncle Owen was my father.' But that would be to miss the point. Luke is meant to be shocked, but also interested – as are we, the audience. Both Luke and the audience are now curious to learn the story of how the relationship came about, and about what will follow from it.

We'll mention a third example of an important biological connection (not mentioned by Velleman). Bettina Goering's father was the nephew of the Nazi leader Hermann Goering. She was born ten years after Hermann's death, and so in no plausible sense can she be linked to the evil of the Nazi regime. Nevertheless, at the age of thirty she decided to have herself sterilised. At the time she did it for what she called 'intellectual' reasons: she felt there were already too many children in the world. But her brother had a vasectomy, and declared it was to 'cut the line'. When he said that, she realised that it might also have been an unconscious reason for her too, and she has been speaking of that motivation ever since.[9] Reading about this, many people will seem torn. On the one hand, her behaviour makes no moral sense, given the complete absence of moral responsibility, given the fact that she was born just as innocent as every other child in her birth year, given the fact that she did not choose her name, and that names are mere labels. On the other hand, her invocation of some kind of inherited moral taint in her 'line' seems like almost a mystical notion: that evil taints can be inherited. And yet she is not invoking any familiar religious metaphysics. Her action, although extreme, is intelligible because it is based on the widely shared understanding of the meaning of biology.

Back to the two questions 'who am I?' and 'where do I come from?', Velleman is writing about a deeper sense of one's life, a way of understanding oneself that goes beyond the merely biographical – something 'higher', and something 'before'. I may feel as if I belong to this group of people here and now, but that has to be more than a mere question of habit and affection, since both are essentially changeable. The word 'family' here is not just the collection of 'me and my siblings and my parents', but stretches back in time, before I was born, to grandparents and great-grandparents. I may have met some of them, I may only have heard of others; some of them might be associated with a building or a town. Perhaps some of the stories are incredible, but even a false story, embellished and revised, contributes to a more extended sense of family and of personal identity, beyond the accident of my entry into the world, beyond the accident of my parents' entry into the world. Missing pieces in these stories – what the adoptees go in search of, or a grandparent whose branch of the family tree is mysteriously blank – can have an impact on our story. Writing about the relationship between grandparents and grandchildren, the psychoanalyst Nicolas Abraham suggests poignantly that 'What haunts are not the dead, but the gaps left within us by the secrets of others' (1987: 287).

Velleman, an American writing in 2005, opens his article with the story of his ancestors travelling from the Ukraine in the nineteenth century, changing their name, learning new languages, growing roots in new places that, however difficult it might be for them to call home, was the place their children and grand-children *took for granted* – in the sense of being granted a meaningful gift. Thus the 'mooring' against radical contingency is not only about necessarily belonging to one's parents, but to a whole line of people into the deep past, a line that leads directly – and apparently inexorably – *to me*. One natural extension of this is the idea of loyalty not only to my parents but to my ancestors. Such a loyalty can be unfair and oppressive, of course; we're not saying it's a good or bad thing, but it is intelligible.

This extended meaning of biological 'family' goes into not only the past, but also the future. It includes the sense in which I will live on, 'in' my biological children, after my death. That does not just mean that I will live on *in their memory* of me – something of my identity will be carried forth in them, whether or not they remember me, and on from there to their descendants who will never meet me.

Thus, my life becomes moored at both ends, and this is a small solace against the sheer brute arbitrariness and indifference of the universe. Again, none of this needs to be religious, nor does it need to rely on any contentious religious metaphysics – it's all built into the meanings and resonances of the biological connection. Two issues here, both of which we address below:

(i) Might the *social* connection be just as powerful, could an adoptive parent leave an equally deep, quasi-mystical mark on her children and grand-children? After all, to 'inherit' something can refer to physical features from my biological parents as well as to behavioural features from my social parents. And we should be wary of thinking that the genetic link determines more than it does.[10]

(ii) Velleman is aware (2005: 362) of the risk that his talk of mythical and symbolic thoughts comes dangerously close to the 'blood and bone and seed' so beloved of eugenicists and racists, not to mention to the honour-killings and the 'sins of the fathers'. Is there not a sense that this language does more harm than good?

Velleman makes an important point about the degree to which this meaning can be articulated. Compare: when I meet a stranger at a party, I can tell them lots of information about myself: what my job is, where I live, what music I enjoy, where I was born – but none of this can ever add to up *me* to the sense I have of *being me*. When I apply for a job at a company, my CV lists my skills and work experience, but the company is looking for a *type* of person, not for *me*. If I am lucky, then it turns out that I tick enough of the boxes that they are looking for. We can call this 'propositional' self-understanding and self-presentation. When talking to the stranger at a party or to a potential employer at a job interview, I will of course mention my origins, but only as a *causal* explanation of my present beliefs, or skills, or perhaps my values. I was born in England and that is why I presently speak English as my mother tongue. My father was a musician; that is who I learned my violin skill from. But that is not essentially relevant to the stranger at the party. What is relevant is that I can speak English and play the violin now, and I can plan for the future on the basis of my present command of English and music. Of course propositional self-understanding is important. But Velleman is writing about a deeper self-understanding, which is more about feeling *at home* in one's life story.

In her response to Velleman,[11] Sally Haslanger quickly admits that she has a personal investment in the matter: she and her husband adopted two children. Although Velleman is not criticizing adoption because it is probably the best *ex post* solution to a pre-existing problem, he clearly thinks that the adoptees are necessarily worse off for not growing up with their biological parents. Haslanger wants to reject this 'bionormative' assumption forcefully.[12] Whilst not denying that biological relations can be a source of deep meaning in the individual's search for identity, they are not the *only* source, nor need they be the *primary* source. Instead, adopted and donor-conceived children can derive enough of a sense of meaning-conferring identity from their non-biological family links, precisely because such social bonds are cultivated before the infant is in a position to choose them. In other words, the child *grows into* such social bonds, to the point where – from the child's point of view – they will seem just as natural and necessary as the biological bonds championed by Velleman; so the child has just as much of a chance of feeling at home in her family as she does in her town or village.

Although Velleman is at pains to deflect accusations of social conservatism and of stigmatizing adoptees, Haslanger sees the threat as undiminished. Instead, Haslanger wants to expand the category of 'family' to the point where any single person or couple can legitimately yearn to have a child, *however* that child arrives in the world. Again, from the *child's* point of view, it makes no difference where she comes from if she can grow into a sense of belonging here with these people.[13] Haslanger's experience of adoption allows her to speak from direct knowledge, but there is an additional element from her story too: she is white, and her children are African-American. Some would argue that adoption should try to align racial identity as much as possible, precisely to maximise the adoptee's ability to identify with her parents. In Haslanger's situation, both the children and everyone else know that they are adopted right from the start. Haslanger is keen to reject the arguments for same-race adoption, since she sees racial identity as just another aspect of identity which her children will have to sort out for themselves. It is important to recognise the philosophical roots of Haslanger's critique: a kind of liberal *non-essentialism* about identity. An essentialist would say that in virtue of that person's essence, X, she must be Y, whether she knows it or not, whether she is comfortable with it or not. Of course, the ugly versions of essentialism include basic racism and sexism. But Velleman is also an essentialist insofar as he believes that one's biological family links are necessarily fundamental to selfhood, and can only be ignored to one's cost. Haslanger, on the other hand, is a pluralist about identity-formation, and refuses all talk of essences beyond the individual's partial self-creation. That is, a particular individual will have essential components to her identity, but these will be a product of many influences *as well as* of her idiosyncratic personal endorsement and repudiation of those influences as she matures.

Daniel Groll (2021) offers a position half-way between Velleman and Haslanger. On the one hand, he agrees with Velleman's condemnation of anonymous gamete donation. On the other hand, he agrees with Haslanger's pluralism about sources of identity. His reconciliation of the two positions has to do with protecting the *option* for the donor-conceived child of eventually looking for her genetic parent, if she wants to. Groll accepts that many donor-conceived adults do not wish to know their genetic origins, and unlike Velleman, he refuses to call this a mistake (i.e. they are not culpably neglecting their deeper interests). But he accepts Velleman's starting point that many donor-conceived adults *do* in fact wish to meet their biological parent, a wish that is perfectly intelligible; but Groll refuses to call that wish a mistake either.

Moral taint

Let us go back to the example of Bettina Goering as an example of 'moral taint'. The concept of 'moral taint' was introduced by Joel Feinberg (1968), but developed most fruitfully for our purposes by Marina Oshana (2006), and we will look at her account in a moment. However metaphysically suspicious the idea of being tainted through a biological connection, the idea is familiar enough to be taken as meaningful when it comes to narratives of understanding. The central idea of moral taint goes back to the Ancient Greek notion of eudaemonia, most commonly translated into English as 'flourishing'. Since eudaemonia is less about subjective happiness or wellbeing and more about an objective state of being, a person's eudaemonia is always vulnerable to all kinds of moral luck. One component of my eudaemonia is the objective quality of my family relationships and the objective quality of my relatives' actions: if a relationship is bad, even through no fault of my own, this will undermine my eudaemonia; and if my great-uncle or sister does something morally wrong, that too will undermine it, even if I made no causal contribution to her act and knew nothing about it.

Bettina Goering was clearly not *causally* responsible for her great-uncle's actions, but her response was intelligible (even if drastic). But it is very common for parents to feel tainted by the deeds of their children. Here there is a crucial difference, of course: not only did the parent bring the child into existence, and therefore bear a kind of ultimate responsibility for what those children go on to do, but the parents can never be sure whether they might have been negligently complicit through some specific act or omission during the child's upbringing. Even if the parent can be completely confident about her parenting, she will still feel tainted; and *be* tainted – that's Velleman's point. If the adult child murders someone, then the parent will be transformed into the 'parent of a murderer'. In fact, a person's eudaemonia is even vulnerable posthumously; however impressive a parent's life appeared to all on her deathbed, its eudaemonic quality can be undermined by her adult children's bad actions long after the parent's death.

Sue Klebold is the mother of Dylan Klebold, one of the shooters at the Columbine school massacre in 1999, and she wrote an autobiography in 2016.[14] Such was her sense of responsibility and taint that she also described herself as feeling a need to atone – she has worked for mental health charities since the massacre. Whatever her status before the killing, Dylan Klebold's actions turned her into the 'mother of a serial killer'. People will buy her autobiography not because of what she has done, but because of who she is.[15]

Now consider 'horizontal' moral taint without causality, between adult siblings. Oshana takes the central example of the more or less estranged adult brothers David and Ted Kaczynski. Ted was the notorious 'Unabomber', who killed three people and injured twenty-three others across the United States between 1978 and 1995 by mailing bombs to people, as part of a campaign to start a revolution against technology. At one point Ted mailed an anonymous 'manifesto' text to the New York Times, who published it. David Kaszynski noticed the manifesto and recognised the writing style and the use of certain words, and informed the FBI of his suspicion that the Unabomber was his brother. This was the key clue that led to Ted's discovery and arrest.

There is a slight problem of terminology here. Oshana suggests that David felt morally tainted by the murderous activity of his brother in virtue of their family relation, and therefore felt compelled to contact the FBI. She distinguishes (2006: 357–9) such a moral taint from two things:

- *Direct moral responsibility* for causally contributing to harm, either oneself, intentionally or recklessly, or via knowing complicity with another;[16]
- *Indirect collective or vicarious liability*, where such liability is incurred through one's voluntary membership in an organization whose other members were causing harm (without my knowledge or contribution to such harm).

In contrast, says Oshana, David was morally tainted because he was faultlessly linked to Ted's wrongdoing through their family 'organization', but he was not vicariously responsible because he did not voluntarily join that 'organization' and could not voluntarily leave. Despite their estrangement, he remained Ted's brother.

Oshana thinks that the concept of moral taint is 'for all practical purposes unnecessary and, moreover, metaphysically suspect' (2006: 354); nevertheless, she is trying to make sense of people feeling shame, but more importantly feeling the urge to atone, for the faults of their family members. David's assistance to the FBI revealed the quality of his experience of being tainted. Importantly, Oshana denies the meaningfulness of the biological connection between Ted and David, and refers to the moral taint as grounded in their common social upbringing. If Ted and David had been separated at birth and grown up in separate foster families, only to rediscover the connection after Ted's arrest, this would clear David of moral taint, thinks Oshana. In this we would disagree with her – separation in time and space has little impact on the shame people may feel in connection with relatives or ancestors.

Part of the taint comes from the retrospective alteration of the significance of events in David's childhood with Ted. For the Ted that David remembers has become the Ted who would *go on* to kill three people. Even though Ted only became a murderer at age forty-three, this changes the story of Ted's whole life, right back to the beginning, for it reveals the fact that Ted 'had it in him' to murder all along – it's just that nobody knew that about Ted's future, not even Ted himself. So David now realises that he spent his childhood with a future murderer.

Biology and naming

There are actually two biological relationships: the *genetic* link between parent and child (Velleman's main interest), and the *gestational* link between mother and child. In the latter case, we're talking about the simple fact that the child grows in the mother, comes out of her, and is made from her flesh. This necessarily gives the mother a deeply intimate relationship with the child. In contrast, the father has to believe in an abstract theory of how reproduction works, without actually being able to *observe* the genetic link, at least until facial and other resemblances start to appear after a few years (and they might not). For all the father can observe, the child that is born really could have come from anywhere; whereas the mother has no doubt at all.

The contrast between the genetic and the gestational may become acute in surrogacy arrangements. Take the case where the surrogate agrees to receive an embryo created from the two gametes of the commissioning couple. The resulting child will have an abstract genetic link to both commissioners, and a gestational link with the surrogate. And this difference might result in an awkward situation where, for example, the surrogate experiences the gestational link particularly strongly, and wants to keep the child. We discuss surrogacy in the next chapter. For the moment, we will stick to a heterosexual couple having their own child through sexual reproduction. And we want to explore this gestational link between mother and child indirectly, by using it to challenge the convention of giving the child the father's surname.

We have to begin with the convention of the woman taking her husband's surname upon marriage. After all, once the two parents have the same name, then the child's surname will follow. Among those women who choose to marry, there is still a large majority who take the new name (Duncan et al 2020). But the vast majority of children are given their father's surname, even when the parents are not married, and even when the married mother has kept her name. A small minority of couples give their child a double-barrelled name. Otherwise, only a small number of heterosexually partnered women (and of course single mothers, and lesbian mothers using sperm donors to conceive) give their own surname to their children.

Whilst there has been a long-standing discussion among feminist philosophers about the rights and wrongs of a woman taking a man's name in marriage, there has been very little discussion about the naming of children. We therefore aim to summarise and develop the philosophical argument for mothers keeping their names and for children being named after their mothers. Our argument is very simple: (i) the mother should keep her name because it is *her name*; (ii) the child should take the mother's name because it grows inside her, comes out of her and is of her flesh, whereas it has no such intimate connection with the father.

Very little has been written on the naming of children by sociologists or lawyers (e.g. Lebell 1988; Johnson and Scheube 2002; Herring 2009), and nothing by philosophers. The entry 'Parenthood and Procreation' in the *Stanford Encyclopedia of Philosophy* does not mention naming at all.[17] One philosopher (Sarajlic 2018) has recently written about government regulation of *first* names; whether the state should permit only those from a certain list (e.g. saints' names) and whether they should reserve the right to forbid certain names such as 'Toilet'. This is a familiar clash between family autonomy and the state's evaluation of the child's best interests. In contrast, we are only interested in children's *surnames* and what the choice of surnames tells us about understandings of the family more broadly. Far more has been said to date about women's surnames. The strongest reason for a woman (or indeed for anyone) to change her surname upon marriage, especially if she and her spouse plan to have children, is familiar: the desire to create a family unit with a single name. Once there is a single name there is also no dilemma about what to name the children. The whole family, including the future children, become known as 'The Smiths'. This is in line with the bureaucratic simplicity of a joint bank account, a joint mortgage, joint utility bills, joint insurance and a joint tax plan.[18] There might also be strong aesthetic reasons for the woman to prefer the husband's name. However, if the 'family unit' argument were the only reason, then one would expect about half of men to adopt the *woman's* surname on marriage. The fact that this barely happens at all suggests the influence of patriarchal norms and male insecurity.

But there are other considerations that may give us pause for thought. Let us look at an example: back when she was a student, Martha Craven married Alan Nussbaum in 1969, and became Martha Craven Nussbaum, going on to become a world-famous philosopher. She divorced him in 1987. On her book covers she is Martha C. Nussbaum. Her Wikipedia page (on which we are drawing for these details) is simply 'Martha Nussbaum', and that is how most people know her. In 1986 she wrote the *Fragility of Goodness*, and this made her name as a major philosopher.

Except that in a way, it (also) made Alan Nussbaum's name. But he didn't write the book, Martha did. And what's more, after their divorce, Martha kept his name because of the success of the *Fragility* book – written under 'his' name. And even though they have not lived together since 1987, all her subsequent books still bear 'his' name. Perhaps he contributed to *Fragility* indirectly, by looking after her as she wrote the book; but even that tenuous connection was lost after the divorce, where he has been reaping in a portion of the credit that is due entirely to her. That credit should have gone to Martha Craven, her name until she was twenty-two.

Maybe others do not feel this awkwardness. Martha and Alan married before the women's liberation movement really took off; since then it has become much more acceptable for women to keep their surname in marriage. And so we can presume most women who do take their husband's name make an unpressured and informed choice that should be respected.

Some insecure men might feel flattered and reassured when the woman 'demonstrates her love' by taking his name. But then why is it so rare for a man to take a woman's name as an equal demonstration? And if a man is secure in himself, and considers his marriage to be between equals, then surely he should resist any desire for her to take his name, precisely because of the outdated subservience it might symbolise. Some will say that the name-change is merely symbolic; but it is a symbol that points in an unfortunate direction – towards keeping the marital assets in the husband's name only, the marital bank account, the household bills.

There is one *indirect* argument that runs as follows: given that the woman has almost certainly inherited her surname from her father, it is less of a loss for her to give it up. Indeed, taking her husband's name is as natural as the shift in her affections from her father to her husband. However, we consider this unpersuasive: specifically, we would disagree with the claim that she has inherited *her father's* name. Once she has received his name at birth, she grows 'into it' over eighteen years, and by adulthood it has become *her* name: her friends know her by that name, her achievements are acknowledged with that name, and all the bureaucratic records refer to her via that name. The fact that the name comes from her father through the original naming ceremony is no longer relevant; in the same way that the historical origins of the word 'America' (the explorer Amerigo Vespucci) are no longer relevant to the name 'United States of America'. Once she is eighteen, she can go out into the world without her father, and the vast majority of people whom she meets will never meet her father or even ask her about him. The question then is whether Martha Nussbaum could claim that, since marrying Alan in 1969, she has gradually made the 'Nussbaum' name *hers*, to the point, indeed, where she is a lot more famous than him. If anything, *he* should feel resentful that she has 'stolen' it from him. He's going to meet people who will say 'are you related to Martha Nussbaum?' and he'll have to explain the whole sad story all over again.

Being given one's father's name is still different, of course, because the baby has no choice in the matter; she had no pre-named existence to move from – as such it cannot be interpreted as a loss or a surrender. Martha Craven had no other name until the age of twenty-two: the name Craven filled up her entire life, and therefore she really was giving up something at that point. Indeed, the whole change of name *reminds* us that her 'maiden' name (what an ugly term that is, too) has been exchanged for her 'wifely' name, with the unfortunate connotation of being property passed from one man to another.

Naming children

Back to the question of naming children, and the patronymic convention. It is surprising how little this is discussed in the popular press (Hardy 2013 is one exception). Let us consider another example to focus intuitions. Eric Roberts is a semi-famous Hollywood actor, who had a string of cohabitational relationships. At one point he was living with Kelly Cunningham, and they had a child in 1991, whom they named Emma Roberts, who went on to become an actor in her own right. Eric Roberts abandoned them soon after Emma's birth. So here you have the absurd situation where the child is named after someone who is *not there* for most of her life. Kelly Cunningham was the only parent to Emma, and yet the child was labelled with the name of someone who chose to take no part in the upbringing, and yet was getting 'credit' for it as a free-rider, just as he is now proud of his successful actor daughter.

But this sounds awkward. Why did Kelly Cunningham not rename her daughter 'Cunningham', once it was clear that Emma's father was not coming back? This case highlights a question about what children's surnames are *for*. Are they to identify the child as a member of a larger family, or as the child *created by* an individual, or as the child *being raised by* an individual?

The answer to this question, as well as the sexism of the status quo can be seen in the following quotation from the 1999 English case of *Dawson v Wearmouth*:[19]

> When the parents are married the child will normally be given the surname or the patronymic of the father, thereby demonstrating its relationship to him. The surname is thus a biological label which tells the world at large that the blood of the name flows in its veins.

As Herring points out (2009: 112), the quotation is interesting because it arbitrarily omits the *mother's* blood flowing through the child's veins. (Technically, of course, there is only one blood in the child's veins, and that is the child's.) The court's recourse to 'biological labels' introduces an important origin-story, generating a present metaphysical link. But once we allow origin stories and metaphysical links into the equation, it seems straightforward that the mother has a far greater claim. We lay out our argument for this below.

Children should be named after their birth mothers, whether or not the mother is married or cohabitating, whether or not the father is present or absent. The child is of the woman's flesh and (as recent work in philosophy of pregnancy and childbirth has taken pains to emphasise[20]) the two are intertwined in a complex physical and psychological relationship. Far from floating in its own private space, the foetus *in utero* is embedded in the wall of the womb, and both foetal and maternal tissues grow into the organ they share: the placenta. Anybody who has seen a human birth realises that it is not the act of gracefully removing a spare tyre from the boot of a car, but an arduous – even violent – disentanglement. The 'coming apart' of mother and child leaves literal wounds as the placenta detaches from the uterus; the uterus must contract quickly to prevent the mother from bleeding out. The name 'labour' is apt for the lengthy, difficult and often dangerous process, which for some women may pass without complications, but for others results in lasting physical and psychic traumas.

Anglophone philosophy has never taken the idea of flesh very seriously. Under the twin influence of Christianity and Descartes, the essence of a person transcended the *mere* body. After all, the body changes radically over the lifespan, it ages, grows, then gets injured and diseased, and dies. Surely *I* am more than the physical: I am consciousness, spirit, the soul, the self. In addition, one of the more pernicious manifestations of sexism is to reduce women to their bodies, to be gazed at and used. Critical disability theorists have also been interested in the purportedly imperfect body as a locus for unfair discrimination.[21] In contrast, Continental philosophers, from Maurice Merleau-Ponty to Simone de Beauvoir, took the idea of flesh (*le chaire*) much more seriously, together with the phenomenon of embodiment and Husserl's distinctions between the physical body (*Körper*) and lived body (*Leib*).

But surely our high school biology lessons taught us that the child is made up with 50 per cent of the genetic material from each parent? True. And we all know this.[22] But there is an important sense in which this truth is too abstract to be directly believable. We believe it *indirectly*, in the sense that we trust the scientists' story. Most of us are not scientists and so would not have discovered this information on our own. Remember that genes were not discovered until the 1950s, and inheritance was only theorised in the nineteenth century. In contrast, we have understood what childbirth is for all of human history. So we are comparing two different ways of knowing. On the one hand is the biological story, abstract, indirect, the stuff of laboratories and textbooks; on the other hand the *direct evidence* of the birth, where the mother brings forth the child in a protracted and bloody labour. This is direct knowledge in that, at the moment of birth, there can be no doubt that this baby came out of this woman, and at substantial cost to the woman. The father is not part of the arduous gestation or birth story at all – his contribution was an act of brief sexual intercourse nine months earlier. And without the biological story, it really is hard to grasp – as opposed to abstractly accept – the causal relationship between *that* sex act in the distant past and *this* child coming out of *this* woman now.

Even if we accept the biological story, the father's contribution is only 50 per cent of the 'design' at most.[23] The bricks and mortar, as it were, come only from the woman. Her body has fed and watered this baby over nine months of increasing discomfort and restriction; she has felt it growing every day; she has felt it kicking inside of her; and she is the first to know that the process of labour is beginning. The fleshly connection has begun even before the birth, as have the psychological processes of bonding and attachment. Our argument is straightforward, then: because the father's link to the baby is not observable and tangible, he does not deserve the huge privilege of naming it after himself and telling 'the world at large', often for the child's whole life, that his blood flows in the child's veins. To take a somewhat blunt analogy: if an author worked on a novel for nine months, only for her husband to sign his name on the manuscript, we would all expect her to be righteously indignant.

Some people might want to suggest that naming is no big deal. If it'll make the dad happy, let him name the child. We think, however, that naming *is* a big deal. As Herring (2009: 105) puts it, in many contexts naming denotes superiority and dominion; it is the most obvious way of denoting property; and certain names such as 'criminal' have strong consequences once formally conferred.

It is of course true that the father may develop a more intimate connection with the child – but later. Signs of biological connection might come through the development of facial and other resemblances, but these won't be visible for several years, and may indeed never be visible. Perhaps the recognition of himself in the child's face will lead to a deeper, more metaphysical bond. More important, we suggest, is the *social* bond that develops over months and years of direct communication and contact – the sheer effort of listening, watching and caring. But it is important that this social connection does not require the biological connection – and many fathers might well develop exactly the same intimacy with an adopted child. Indeed, we suggest that a truly loving father would see his child as a gift, and would not care about the origins of the gift: from his wife, from another woman, from a stork or from God. Indeed, we would argue that the genuinely loving father should not even care if he learns that the biological father is the postman; that is, such knowledge should not affect his deepening social relationship to the child, even if it might harm the relationship to his wife (and to the postman). We come back to this problem in Chapter 7.

It might be argued that the father's improving social relationship with the child might eventually bring him to parity with the mother's relationship; in which case the child should be named after both parents. This is certainly better than the father's surname alone. But the double-barrel brings new complications. First of all, as in the case of Martha Nussbaum, unless the maternal name is legally incorporated into the surname, then it is more likely to remain secondary – just as Martha Nussbaum reduced the 'Craven' to a mere C on her publications. Second, the obvious problem will be when the double-barrelled person has a child of his or her own.[24]

Maybe all the above can be true, but there remains one argument for naming the child after the father. Precisely because the father lacks the tangible fleshly connection, precisely because the insecure father might not be sure whether the child is a causal product of his loins, then the name – his name – serves to reassure him as well as to remind him of his responsibilities, and keeps him around to look after wife and child a little longer. As things stand today (as indeed in the past), many fathers abandon the mother when the business of child-rearing gets difficult and boring; and many fathers refuse to contribute financially after their departure. If the child were named after the mother, the lack of symbolic connection might make it easier still for the father to dump 'her' child on the mother.

On the other hand, this would seem to be an argument for better state infrastructure enabling the enforcement of child support, rather than trying to coddle fathers into honouring their responsibilities. Designing a system with a view to the worst possible outcome is sensible for an airline or a hospital or a bank. And maybe from the perspective of a social worker who has seen too many single mothers struggling to cope, the pragmatic concession to male insecurity might help. But from the point of view of two individuals entering marriage and entering parenthood with sincere mutual respect and faith in their equal status, then naming the child after the father as a pragmatic concession comes *too early*. The birth of a child is a time of renewed hope for the future, when it would be inappropriate to speak about things going wrong. 'We should name him after you in case you decide to run off' is not generally what a new mother wants to tell the father. As Hale LJ put it, in *re R (A Child)* [2001]:[25]

> It is a matter of great sadness to me that it is so often assumed, and even sometimes argued that fathers need that outward and visible link in order to retain their relationship with, and commitment to, the child. That should not be the case. It is a poor sort of parent whose interest in and commitment to his child depends upon that child bearing his name. After all, it is a privilege which is not enjoyed by many mothers, even when they are living with the child. They have to depend on more substantial things.

Divorce and remarriage

We have been discussing the initial *naming* of the child. We now want to consider a slightly different situation, the possibility of *renaming* the child after her parents' divorce. To fill out the situation a bit more: the child is born, and given the father's surname as per convention. The parents divorce when the child is still a minor, and a court awards main custody to the mother. If the mother remains single, she might want to rename the child with her (maiden) name (so Emma Roberts might have become Emma Cunningham); if the mother remarries, she might want to rename the child with the new husband's surname – and the biological father might object to this. Normally in such a situation, the matter goes to court, who will rule on the basis of the child's best interests. The recent case of *R v P* [2019][26] is a good example. The parents were both Lithuanian, were married in Lithuania, and a child was born in 2010 in Lithuania, and given the patronymic. The parents divorced in 2012, and this was followed by three years of violence and threats against both mother and child. In 2015, the mother and the child (now five) moved to the UK, but the father made an application on the basis of the Hague Convention on Child Abduction, and the British court refused on the basis of the continuing danger that he posed to both mother and child. The mother remarried and had a second child with the new husband. The second child was named after the second husband, and in 2018 the mother applied to the English courts for permission to rename the first child with the second husband's name (with the first husband's surname as the child's middle name). In addition, the child (now eight) herself wanted to change her name. As a final argument, the mother argued that it would be easier and safer for her to visit Lithuania in the future if the child bore her step-father's name.

Our first point in response to such a case is: how much simpler for everyone, but above all for the child, if she had been given her mother's maiden surname at birth, and retained it all her life. However, given that she was named with the patronymic, what should be done when her mother remarries?

In the end the application was refused on the grounds that it would not be in the child's best interests, because the name-change would be confusing for all, and because the name-change might undermine the relationship with the biological father. Despite the father's violent history, there was evidence that he was repentant, and that he wanted to start sending gifts to the girl. Otherwise, there were no other symbols or reminders of the father's existence in the new family home. Despite rejecting the application, the judge allowed that the situation could be reviewed at a later date, once the child had more knowledge of the father and the paternal family, and once there was more evidence of the father's repentance.

In our view, this judgement is completely mistaken. The case is even clearer because of the father's violent threats in the past, and we would interpret that as him effectively forfeiting all future claims to the child until the child is eighteen, at which point she can make her own mind up about what name she wants and about what sort of relationship she wants with her father, if any. No society has yet taken domestic abuse sufficiently seriously, as we go on to discuss in further detail in Chapter 9. As such, any bias in favour of the father in this context can only undermine wider gender justice. As Priscilla Ruth MacDougall (1985: 99) puts it, retaining the father's surname 'tells children that their mother's importance remains secondary to that of their father's even after their parents are divorced'.

But even if the father had not been violent, and even if the divorce had been amicable, we would support the unilateral renaming of the child *given* the original custody decision, given the interests of the child in integrating as much as possible into its new family. As to the risk of confusion, we think that renaming the child may well make things less confusing in the longer term, as she grows into her new family.[27] We are not suggesting that the violent biological father be erased from the girl's biography. We agree with Velleman about the importance of the origin story, and of the child being allowed to make contact with him if and when she chooses. It should also be remembered that the court proceedings will usually leave the father with some visitation rights, and that should be enough to provide the substance of any ensuing relationship between father and child, not some stamp of spurious ownership.

Finally, it is troubling that the court in *R v P* did not grant any weight to the child's wishes. If the child has its father's name *forced* on her against her will, it is hard to imagine that this will help its relationship with the father! But as the child gets older, her opinion should carry more and more weight, and could even be determinative at the age of sixteen, at which point she is considered old enough to competently know her interests in many other contexts.

6 Adoption, surrogacy and assisted reproduction

The last chapter explored the meanings – social, legal and philosophical – of the biological family. In this chapter, we consider the ways in which people construct families when normal procreation isn't possible. We discuss various moral questions about adoption and assisted reproduction, some of which have been with us for thousands of years, and others that have arisen only recently, as modern medicine has produced novel ways of bringing the requisite 'ingredients' together to allow people to have children.

Adoption

In law, adoption is the process by which an adult becomes the legal guardian of a child and acquires all the relevant legal parental rights and responsibilities. Even if the child has one or both birth parents still living, then 'where a person is adopted by a couple or a partner of his parent, he is to be treated as if he had been born as the child of the relationship of that couple'.[1] Except in the few countries where private adoption contracts are legal prior to birth, adoption is always a post-facto affair, responding to and directed by (in theory) the best interests of a child in need of parents. However, when there is a shortage of suitable prospective adopters, or when the administrative and legal systems that match children and adoptive parents are slow, children end up in the care of the state. There are currently vastly more 'looked after' children in the care of local authorities than there are adoptions of such children. In the spring of 2021, there were 104,989 children in care across the UK; in the preceding year, there had been 3417 adoptions from care, representing 3.26 per cent of looked after children.[2] The gap represented by these figures might be a sign that there aren't enough prospective adoptive parents, that many prospective adopters are rejected by the adoption system, that the adoption applicants are too fussy, or that this system simply works very slowly, resulting in a backlog of children waiting for parents.[3]

Adoption or procreation

Even today, many people feel a duty to have children (whether this is a duty to give their own parents grandchildren, to invest in the future of society, or some different framing).[4] As we've noted already elsewhere in this book, women who stay childfree by choice continue to report being questioned and criticised as 'selfish' for refraining from parenthood (Daum 2015; Gotlib 2016). That aside, many people today would agree that we don't have a general moral responsibility to become parents – it's fine to choose to stay childfree (whether as an individual or in a couple) and to focus on other life projects such as career, friendships and other forms of family. If there isn't a general duty to become a parent, then it follows logically that we can't have a general duty to adopt children. On the other hand, if somebody already wants to have children, it's been suggested that there may be a moral duty to adopt rather than to have biological children (and especially rather than having biological children by means of expensive and uncertain assisted reproduction). Tina Rulli (2016) makes this kind of argument, observing that millions of children around the world are in desperate need of caring parents, and prospective parents have a *pro tanto* duty to adopt, analogous in many morally relevant aspects to other situations in which we would accept a general duty of rescue. Rulli examines various reasons that people might give to prefer a *genetically* related child to an adoptive child. For example, people might want a child with whom they share observable family resemblances ('you've got your mother's curls'), or who is psychologically similar to them ('she has her father's taste in music'). They might see the child as an embodied expression of their love for their partner, or a way in which they can 'live on' after death. Rulli argues that these reasons, and the others that she considers, 'are either too trivial, presuppose the value of the genetic connection in question, are constrained by plausible, normative parental requirements, or fail to distinguish adopted children from genetic ones' (2016: 671–2). As such, they cannot defeat the duty to adopt.

Of course, there may be people whose strong desire for biological children persists *despite* acknowledging that the strength of one's parent-child relationship, the wellbeing of one's child and the cost of rearing children are not significantly different between adopted and biological children. They simply want 'their *own* child'. Here, Friedrich concedes that there won't be a moral duty to adopt – not only because the emotional and financial cost of adopting in place of having a biological child may be too great for the person in question, but moreover because 'given their psychology they are likely ill-suited to optimally care for the emotional needs of an adoptive child', i.e. without the biological link as extra motivation during the rough patches (2013: 31).

It might be argued that parenting biological children amounts to a special project, such that we don't *need* to overcome a duty to adopt to justify procreating instead. Luara Ferracioli, for example, argues that prospective parents have a 'compelling interest' in procreative-parenting (i.e. having a biological child to parent, as opposed to parenting in general). This interest doesn't have to outweigh all other interests, like those of future generations who might be negatively impacted by climate change, or those of orphans currently in need of parental care. As long as a person's own projects and relationships are 'an important ingredient of their conception of the good and have *non-trivial* value', they are allowed to give some priority to those projects and relationships, even when they conflict with the demands of morality (Ferracioli 2018: 80).

The non-trivial value that Ferracioli locates in procreative-parenting is in 'a deep, and robust, loving bond between the child and her parent' – a love for which, she argues, the fact of procreation provides a weighty *pro tanto* reason. But many would reject the claim that procreative-parenting gives us significantly greater reason for, or possibilities of, this kind of deep parent-child love. Rulli is one of these; she agrees with Ferracioli that personal interests can sometimes defeat *pro tanto* duties like the duty to adopt, but denies that procreative-parenting fulfils any non-trivial personal interests in a way that adoptive parenting cannot.[5] Daniel Friedrich is also one of these people. He acknowledges that many people's ambitions in life include parenthood and that many of these have a particular desire for their own biological children. However, he suggests that this desire is likely to be grounded in a number of false beliefs about both adoption and biological parenthood: 'as a result of these false beliefs many think their innermost desire is to have a biological child when in fact their desire has a broader content and can also be satisfied by raising an adoptive child' (2013: 28). Some of these beliefs include the belief that one will find it harder to love an adopted child, that one's own children will have superior genetic outcomes, that adopted children are 'damaged goods' and that adoption is significantly more expensive than having one's own child. These, Friedrich argues, are simply false. Insofar as the choice of procreation over adoption is based on these beliefs, it therefore isn't justified. Some of the beliefs mentioned by Friedrich are not only implausible, but verge on vanity or undesirable perfectionism – for example, the desire to procreate specifically because one believes that one's own genes are superior to others' and so should be passed on to the next generation.

The role of the state

We've seen that there is very little stopping someone from becoming a parent if they do it simply by procreating (though in Chapter 1 we consider whether this should be more difficult, looking at the debate over parental licensing). It is more widely accepted that there are constraints on one's liberty to become an *adoptive* parent. If someone wants to adopt children, there are practical, legal and moral limitations on the methods by which she may do so. The state plays an important role in this process; there are few countries in the world where private adoption is legal, and so everywhere else, state agencies undertake the work of screening and matching prospective parents to available children. Stereotypes of the adoption process generally suggest that the screening element is overly intrusive and complex, and that candidates with imperfections will be rejected. As Anne Moody observes, however, 'It actually is difficult, both ethically and legally, to deny a family the right to adopt. There is no end of good ways to be a parent, and any worthwhile adoption agency or counselor understands this' (2018: 60). Whilst recent data on adoption application success rates are not publicly available, Ofsted published a report in 2012 giving an overview of adoption statistics in England. Of 4145 applications for formal adoption, only 23 (0.6 per cent) were refused.[6] This is comparable to the success rate for fostering applications, more recent data on which are available: a UK government report covering 2020–21 shows that only 0.8 per cent of fostering applications completed in this time period were rejected.[7]

Even where private adoption *is* legal, and parents can arrange the social part of the process themselves (e.g. by choosing the individuals to whom they want to give up their child for adoption), the state isn't out of the picture: adoptions still have to be legally formalised, the appropriate paperwork signed, and the relevant legal rights and responsibilities terminated or transferred. Likewise, if a child's parents are no longer able to look after her, relatives such as grandparents still have to have institutional approval to take over as the child's guardians (though in most cases, they will have a much easier time getting this approval than strangers wishing to adopt the child).

The state's role in adoption isn't just in conducting background checks, rubber-stamping applications and sending new families on their way – social workers are also sometimes responsible for the initial decision to temporarily or permanently remove children from their original parents or guardians, and to find a new home for them elsewhere in the latter case. Terminating parental rights entirely is meant to be justified only by the best interests of the child, and is generally seen as a last resort in the case of severe abuse or neglect.[8] This means, however, that children whose parents are merely incompetent, or who are not considered abusive 'enough' by social services or courts, can end up suspended in a kind of limbo. Former social worker Anne Moody describes the repercussions of this for some children on her caseload: 'Their parents' problems proved serious enough to keep the children in foster care but not serious enough for the courts to terminate the parents' rights and free the children for adoption. The ensuing stalemate had these kids essentially growing up in foster care' (2018: 21).

It should be noted that the termination of parental rights, and placing of children in institutions or with foster/adoptive parents, has not been a politically neutral practice, currently or historically. Concerns are often still raised regarding the influence of racial and class biases in social worker recommendations and family court decisions. In the UK and elsewhere, assessments of parent 'unfitness', and the availability of support and resources to help families stay together, may vary significantly depending on income bracket, education, geographical area, mental capacity and race (Roberts 2002; Bywaters 2015). Despite formal concern with the child's best interests, 'child-centric' social frameworks have been criticised for paradoxically emphasizing the importance of parenting whilst neglecting to understand or engage with parents as people: 'Parents are seen as impacting upon children rather than being in relationships with them and with each other, thus practices focuses on how their actions/inactions do or do not affect children' (Featherstone, White and Morris 2014: 9). Whilst separation from parents will indeed be necessary for child protection in some cases, as we saw in Chapter 1, heavy-handedness by social services may sometimes be experienced as cruelty (14).

However, social services and family courts must also grapple with the opposite problem, represented by cases where children are left for too long with incompetent, neglectful or abusive parents (or lingering in foster care for many years, as we saw above) on the grounds that family relationships should be protected above all. Commitment to the protection of children's interests, biological family bonds and the rights of parents can give rise to seemingly impossible dilemmas, as Moody describes:

> Do we risk leaving [children] in dangerous situations in order to preserve their bonds to abusive parents? Should we immediately terminate parental rights when a baby is born to a mother whose long-term mental illness makes it impossible for her to safely parent? Should we set rigid rules about just how long a baby can be in foster care before the parent's rights are terminated? And what would the magic number of weeks or months or years be before too much harm had been done? For that matter, how would we decide how much harm is too much? (Moody 2018: 47)

Not all children who are looked after by the state have ended up there due to interventions like those described above. Some children will be placed in care because they've been orphaned, and others will be adopted as infants on the back of their mother's decision during pregnancy. A woman might make it known to authorities that she wants to give up her child for adoption before giving birth (or shortly afterwards), and in countries like the UK, her legal rights and responsibilities can be terminated by a court six weeks after the birth. However, in some countries, she might also place the child in a 'baby hatch'. These hatches (or 'foundling wheels', going further back in history) provide a warm and closely monitored space where new-born babies can be left anonymously by parents who cannot or will not care for them, and have reasons not to use the state adoption system to give them up. One such reason might be stigma attached to single motherhood or pregnancy out of wedlock, whilst another might be fear that the child (if given up for adoption formally) would eventually track down their birth parents through public records.

Baby hatches have seen a resurgence in some European countries (such as Germany, Czech Republic and the Netherlands) but are illegal in the UK, where abandoning a child below the age of two years old is a criminal offence. Abandonment happens nevertheless, with a yearly average of sixteen children aged two or lower abandoned in the UK between 1998 and 2005 (Sherr, Mueller, and Fox 2009). An insistence on formal procedures for the termination of parental responsibility might be motivated by a belief that biological families should stay together where possible, or by a belief that parental responsibilities are too weighty and important for people to be able to discard easily. On the other hand, where parents are unable or unwilling to care for their children, most would think that the best thing for the child is to ensure their placement with keen and vetted adoptive parents as quickly as possible.

However, the appropriate practical response will vary depending on the reason for abandonment: post-partum depression, fear of social stigma, fear of an intimate partner's actions, a desire to avoid being recorded as the child's parent or something else entirely. Baby hatches may not be the best solution to some of these reasons; they have been criticised for providing only the semblance of protection for vulnerable women and their infants, especially on the grounds that the hatches encourage childbirth in private at home, or even in secret, without any assistance.[9] An alternative approach, which might more appropriately address some of the reasons for abandonment listed above (and without the medical risks associated with using baby hatches) is the introduction of anonymous delivery. This would mean allowing women to access prenatal and postnatal care, and of course assistance in childbirth, without having their identifying information recorded. This remains illegal in most countries, but the implementation of a law allowing anonymous delivery in Austria in 2001 was linked to a significant decrease in police-reported neonaticides (Klier et al. 2013).

Giving up children

Whether we think it's morally acceptable to give up a child is likely to be influenced by our beliefs regarding (a) abortion, (b) the state of the fostering and adoption system, and (c) the moral obligations of biological parents. In a situation in which a woman has access to safe, affordable abortion care, and where we think that abortion is morally permissible, many people might think it's wrong to bring the child into being and place her in the care system *rather than* terminate the pregnancy. Individuals' moral intuitions about their own choices likewise reflect the weight of these different factors. For women who express anti-abortion beliefs, intuitions might swing either way: they might say that adoption to a caring, vetted couple will always be better than abortion; or they might say that giving up a child for adoption – even an unwanted child – is largely irresponsible compared to accepting the unexpected labour of parenthood (Cannold 2006).[10]

In states like the UK, biological parents are (legally) allowed to give up their default parental rights and responsibilities by entering into the state adoption process or surrogacy process. However, they aren't allowed to give up or give away their children by any less formal route, whether that's by putting them in a baby hatch or by giving the child to kindly neighbours who are desperate to parent. Parents can't even give their children to relatives to raise without the approval of the relevant institutions (although as we've noted elsewhere, relatives are nearly always given priority over strangers in applications for formal adoption or special guardianship orders).

Even if we don't think that biological parenthood comes with an automatic child-rearing obligation, we would still probably think there are some circumstances and ways in which it's more or less morally permissible to give up one's children. For example, we'd have far less sympathy for someone giving up their child for adoption because of its appearance than someone giving up a child for adoption due to serious financial strain. In that sense adoption is not really an *option* among others that can be assessed dispassionately in terms of likely costs and benefits and then rationally selected; it is not as if a hospital midwife will tell a nervous new mother: 'try out this parenting thing for a few weeks, and if it doesn't work out, you can always give the child up for adoption.' As such, a woman does not really *decide* to give the child up, 'all things considered'; it is more often a last resort in a desperate situation.

On the other hand, we might think that it's in the child's own interests to be adopted in such a situation, rather than raised by shallow and vapid parents. David Velleman argues:

> Of course, parental obligations must sometimes be transferable in practice. A child has a right to grow up in the care of parents who are willing and able to care for it. If its biological parents do not rise to the task, then the child has a right to adoptive parents who are willing and able to take their place. Thus, the mere unwillingness of biological parents to discharge their obligations may be sufficient to ensure that those obligations may be transferred to others, in deference to the rights of the child. (Velleman 2008a: 252)

However, he goes on to argue that this 'practical accommodation' can't give parents carte blanche to give up their children, and their responsibilities to those children, at will. Whilst they may be transferable in practice, this is 'only under exigencies that make their transfer beneficial for the child rather than convenient for the parent' (Velleman 2008a: 252). Partly, this is because parental responsibilities are too morally weighty to be discarded at will; partly, it is because these responsibilities arise in the context of a personal parent-child relationship; and partly, it is down to the nature of parental responsibilities. As we saw in Chapter 5, it follows from Velleman's view of these responsibilities that biological parents are best placed to fulfil them. However, those who (like Velleman) want to hold biological parents accountable whilst prioritizing the child's interests must consider how much time we give the parents to 'rise to the task'. Whilst it might be argued that most parents who are initially unwilling to parent will learn to love the child, the usual consensus regarding adoption is that the earlier a child can be adopted, the better.[11]

Assisted reproduction

Many couples want children, find they are unable to conceive, and therefore seek assistance. Many others know from the get-go that they will need assistance in making a baby; same-sex couples, for example, either require clinical assistance and the cooperation of gamete donor and surrogate mothers, or may explore co-parenting arrangements with other individuals or couples in a similar position (see e.g. Herbrand 2018). In the clinical context, 'assisted reproduction' can mean a range of different procedures, including interventions to treat blocked fallopian tubes or endometriosis, to treat a blocked epididymis or to prompt ovulation; artificial insemination using a partner's sperm; collaborative reproduction with a sperm, egg or mitochondrial DNA donor or surrogate mother; and *in vitro* fertilization (IVF), which may or may not be performed in conjunction with pre-implantation genetic diagnosis (PGD) and embryo selection. Newer reproductive technologies and procedures (like womb transplant) have been developed and trialled only very recently, whilst others (like synthetic eggs and sperm made from body cells) are slowly emerging over the scientific horizon. With all these procedures, there is then a second question of whether the state will provide it within the context of a national healthcare system, and if so, under what conditions.

Even putting aside the earlier debate regarding the duty to adopt, plenty of other social, ethical and legal questions arise in relation to assisted reproduction. One debate focuses in particular on the morality of assisted reproduction using other people's sperm, eggs or wombs, and is rooted in the debate over how we acquire parental responsibilities. Some philosophers think that procreation carries heavy moral responsibilities that we cannot simply delegate away to others: biological parents have 'permanent and nondispensable duties' to care for their offspring, including any offspring that are brought into being with their gametes (Callahan 2012: 225). This view leads to the conclusion that gamete donation and surrogacy involve someone – specifically, the donor or surrogate mother – shirking heavy moral responsibilities. As Velleman points out, 'we don't think that adults are permitted to conceive a child with the prior intention to put it up for adoption' (2008a: 252). Why, then, do we think that it's alright to conceive a child (or contribute to that process with one's eggs or sperm) with the prior intention of having nothing to do with his/her upbringing? And why does the legal system allow donation without any legal consequences?

Of course, one key difference between these two things is certainty regarding the child's care. As we saw in the last section, for a child to be given up at birth and put into the care system will often mean some time in the care of foster parents or state institutions. Whilst infants are the most in-demand group for prospective adopters, the wheels of the adoptions system still move slowly, and there is no guarantee that a child given up to 'the system' will be taken in immediately by a loving (and permanent) family. On the other hand, sperm and egg donors can say with much greater certainty that any child born from their genetic contribution will be born *to* one or more specific parents. Furthermore, it might be argued that these will be parents who are motivated enough to expend quite a bit of effort (and possibly money) to conceive that child, and so are likely to have given the project greater thought than those who conceive by accident.

Supporters might point to a further difference between sperm/egg donation and giving birth to a child with the intention of giving it up: if I donate my gametes to an IVF clinic, there are a lot more steps that have to be taken before someone has a baby from those gametes. It is not unheard of for couples to conceive – whether deliberately or not – and then separate, leaving the responsibility of childrearing mostly or entirely with one party. If single parenthood and recombined families are morally acceptable ways to deal with parental obligation, then arguably, it would seem illogical to reject gamete donation.[12] On the other hand, we could follow this line of thought in the other direction, arguing that absent parents and gamete donors alike shirk their natural obligations to their genetic children. We find this approach in Daniel Callahan's (particularly scathing) indictment of sperm donation: 'It is as if everyone agreed: Look, males have always been fathering children anonymously and irresponsibly; why not put this otherwise noxious trait to good use?' (2012: 229).

Regulating reproduction

Who should have access to assisted reproductive technologies/treatments (ARTs), and for how many 'attempts'? Should the state provide subsidised (or even free) access to ARTs? How should ARTs be regulated?

Some of these are questions about resource management and prioritization – obviously, if a healthcare system has limited funds, it may not be possible (or justifiable) to use funds for ARTs instead of some other needs. Part of this will depend on the status of infertility. One view would be to say that infertility is not an injury or a disease that impedes any 'activity of daily living', and therefore it should always take second place to hip replacements and cancer treatments under a limited NHS budget. One implication of this view would be to encourage infertile couples to adopt (since there are *always* kids waiting to be adopted), or to come to terms with their childlessness. The opposing view would be to see infertility as a physiological dysfunction *like any other*, and moreover one that is causing the couple a great deal of distress, and as such IVF should be eligible for state funding in the normal way. The message here would be pronatalist, and could even be couched in terms of a citizen's 'right' to strive for genetically-related children. In the UK, the NHS adopts a compromise, by offering a limited number of IVF attempts (without payment) to a limited number of eligible couples or women. Different countries will offer different compromises. Throughout this debate there is also the question of social justice: if the NHS refused to subsidise IVF, then only wealthier couples would be able to attempt it, through private clinics.

Other questions are less concerned with economics and lie more clearly in the realm of ethics – it was this area of debate that the Warnock Committee made their primary concern. This was a group (led by philosopher Mary Warnock) whose recommendations shaped the development of the *Human Fertilisation and Embryology* (HFE) Act 1990, as amended with the HFE Act 2008, and the establishing of the Human Fertilisation and Embryology Authority (HFEA) in the UK. The HFEA is an independent regulator – meaning that it works on behalf of the government but isn't part of the government itself – concerned with both fertility treatment and scientific research using human embryos. They provide guidance to, and inspect, embryology research institutions and fertility clinics to ensure compliance with the HFE Acts.

Another body, the National Institute for Health and Care Excellence (NICE), was created to offer evidence-based guidance on particular medical treatments. NICE suggests that IVF should be offered to couples who have been trying to get pregnant (by regular unprotected sex) for at least two years. At which point they recommend offering at least three cycles of IVF to infertile couples where the woman is under the age of forty.[13] In practice, however, IVF availability in the UK depends on a postcode lottery; some integrated care boards (ICBs) have no IVF provision, some will only offer one cycle, and some have stricter or laxer conditions for NHS-funded IVF.[14] For example, in Hertfordshire and West Essex, IVF is available only to couples (but not single women) who fulfil the following requirements:

- They do not have any children already (with each other or with previous partners), including adopted children;
- They have not had previous IVF treatment, whether private (self-funded) or provided on the NHS;
- They have not been sterilized in the past, even if that sterilization procedure was reversed;
- Both partners have a healthy BMI and do not smoke; and
- Female partners are aged 23–42 and meet a specified Anti-Mullerian hormone (AMH) blood level.

For couples experiencing unexplained subfertility (where some unknown factor is delaying conception but where conception is still technically possible) there are even more stringent conditions on access to IVF in this area. For example, if a couple does manage to conceive and the woman has a miscarriage, the couple has to wait another three years of unexplained subfertility from the date of the miscarriage to be eligible for IVF on the NHS.

Some requirements/restrictions, such as maternal age and AMH levels, might be justified on the basis that some prospective IVF patients simply have a too-small likelihood of success to make the use of state funds worthwhile. Whilst birth rates have improved significantly since the development of IVF, this treatment remains an option offering relatively narrow chances of success – the HFEA's data for 2018 shows that the average birth rate (per embryo transferred to the patient) was 23 per cent, with rates below 5 per cent for patients over the age of forty-three. However, other conditions for access to state-funded IVF treatment can be criticised on social justice grounds. The requirement that a couple 'prove' themselves infertile by means of two years of unprotected sexual intercourse is naturally applicable only to heterosexual couples. Until recently, lesbian couples had to prove their eligibility through expensive private donor insemination treatment, even though natural conception as a couple is clearly not feasible. In addition, their desire (biological parenthood) is the same as that of the heterosexual couple, and their need (assistance to achieve this goal due to a fertility impediment) is likewise the same.[15] As Murphy points out, 'same-sex couples will be like everyone else in being interested in the rewards culture and the law confer on genetically related children. Genetically related children still amount to a cultural gold standard as an aspirational ideal' (2018: 823). He describes this standard as a 'social good' to which all should be offered the same level of access.

This might lead us to question what the social good of IVF is that justifies state provision or subsidies. Does the state provide IVF because it is a form of healthcare? Is it because it enables genetic parenthood? Is it because it enables parenthood per se? Is it because it allows someone to reproduce with their chosen partner? Depending on the answers we come to, we might criticise the exclusion of those who have had children with previous partners, those who have adopted children and those who have reversed earlier sterilizations. If Andy and Beth want to have children together, it seems terribly unfair to Beth to be denied the opportunity to (a) become a biological parent, and (b) become a biological parent with her chosen partner, just because Andy had a child with his ex-wife. Likewise, parents who aim to have both adopted children and genetic children are excluded from NHS IVF provision if they adopt first, but will not be excluded if they plan to adopt later on.[16]

Choosing children

One important area in which the HFEA exercises control regards the distinction between technologies allowing people to have *some* child (i.e. with the same degree of chance as natural conception), and technologies that allow people some small degree of choice about *which* child to have. IVF may allow a couple to conceive, but PGD gives couples greater control over which embryos are implanted.[17] IVF routinely involves the attempt to fertilise, say, ten eggs at one go, on the assumption that two or three will fail. Of those, we could choose one at random to implant (and if the first implantation fails we could choose a second, again at random.) Alternatively, we could distinguish among the seven fertilised embryos on the basis of some criterion. This is where PGD would enter the picture. PGD involves the removal of a small handful of cells from the embryo, and the testing for certain genetic markers. This is especially relevant when one of the parents is a known carrier of a serious genetic disease. In such a way, the genetic marker for, e.g. Duchenne Muscular Dystrophy (DMD) can be identified and that embryo discarded. There are four main sets of ethical questions arising in relation to PGD:

(i) Whether to select against serious genetic conditions (such as DMD);

(ii) Whether to select against less serious genetic conditions (which are easily treatable or operable) such as diabetes or cleft lip;

(iii) Whether to select for a certain sex, unrelated to genetic disease; and

(iv) Whether to select for certain desirable inherited traits such as intelligence or height, assuming that this is enabled by future technological developments.

The first two questions are already familiar from the debates surrounding abortion. Many countries allow late-term abortion in the case of serious disability or foetal malformation, which we might take as a moral parallel to (i). However, both legal regulations of and social attitudes towards abortion in the case of less serious abnormalities or disabilities – paralleling (ii) – are stricter, with many taking far less sympathetic view of those who choose to terminate in such cases. In the UK, the abortion of a foetus with cleft palate (crucially, *after* the 24-week cut-off point, after which abortion due to foetal abnormality is only allowed in the case of 'serious handicap') led to an (unsuccessful) demand for judicial review (Dobson 2003). With regard to (iii), it's widely accepted that sex is not an ethically sound basis either for abortion or PGD, except for sex-linked serious genetic disorders.[18] Question (iv) brings us to the debate surrounding procreative beneficence, which we discussed in Chapter 2. As we move from (i) to (iv), we move away from parenthood of a given child as something given over entirely to chance, and more towards a state of affairs in which parents can choose more of their child's characteristics.

To what extent should the *state* control this? The UK currently allows PGD only in order to screen for, or avoid passing down, specific (pre-approved) diseases and genetic conditions. But as we saw in Chapter 2, some views of parental love and duty imply that ARTs that allow parents to select *which* children to produce are inconsistent with the kind of unconditional openness and acceptance we expect from prospective parents. Worries about parents being motivated by forms of perfectionism that conflict with this normative standard of parental love (and concerns about 'designer babies', spurred on by sci-fi) partly underpin regulations that restrict access to these ARTs to those with medical reasons for using them. But does reproductive liberty mean that everyone should have the same entitlement and access to any form of assisted reproduction?

In principle, anybody *can* use private IVF if they're willing to pay for it. But private clinics are just as bound by HFEA regulations as NHS clinics, and so if the state restricts use of a particular technology (e.g. using a 'medical necessity' condition), this applies across the board (unless one is willing and able to travel abroad to use an IVF clinic governed by much looser regulation). However, rules that restrict access to fertility treatments to those for whom such treatment is medically indicated have themselves been subject to critique and debate. For example: mitochondrial DNA (mtDNA) donation is currently allowed in the UK only where needed to avoid passing on a specific disease carried in the intended mother's mtDNA.[19] This constraint is justified on the basis of a perceived distinction between *therapeutic* and *non-therapeutic* uses of this technology, and the belief that only the former is justified. A lesbian couple seeking to use mtDNA donation to create a child to whom both mothers have a genetic link would be barred from doing so. But Cavaliere and Palacios-González (2018) argue that mtDNA donation is not therapeutic: it doesn't cure anyone of a disease. Rather, it allows us to *prevent* an individual with the disease coming into existence, and to *choose to create* an individual without that disease instead. The hypothetical lesbian couple would have the same goal as the straight couple where the female partner has (or is carrying) a mitochondrial disease: 'both types of uses could be considered "eugenic", rather than "therapeutic", in the sense that they aim to bring a particular kind of individual into existence: healthy people who are genetically related to their parents' (2018: 840). Considerations of equality therefore suggest (according to Cavaliere and Palacios-González) that we should allow access to this ART to all, if we allow access to anyone.

Desperation for children

We have been assuming that some couples (or individuals) want children, and are distressed enough by natural failure that they are willing to undergo the effort, expense and anxiety associated with repeated assisted reproduction. In most parts of the UK, the NHS offers three cycles of IVF, and it might be possible to try these without much emotional investment. But some couples and single women (the latter using IVF with donor sperm) are unsuccessful after these three cycles and want to try again, in which case they have to go private; others do not fulfil the NHS conditions and go private directly, or they live in a jurisdiction (like Ireland) that does not provide any free IVF; and others may be desperate enough to pay a lot more money for experimental treatments in other countries. How do we respond to such cases?

As we have seen, one response may be to tell them that they have a moral duty to adopt, given the sheer numbers of looked-after children in need of parents, both in the UK and over the world. They should accept their own biological limitation, give up on the genetic link and accept that they can have a perfectly good family through adoption. Nevertheless, the couple or the single woman might complain (with some justification) about the hurdles to adoption, or they might just insist they want their 'own' genetic child at all costs. At that point the liberal has to say: 'OK, it's your money, your free time, your emotional investment, you spend it as you please, as long as you don't harm anyone.' But beyond that liberal reaction, there are two deeper responses to these more extreme cases that pull in different directions.

One response is to recognise the depth of such people's distress, as *proven* by their willingness to spend so much effort and money on such a low chance of success. One can only sympathise deeply with such distress. It seems clear that people in this situation do not want their own children for an independent 'purpose' – e.g. someone to whom to pass on the farm. Instead, the craving for children is something very deep and very primitive, beyond reason.

The opposite response is to say: 'even if it's their own money, this is an insane way to spend so much of it, compared to all the other ways to spend it.' In saying this one does not necessarily blame them for spending the money on themselves as opposed to giving it to charity – but rather, there must be better ways to spend it on themselves, or on their friends. As before, the concern here is that some couples/individuals have internalised unhealthy norms of what 'proper' families should look like (especially in the media) and feel pressured (more or less overtly, more or less intentionally) into parenthood, by their own parents, by peers, by work colleagues.[20] We would therefore support the normalization of voluntary childlessness, and, in the case of couples or women who are ambivalent about parenthood, we would support a fatalistic view of infertility that would lead them to refrain earlier from IVF, in order to steer their lives into other projects. The worst thing is to think in terms of a 'duty' to have children, the related thought that one has 'failed' as a couple or as a woman without children, and their concern that they will be seen as 'selfish' for being childless.[21]

Surrogacy

Elizabeth and William long to have a child, but whilst they are both fertile, Elizabeth suffers from multiple sclerosis, making pregnancy a serious potential threat to her health. The couple pay Mary Beth $10,000 to conceive a child using Mary Beth's own egg and William's inseminated sperm, with the agreement that Mary Beth will give that child up to them at birth.

The idea underpinning this arrangement is not that William and Mary Beth are the parents, or that Mary Beth is giving her child to the couple to adopt. Rather, the idea is that Mary Beth is a 'surrogate' standing in for Elizabeth and would thus be giving birth to *Elizabeth and William's child*. Mary Beth would be doing no more than providing a service, in exchange for money. The word 'surrogate' denotes a person deputizing someone else in a particular role. It's synonymous with 'substitute', 'proxy', 'stand-in' and other similar terms. In the reproductive context, a surrogate mother is understood as standing in for, or substituting for, part of the maternal role.[22] But what does it mean to stand in for someone else? For some person *x* to be a substitute or stand-in for another person *y*, it is a matter of common sense that the role in question belongs to *y* originally. It's not a matter of sharing the role, or one person taking over from another. So, for Mary Beth to be a *surrogate* mother, it follows that Elizabeth must have independent grounds for being the *original* or *true* mother of the child. In this case Elizabeth did not supply an egg, and so cannot claim a genetic link to the child. However, she and her husband launched a process, resulting in a child, such that without their launch that child would not have come into being; in that sense they are the *causal originators* of the child, as if they had brought about its existence through sexual intercourse.

Let's consider an analogy: substitute teachers are those who stand in for permanent staff when, for example, they take sick leave. If I ordinarily teach Maths, but Ms Smith covers my classes whilst I have the flu, it makes sense to describe her as substituting in for me. Someone who visits the school may ask 'Who is the Maths teacher at this school?' and it would be reasonable to answer that I am, I have a permanent contract with the school, but that Ms Smith is standing in for me. If, on the other hand, Ms Smith teaches Maths at a school for one academic year and I am then hired to teach Maths for the next academic year, neither of us is standing in for the other: it is simply the case that Ms Smith *was* the Maths teacher, and now *I* am the Maths teacher. This is analogous to the transfer of parental status in adoption: neither set of parents is standing in for the other. Rather, we view adoptive parents as taking over this role from the birth parents of the child.

So, for it to make sense to say that the woman who gives birth to a child is a *surrogate*, we must show that there is someone else who already has a claim to 'true' parental status. Common descriptions of surrogacy certainly imply that, and this idea plays an important role in defence of surrogacy as a practice. It could be argued (and has been, by many opponents) that commercial surrogacy is morally wrong in that it amounts to baby selling. And indeed, with a narrow enough description of the events, there will be a moment where a child is handed over in exchange for an agreed sum. This argument has pushed many jurisdictions (including the UK and all EU member states) to prohibit commercial surrogacy.

However, defenders of the practice such as John Lawrence Hill argue that commercial surrogacy cannot be considered a form of baby selling because the baby is not the surrogate mother's to sell. She is paid for the service of gestation, and not for the child; and the intending parents cannot be 'guilty of buying their own baby' (Hill 1991: 356). Similarly, Barbara Hall claims that the surrogate mother 'use[s] her body to give birth to someone else's baby' (1985: 423). The analogy is with craftsmanship: the surrogate is provided with the design and with an advance payment, and she builds the furniture according to that design. The furniture is already paid for, and it belongs to the client from the start, regardless of whether the craftsman becomes fond of the furniture during its assembly.

There are two key ideas at play here: for birth mother Mary Beth to be a genuine *stand-in* for intending parents Elizabeth and William, it isn't enough to show that Elizabeth and William are parents in their own right. We must also show that Mary Beth is not *also* a parent in her own right. It seems clear that only if both of these conditions are met can we say that she really gives birth to 'someone else's baby'. But then the question is: what makes this baby *my baby*?

In the case described here – the infamous 1988 'Baby M' case – the 'surrogate' mother, Mary Beth Whitehead, gave birth to 'M' but then changed her mind about giving up the child, leading to a kidnapping, a protracted custody battle and media furore. Whilst the judge presiding over this case ruled that the surrogacy contract wasn't valid, he nonetheless recognised the paternity of William Stern (the 'commissioning father'), and decided that it was in the best interests of 'Baby M' to be raised by the Sterns, but with Mary Beth having visitation rights on the basis of her being M's *genetic* mother. Since that case, debates have continued across the globe over whether surrogacy agreements should be allowed at all; allowed and legally enforced; allowed across borders or only domestically; allowed in commercial or in expenses-only form, etc.

Debates over surrogacy

Some of the most vociferous objections to *and* defences of surrogacy have been made by appeal to feminist principles. Those critical of surrogacy have argued that the very idea of surrogacy reduces women to living incubators, denigrating the unique maternal-foetal relationship whilst inflating the importance of genetic parenthood (especially paternity). Commercial surrogacy in particular allows vulnerable women to be commodified and exploited by individuals and couples in more privileged economic positions. Not only is the surrogate objectified, but it constitutes the most intimate possible invasion and use of the female body. Moreover, it is not ordinary work for the simple reason that the worker cannot get away from the workplace, not even at night. A surrogate mother cannot detach the foetus for a couple of hours to go to the pub after work – her 'workday' is nine months long. For some, like Kajsa Ekis Ekman, even altruistic surrogacy is objectionable, because it reinforces gendered expectations of generosity and self-sacrifice as intrinsic and normal parts of female 'nature' (2013: 181–3). Some feminist arguments against surrogacy have also objected to the practice as a way in which wealthier women have been able to outsource gendered labour. Here, surrogacy is framed as a way in which privileged women can 'escape' the roles pushed onto them by patriarchal social norms, without doing anything to fight those norms, by simply passing those roles onto other women. Like the outsourcing of housework and childcare to poorer women (a debate we discussed in Chapter 3), surrogacy provides an individualistic solution to a systemic problem – but a solution only available to the upper classes.

On the other hand, liberal feminists would argue that we should not be telling women what to do and not to do – as long as there is no coercion or deception, then the freedom of association and freedom of contract are the best ways to respect women as autonomous adults. The prohibition of surrogacy effectively denies women bodily autonomy, reinforces biological essentialism by equating pregnancy and childbirth with the social role of mother, and (in the case of commercial surrogacy) unjustly prevents women from using their bodily capacities to choose to support themselves and their families. They might argue that yes, perhaps it is more exploitative – and potentially more dangerous – than housework and childcare, but, in those areas where commercial surrogacy is legal, it has turned out to be a sufficiently attractive option for low-income women if the price is right. Whilst surrogacy may, of course, present physiological and emotional risks for the pregnant woman, the liberal feminist argument defends a woman's individual choice to make her own risk-benefit calculations. To make an exception for surrogacy, when we do not prohibit other consented risky activities, would present a particularly sexist form of paternalism. Sophie Lewis criticises the 'moralizing' narratives employed in discussions of both surrogacy and prostitution: 'There is fretting about what "these technologies" will do to "the children", excess villainization of bioengineers, and hefty amounts of pity toward the impoverished girls "selling themselves"' (2019: 42).

The debate over payment for surrogacy occupies a lot of the 'centre ground' between these opposing sides. Many of those who want to defend women's freedom to do as they like with their bodies still balk at the idea of bringing money into the mix, since this raises difficult (and potentially uncomfortable) questions about what exactly this money is paying for. Is the woman's body being paid for, or her labour or the child herself? As Elizabeth Anderson points out, 'the prospect of reducing children to consumer durables and women to baby factories surely inspires revulsion' (1990: 71). This concern underpins one of the key differences between different states' approaches to surrogacy (after prohibiting or allowing surrogacy at all). Of those that *do* allow surrogacy, the majority of countries allow only 'altruistic' arrangements: any money that changes hands must be limited to 'reasonable compensation' for expenses the surrogate mother incurs as a result of pregnancy and childbirth, such as lost wages, doctor's appointments or maternity clothes.[23] As a result, the few countries that allow commercial surrogacy – such as the United States, Ukraine, Russia and (until 2022) India – are popular destinations for 'reproductive tourism'.

Some philosophers have argued that surrogacy is unethical regardless of whether it is paid or unpaid, and for the same reasons as private adoption. These views may be rooted in a particular view of parental rights or of parent-child relationships, or in a belief that commodification can happen even without the exchange of money incentives. Donna Dickenson notably argues that a child is commodified by being given away as a gift just as much as when it is given up in exchange for a surrogacy payment (2017: 77). The language of 'gift-giving' and 'generosity' so prevalent in the surrogacy context (including in the sphere of commercial surrogacy) implies that the child's birth parents – and particularly, the birth mother – have a right to dispose with that child at will in the same way as other commodities.

Anca Gheaus takes a slightly different approach in her objection to both private adoption and surrogacy, though arriving at the same conclusion as Dickenson. Gheaus sees parental rights as *privileges* to care for a child: parents' rights to control and custody are grounded in the fact that it's in the child's best interests, contingently, for them rather than someone else to have those rights. However, such privileges cannot then be sold or gifted to others. They can only be transferred where it would be in the child's best interests, and *because* of those best interests (Gheaus and Straehle 2024). This argument goes further than the view (shared by those who support altruistic surrogacy, but not commercial surrogacy) that children should not be bought and sold. It implies that the only justification for a gestational mother surrendering her child to the care of others is that child's best interests. Private arrangements involving the handover of the future child would introduce the interests of adults (the birth parents and the hopeful adoptive parents) into the mix, and so the gestational mother should only be allowed to give the child up to a state adoption agency acting directly in the child's interests.[24] Supporters of altruistic surrogacy might respond by arguing that at least intra-family arrangements (e.g. a woman acting as a surrogate for her sister) should be permissible. First, whilst this would involve the private transfer of a child, it would not be to strangers – the child would remain within the family. In such a case, the surrogate mother would be in an excellent position to judge the prospective parents' suitability, having known at least one of them for most of her life; and more than likely the surrogate would remain in the child's life. Second, it would presumably be in the child's best interests for such an arrangement to be approved by the court, rather than risking the family schism resulting from a denied application (or worse, the re-allocation of the child to prospective adopters outside the family).

In answer to the first objection, Gheaus and Dickenson (and others sympathetic to their view) might argue that moral rules grounded in the child's rights, dignity and interests will be constant, regardless of the identity of the intending parents. If a child is commodified by being given as a gift, then I commodify a child whether I give her to my sister or to a couple I've never met. We have to note a crucial distinction here, however. It may well be that X is the best solution to situation Y, but it doesn't follow that one is entitled to bring about situation Y as part of a plan to achieve X. In the light of the relevant family situation, the expectations of the gestational mother, and the likely alternatives (including entry into the state adoption and fostering system), the surrogate-born child's interests *post facto* will usually justify a court giving their approval for the intended custody transfer. But if children's interests *in general* are undermined by private transfer, it may still be impermissible to make that kind of plan to begin with.

Surrogacy, law and contracts

What happens when different states disagree with one another about surrogacy? This is not an issue that arises for parents who use domestic surrogacy arrangements, but those who want to use a surrogate mother in another country may run into a sticky situation if there's a conflict between the two relevant sets of laws. This was the problem in the case of the Balaz twins: children caught between the differing legal approaches to surrogacy of Germany and India. All surrogacy is banned in Germany, and the country does not acknowledge legal parenthood of children born to its citizens through surrogacy abroad (even if those citizens are the genetic parents of the children). Hospital records showed that the surrogate mother was the birth mother of the twins, but the Anand Municipal Registrar recorded the commissioning mother as their mother. Germany rejected the birth certificates as a basis for filiation of the twins, and recognised the surrogate mother and her husband as the twins' legal parents, making the twins (according to German law) eligible for Indian, and not German, citizenship (Ergas 2013: 128).

How do we address this kind of problem? On the one hand, we ordinarily expect states to recognise relationships legally established beyond their own borders. For example, even if a country does not allow same-sex couples to adopt children, they would have to recognise the legal parenthood of a same-sex couple from another country visiting with their adopted children. On the other hand, there is something dubious about insisting that a state accommodate acts that are illegal in their country as long as their citizens hop across the border to commit them. Indeed, we would probably think that a state that did so was hypocritically outsourcing ethical issues to other countries. The case of the Balaz twins was eventually resolved when the commissioning parents adopted the twins in Germany, according to German adoption law (Ergas 2013: 131). This might seem unfair to the commissioning parents – particularly to the genetic father, who had to adopt his own progeny – but might at least be considered more consistent than the approach of countries that recognise surrogacy contracts made abroad whilst banning them on their own soil.

There are many countries where surrogacy is either illegal or not legally recognised. In those countries, *de facto* surrogacy arrangements may still take place, but they have to be processed differently (and sometimes quite carefully, in order to avoid potential prosecution). For example, they may have to be legally processed as an adoption agreement, or as a custody matter between unmarried biological parents. Or a couple may come to an informal agreement with a surrogate mother in which she conceives a child using her own egg and the commissioning father's sperm, using at-home artificial insemination. When the child is born, she can declare that the commissioning father is the genetic father and have his name placed on the birth certificate, and then request that her own parental rights and responsibilities be terminated, leaving him with full custody. His partner or spouse can then petition to adopt the child as a step-parent.[25]

In the UK, altruistic surrogacy agreements are both permitted and recognised, with an institutional system in place to process these agreements. Whilst the child's birth mother is still the legal parent by 'default' (and her spouse/civil partner likewise, if relevant), she can sign over those rights and responsibilities to the commissioning parents six weeks after the birth, if a court approves the commissioning parents' application for a parental order. However, surrogacy agreements are not legally *enforceable*. That means that if either party changes their mind about the arrangement, current law states that parental responsibility stays with the gestational mother. That is, the system reverts to the 'default position' by which legal parenthood is assigned: by reference to the fact of birth to a particular woman.[26]

Let's consider a surrogacy break-down like that in the 'Baby M' case we described above, where the gestational mother does not want to give up the child to the commissioning parents after birth.[27] Should the surrogacy contract be enforced? And what does enforcement mean? As Debra Satz notes, in most ordinary contracts to provide a service, if the service provider reneges on the contract, the other party can demand compensation, but they can't demand 'specific performance' (1992: 126). For example: If I hire you to come and replace my windows, and you then decline to do so, a judge might approve my demand for payment for breach of contract, but the judge won't force you to come and do the windows. Applying this norm in enforcement of surrogacy contracts would mean that the surrogate mother who reneges on the contract might have to pay monetary compensation – returning all payments to date, in addition to a contractually specified fine – to the disappointed commissioning parents. She would then, however, be able to terminate the pregnancy or bring the child to term and keep custody, or give it up for adoption. But usually, debates over enforcement of surrogacy contracts depart from this norm; they are precisely about whether the original agreement about *custody* should be enforced.

Richard Epstein argues in favour of full enforcement on the grounds that the 'commodity' in question is special. Specific performance is 'unnecessary in those cases where the contract in question calls for the sale of a fungible commodity that can be covered in the market' (1995: 2337). For example: I can find someone else to replace my windows. But in the case of surrogacy, the service or product is something far more unique, that the market can't just step in to replace. For one thing, the child is still out there, somewhere. For the surrogate mother to keep and raise the child on her own (or with her partner), 'the [commissioning] father would still be required to abandon all parental rights, and to sever all connections with his own biological child' (2337).

Of course, if the surrogate's husband or civil partner becomes the second legal parent by default, then the genetic commissioning father cannot be pursued for child support; but the issue with which Epstein is more particularly concerned here is the lack of connection to the biological child. Whilst we might agree that this consideration makes it harder to treat surrogacy contracts like any other kind of contract, we might also note that Epstein's argument can also be applied in the opposite direction: enforcing the surrogacy contract completely would likewise require the gestational mother to abandon all parental rights and sever connections with her own biological child, against her present will. (Remember that a 'biological' link between mother and child can be either genetic or gestational – but the point is that the surrogate might well bond closely with the child.) The problems connected with the enforcement debate have led some people, like George Harris, to conclude that we shouldn't allow commercial surrogacy contracts at all. Whilst giving up the possibility of having a genetically related child and adopting instead may be deeply disheartening for some couples, Harris argues that this is still less difficult than the potential struggles involved in surrogacy: 'too much is lost with surrogacy, and some of what is sought by it can be retained through adoption' (1992: 265).

7 Family history and fertility fraud: A case study

In May 2022, Netflix released a documentary entitled *Our Father* (directed by Lucie Jourdan), about fertility doctor Donald Cline in Indianapolis, US. Cline opened one of the first fertility clinics in Indianapolis in 1979. This was before IVF and before sperm freezing, so he was mainly offering artificial insemination with fresh donor sperm, as well as various drug therapies and other gynaecological interventions. Cline's clinic was successful, and he developed a good reputation; soon, other practitioners were recommending him to patients seeking fertility treatment.

Jacoba Ballard was born in 1980. She knew she was the product of donor sperm, but as an only child, was mainly curious about her half-siblings from the same donor. In 2014, she made use of the genetic testing company 23AndMe to discover seven half-siblings living nearby, and after further investigation, she eventually discovered that Cline was the father of all of them. Since then, she has been receiving an automatic notification with every new half-sibling. Cline had covertly used his own sperm to inseminate at least ninety-four women between 1979 and 1986.

The documentary raises many fascinating philosophical questions, and yet, given the target audience (and the primary intention to shock and thrill that target audience) the documentary does not delve beyond the surface of these questions. Our aim in this chapter is to do that. We use the scandal as a lens for a discussion of fertility fraud (a legal concept only recently created, due to cases like that of Cline) and its impact on family relationships and the individual's sense of self. Themes we've discussed in some of our previous chapters – especially the meaning of biology and the non-identity problem – play important roles in this case study. We do not defend Cline's deception or question the genuine harm he has caused; rather, we will enquire into the exact nature of the deception and the harm.[1]

The sources of identity

Perhaps the most distressing part of Cline's deception was the effect it had on some of the Siblings' sense of identity. Their testimony raises a number of wider issues about the nature of identity and the role of biology in it. Rather than revealing the moral significance of genetic ties *per se* for our sense of identity, their testimony demonstrates the importance of explanatory narratives in the way in which we build our personal identities and our family identities.

A useful place to start here is to segue back to David Velleman, whose provocative claims about the meanings of biology we discussed in Chapter 5. Velleman argues that biological ties are fundamental to the task of understanding oneself and understanding others; indeed, he suggests that they are fundamental to understanding works of popular culture. As a result of this, Velleman declares it immoral to deliberately seek the creation of a child using one or two anonymously donated gametes, for in such a situation it would be impossible for the resulting child to find out enough of 'where' she came from, and therefore where she belongs, thereby unacceptably increasing the risk of a distressingly unmoored identity. Sally Haslanger, we recall, accepts that the biological origin story can play a strong role in healthy identity formation; but equally, if not more important is the determinate *social* component of identity. According to Haslanger, it is perfectly possible for an adoptee to acquire, over time, a robust identity based on a sense of belonging to her adoptive parents (and their extended family relations), regardless of any biological connection. In the same way, a couple can raise a child conceived through anonymous donor gametes and *make* her their child.

With this debate between Haslanger and Velleman in mind, let us look at the case of Dianna Kiesler, the mother of Julie Harmon (Sibling #14). This case involved a clear deception: Kiesler explicitly wanted to be inseminated with her husband's sperm, but Cline discarded the husband's sample and used his own instead. Harmon's reaction to the news is striking: 'You go back to everything you've known about yourself. It just completely washes away your identity. And you really have no idea who you are anymore.'[2] We can appreciate her saying that in her first response to the news. But in making the documentary, she had plenty of time to think about it more, and to decide what sort of understanding she wanted to present. And we find this a bit perplexing. Does the news really wash *all* of her identity away? First, the most obvious question: what about that part of her identity grounded in the (fully biological, as well as social) relationship with her mother? Surely she has no doubt that she is her mother's daughter? Second, how does this revelation invalidate *any* of the social relationship between Harmon and the man who raised her, composed of unchangeable historical facts?

The documentary lingers over family album pictures. We can presume the pictures depict Harmon as a young girl, embraced by a man who was presumably her 'social' father. Surely that relationship was based on real love, care, shared values and activities, as manifest in the family album, *rather than* based in the biology. Some might think that Harmon's statement that her identity has been washed away by the news is a remarkably cruel thing to say about her social father. After all, it is not as if *he* has been revealed as any different to what he has always been: he is not a secret terrorist or adulterer, for example. We can assume that he has always been sincere and open in his assumed role of father.

In the end it is left to a different Sibling to reach a conclusion similar to this. Todd Foster was able to redescribe the situation in more promising terms:

> [Cline is] just DNA content. He gave us the biological blueprint for what we could become. But it's our experience, our lived environment, that's what made us. So those people who raised us, they are the ones who … he might have provided the blueprint but they built the building.[3]

Perhaps Harmon herself comes to recognise this: later in the documentary, she declares 'I may share half of his DNA but he [Cline] is not my father and he never will be.' This aside, when Kiesler (Harmon's mother) is interviewed, she describes telling her husband the news: 'We're just now finding out that Julie is not yours.' Of course, we can fill in the gaps and realise that what she means is 'Julie is not *genetically* yours.' But regardless of her genetic origin – that is, regardless of 'whose' she was in infancy – Harmon has surely *become* 'his' over their thirty-five years together, especially during the particularly intimate parent-child relationship of her formative years. If we ask 'Who is Julie Harmon?' the image that pops into our head is not the neonate just out of Kiesler's womb, where there *might* be questions about causal contributions, but *this 35-year-old woman,* and the sum of the events and relationships that contributed to her life since birth, as represented by the photo album.

Let us compare Harmon's reaction to that of her father. In response to the revelation, Kiesler tells us that her husband started crying, and said (of Cline), 'He's taken everything away from me.' What does this mean? Julie Harmon has not been taken away from him, nor have thirty-five years of shared activity together. And why think that it is *Cline* who has taken anything away from anybody? Presumably they have not had much to do with him in the last thirty-five years. In another context, Harmon's social father is described as follows: 'For her dad, Julie has always been special. When she was little, he braided her hair before school. And he's still really involved in her life, and her kids' lives.' One might see this as reinforcing the primacy of the social relationship over the genetic-causal origin story, and again, one would hope that, between the revelation and the making of documentary, he could have reached a position of *stipulating* that Harmon was and always had been his daughter.

Why, then, does Harmon's father respond in this way? We might be tempted to explain his thought process in two ways. The first has to do with the inappropriate language of property and possession; that he, as the presumed biological parent, thought he 'owned' Julie and now he finds out that she has been 'taken' from him. The second is the inappropriate language of macho achievement; that he had been the manly and virile depositor of the seed, and now he has been made a fool and a cuckold by another man. It surely does not need stressing that both these thoughts are essentially corrupt. Not only are they too closely linked to patriarchal domination and male insecurity (and all the damage wrought by both over the centuries), but they fail to acknowledge that the most appropriate relationship with one's child is a trusteeship, informed ultimately by the child's best interests (Herring 1999). However psychologically difficult misattributed paternity might be for some fathers, surely there is room for an ideal of the secure, loving father who is genuinely indifferent to the causal origins of the child, and content in the actual relationship with her.

This paternal ideal is already present, after all, in the ideal of unconditionally loving *whoever* comes out of the womb, regardless of their properties (Vehmas 2002; Asch and Wasserman 2005).

Both Harmon's reaction and her father's (not to mention the other Siblings and their families, who express similar feelings of shaken identity) are more understandable when we understand personal identity as an integrated narrative built originally on certain foundational beliefs. One of those beliefs was 'I am the product of these two people; many of my characteristics originated with them.' Harmon will likely not have thought too deeply about whether such a 'product' is biological or social or both. She may, during the course of her life, have come to understand many of her own traits and tendencies by reference to those of the people who raised her (with frequent reference to other close family members too). Socio-psychological data indicates that both adopted and donor-conceived children who are informed earlier about their origins are better-adjusted than those who find out later; this would provide empirical support for the importance of constructing this integrated narrative early on (Jadva et al. 2009; Ilioi et al. 2017). We can also observe this kind of narrative process in parental identity formation, in the strategies used by adoptive parents and parents of children resulting from assisted reproduction to affirm their connection to their child (Dorow 2006; Newman 2019; Tober 2019).

This view of the vague moral significance of biology sits somewhere between Velleman and Haslanger's accounts: biology can indeed be very important to identity formation, *as can* one's social relationships. However, the way in which we navigate the relationship between the two, and the ways in which we narratively construct our identity, relies on early possession of some foundational beliefs. This account explains why so many of the Siblings described experiencing the paternity revelations as a blow to their *whole* identity. Sibling #16, Alison Kramer, stated: 'To find out that the man I looked up to and emulated from the time I was small was not my biological father was crushing.' If we presuppose that her parent-child relationship and familial identity are made up of different component parts, of which one has been lost, we might consider this melodramatic (not to mention hurtful to her father). However, when we consider that she constructed and understood her identity as her father's daughter *through* the lens of (presumed) foundational biological relationship, her reaction is more intelligible.[4] The same can be said for both Harmon and her father: we may be perplexed about their responses, given everything that remains intact after the revelation, until we understand that one's entire integrated sense of self can be challenged if an early sense-making foundational component has been removed.

This brings us back to deception as the root of this particular harm caused by Cline. By leaving the Siblings and their families to navigate and construct their personal identities and relationships on a false foundation, he exposed them to the risk that these narratives would suddenly crumble in unforeseeable ways. Rebuilding is of course possible but takes time and care. We should not be quick to judge as "irrational" those whose original sense of self (or of their family relationships) is shaken when a central pillar of their story has suddenly been removed.

Regret and gratitude

Deborah Pierce was told by Cline that he was using the sperm of a medical student; instead he used his own. The result was Jacoba Ballard (Sibling #1). And we see Pierce's strong attachment to Ballard: 'she's my everything. I love that child more than life itself.' There is of course a question of what Pierce would have done if she had discovered Cline's deception whilst she was still pregnant – whether she would have not been grateful for *this* child then, to the point of aborting it. As it stands, though, there is an asymmetry here: the Pierce parents would probably have been just as grateful to have received *any* child, regardless of whether the sperm came from Mr. Pierce or from any of the several anonymous medical students available to Cline on the day of Mrs. Pierce's visit to his clinic. In contrast, Ballard cannot speculate about such counterfactuals. She and the other Siblings simply would not exist without Cline's actions. They also indicate (by talking about their love for their social parents, happy childhoods, etc.) that they are content with existence. However, Ballard and the other siblings also express their vehement condemnation of Cline's actions. Is there a contradiction here?

The case of the Siblings is not a standard non-identity case, since a significant harm that they experienced and for which they blamed Cline is the harm discussed in the last section; this harm was *not* identity-linked, and we can imagine possible worlds in which Cline revealed his actions shortly after conception or birth, allowing the affected families to integrate this knowledge into their sense of self and of their family relationships. It is worth observing here that most articulations of the non-identity problem focus on the individual whose existence hinges on the action considered to be wrong. However, the Siblings are clearly not the only ones who can claim that they were wronged; as we saw in the first section, the harm to their sense of self and of family identity is a harm to which both the Siblings and their parents were exposed. The parents' gratitude and their condemnation of Cline's actions can also coexist without as much apparent metaphysical conflict as that experienced by the Siblings. Nonetheless, the parents – and especially the mothers – of the Siblings were harmed in *further* ways at the time at which Cline carried out these procedures.

Clearly Cline did something wrong to his patients, but it's surprisingly hard to spell out the precise contours of that wrongness. First, recall that we are dealing with two kinds of case here: Kiesler thought Cline was using her husband's sperm when in fact he used his own; Pierce thought that Cline was using the sperm of an anonymous medical student when in fact he used his own. The former is clearly a straightforward case of deception, and of medical malpractice. But in the latter, we could say that Pierce was seeking, and consented to, artificial insemination by donor – and that's what she got.

It seems that Cline did not offer Pierce any other information about the (fictional) medical student, and Pierce did not seek any; nor did Cline offer to arrange a meeting with the medical student, nor did Pierce seek a meeting. All that Pierce could assume was that the medical student was evidently smart enough and healthy enough to get into medical school – so, it might seem, these are the only positive criteria that she could have asked for. (She may also have reasonably inferred that the medical student would be *young*. Although that would not normally make a difference to the quality of the sperm, it is clearly up to the client to set her terms.) Unbeknown to Pierce, Cline went into another room to 'get the sample', but came back with his own sperm, which he then injected into Pierce. It is straightforward that Cline lied about the origin of the donor sperm, and this is confirmed by the counterfactual: Pierce states explicitly in the documentary that had Cline offered to be the donor, she would certainly have declined. However, the fact that AID was sought and AID was provided was taken by Tim Delaney, Marion County Prosecutor as a reason not to bring charges. As he put it in the documentary, 'the jury is going to say "this woman consented to insemination. This woman wanted a child"' (Jourdan 2022).

For this second kind of case – that is, where a woman went to Cline seeking AID – we argue that the wrong of Cline's actions goes beyond the 'mere' lies about the identity of the donor. Rather, we want to make the further point that anonymity, a crucial aspect of the AID process sought, goes two ways. We can assume that Pierce wanted to have a donor whom she did not know, and who did not know her, and a donor who was not famous in the community.

In addition, Pierce also knew that the donor would have to masturbate into a cup; this piece of information could be ignored if the donor was unknown and the masturbation taking place elsewhere. If she had known that *this man*, Cline, was going to go into the room *next door* to masturbate, and that *he* was also going to inseminate her with his own sperm, that description approaches the thought of Cline injecting his sperm the 'natural' way, i.e. with donor, donation and insemination all part of a single action. As journalist Sarah Zhang puts it:

> But artificial insemination still requires an exchange of bodily fluids that can be procured only through sexual stimulation. (Consider: the stereotypical drawer of porn magazines at the fertility doctor's office.) To have your doctor masturbate in his office and then to have that same doctor sit between your legs, injecting his sperm inside you – the edifice separating the clinical and the sexual breaks down completely.[5]

Those who seek out donor sperm today routinely take measures to 'de-sexualise' the process. We can imagine that in the very earliest days of sperm donation and artificial insemination – recalling that this was a novel procedure provided by Cline's clinic – patients would likely have been even more concerned about the potential sexual connotations of AID. The expectation of two-way anonymity therefore has importance on multiple levels. The moral significance of this asymmetry in knowledge is made clear in a slightly different context by Sibling #61, who was actually treated by Cline as her gynaecologist. She was horrified to learn that he had carried out intimate examinations on her whilst knowing that she was his genetic daughter: 'I *don't want someone that is biologically related to me touching me in that way [....]* I didn't get to have that knowledge. He knew.'

So in Pierce's case we have three loci of consent against which to evaluate Cline's actions. The first invokes an explicit description, on which Pierce consented to insemination with sperm from a medical student. This was not the intervention carried out. The second invokes Pierce's reasonable inferences and presumptions – that the sperm was coming from a smart and healthy stranger, probably young, under the important condition of *bilateral anonymity* – and her putative consent under that inference was likewise seriously undermined. The third is the counter-factual, where Pierce states clearly that she would not have agreed to Cline doing what he did if he had offered explicitly – she would not consent *either* to Cline as mere donor (with the insemination carried out by someone else) *or* to the actual series of events that Cline performed *as the donor*.

Wrongful life

So, against concerns raised by the non-identity problem, both the Siblings and their parents can consistently condemn Cline's actions without regretting the Siblings' conception. But what about cases in which a child does wish she had never been born? Or when her parents claim to regret her birth?

'Wrongful life' lawsuits are suits brought by a child or on the child's behalf, or sometimes by the parents of a child, against medical practitioners involved in prenatal care. In a paradigmatic case, a child with severe congenital disabilities might sue a doctor for negligently failing to discover their condition during pregnancy. In most cases, early discovery wouldn't have enabled medical practitioners to *cure* that condition. Rather, their negligence is in failing to inform the mother of the foetus' condition, and thereby preventing the mother from choosing to abort the foetus. Typically, in Shiffrin's words, 'the child charges that he has been born into an unwanted or miserable life' (1999: 117). So the suit seems to involve the wish never to have been born. How coherent is that?

Such lawsuits have 'only mixed, mostly negative, success' (118). This, Shiffrin suggests, is because many people regard it as implausible to resent or regret one's identity-linked disability – and by extension, resent or regret one's existence – if one's life is overall tolerable. The paradoxes we outlined in our introduction of the non-identity problem (see Chapter 4) come together to undermine a claim that one's birth was harmful. To recap, the first paradox is that I cannot be harmed by something that was necessary for my existence; the second is that I cannot robustly condemn any act that was necessary for my existence, since to do so is implicitly to wish it hadn't happened.

However, Shiffrin argues that when a person suffers because of their disability or condition, this can be identified as a harm *even if* that person couldn't have existed without the condition. Addressing Joel Feinberg's argument – in which he compares wrongful life suits to prosecution of a rescuer for injuries caused in the process of saving a person's life – Shiffrin argues that harm and benefit are not calculable in a way that makes one cancel out the other. Even if you saved my life by giving me CPR, the ribs you had to break in the process nonetheless cause me great pain, and that is a harm itself requiring treatment. It would be unreasonable in most cases for me to demand that you, my rescuer, pay for that treatment; but the broken ribs are a harm nevertheless.

Furthermore, bestowing existence itself 'rescues' no-one from any specific harm. The broken ribs you cause whilst giving me CPR are a harm incurred in pursuit of rescue from an even greater harm. Non-existence isn't a harm we rescue children from by conceiving them. Even if life is a *benefit*, causing harm in the course of bestowing an un-asked-for benefit is (Shiffrin argues) far less justifiable than causing harm in the course of saving someone from a *greater* harm. For this reason, she continues, we can say that even identity-linked conditions are harms if they cause suffering. But further, we can reasonably hold parents and medical professionals liable for at least some of the associated costs if they made the decision to bring a child into the world, 'even in cases in which the life is worth living and in which those responsible for creating did not have, nor should they have had, special knowledge that the child's life would feature unusual or substantial burdens' (119).

Amos Shapira takes a similar approach, arguing that irresponsible or negligent treatment can be identified, and redress demanded, without having to claim to wish you had never been born. The right to redress is grounded in negligence that 'effected two simultaneous results: the child's actual birth and his or her inevitably handicapped condition. Though logically these two realities are unequivocally intertwined, a conceptual distinction can be made. The impaired child brings a suit for his or her handicapped condition, not for being brought into existence' (1998: 373). We can take this kind of split approach to regret and condemnation in other non-identity cases.

In closing, consider again the case of Julie Harmon, Sibling #14. Her parents clearly love her deeply, whilst still wishing that their family had not been subjected to Cline's fertility treatment. Their regret is not necessarily mutually exclusive with genuine love for their child and their gratitude that *this child,* Julie Harmon, came into the world. Logically, of course, this particular woman's existence is 'unequivocally intertwined' with her genetic father's crimes – she could not have been born from any other sperm. But one can regret the circumstances under which one's child is born without saying that one is logically barred from loving the child.

8 Marriage and commitment

Any book about the family has to talk about marriage. Most family relationships are unchosen; marriage is the big exception – and that choice is very interesting. And although 'starting a family' normally means having children, we don't see any problem in calling a childfree marriage a 'family'. Right away, however, we have to say that we are not 'pro' or 'anti-marriage': we tend to think that individuals can be left to make up their own mind about whether to marry in a church and/or marry in a registrar's office, or not marry at all, but live in an indefinite long-term relationship, whether cohabiting or not, whether with children or not. We can understand those who do not wish for a 'piece of paper' to legitimise their union. And as we mentioned in the Introduction, we will certainly not follow the social conservative agenda, to complain that marriage is 'under threat', to argue that children grow up best in a marriage, to argue against open marriages and same-sex marriages. What interests us more in this chapter is the idea of a formal public commitment to spend the rest of one's life with a single other person (of either sex). In principle, two people could still make a semi-formal public commitment in front of their families and friends, without any legal status, and without any implications for their sex life. With the proviso in mind, we will still use the word 'marriage' in this chapter as a shorthand.

As it is, fewer and fewer people in England and Wales are getting married.[1] The year 2018 saw the lowest numbers on record, with 20.1 marriages per 1000 unmarried men and 18.6 marriages per 1000 unmarried women. Along with this trend, those who do marry are leaving it later and later: the average age is thirty-one, compared with twenty-three in 1970.[2] For those who take this route, however, the law is pretty clear in its definition of marriage, and this is important because of the range of benefits offered to married couples (whether heterosexual and homosexual). We start with Claudia Card's (1996) argument that marriage should be a private affair, and the state should not be involved at all. One reason is that the state's involvement inevitably reinforces the oppressive norms of 'good wife' and 'good mother'. Next we ask – if the law does recognise marriage – whether it should paternalistically *insist* on a more robust contract between the parties, either in the form of what is known as a 'prenup', or something wider-ranging. In the third section, we look at the marital vow: from one point of view, it appears profoundly foolish or non-sensical, or both, to promise to love someone else for the rest of one's life. This paradoxical status is compounded when we ask whether someone can utter such an unconditional vow *a second time*.

The state's blessing

Claudia Card's (1996) account starts with a simple liberal position: if two people want to get 'married', and there is no coercion or deception, then let them. But, she asks, why should the state be involved? If they want to make a public moral commitment in front of their friends and family, then fine. If they want to make a public *religious* commitment, then fine. If they want to just keep going, day to day, year to year, and end up in some marriage-like state, fine. But why do they need the blessing of the state on top of that? Obviously the state would still have to be involved in protecting individuals from domestic abuse, as well as settling disputes about jointly owned property and jointly parented children in the event of separation: but there are enough rules about those situations to govern the process fairly even without the categories of 'marriage' and 'divorce'.[3] And why should only married couples have the tax advantages, pension advantages, inheritance advantages, health insurance advantages, etc.? The traditional answer to this is that the state offers them as incentives to form and remain in marriages, since stable long-term marriages are good for the participants, good for any children living with them and good for clear flows of family money across the generations. But if stability is the point, then it is not so much *marriage* that the state should be supporting, but all *long-term caring relationships*, whether sexual or not, whether cohabitational or not. The worry then would be about any definitions and conditions, including self-definitions: should two people be asked to register their caring relationship with the state in order to avail of its benefits?

This is an on-going theme in the work of philosophers like Jonathan Herring and Christine Overall, and it echoes the point we made about the definition of 'family' in the introduction to this book. We can take Card's scepticism further: surely the blessing of the state not only risks corrupting the love, but may also undermine one fiancé's confidence in the other's motivation? True love should be driven from within, not pulled from without, shouts the Romantic from the rooftops. However, the defender of marriage would say that embarking on a new legal status, launched by a serious ceremony before witnesses, focuses the mind and reinforces the *commitment*. The whole point of commitment is to bind oneself to stay with the other despite the future ebb and flow of capricious feelings and despite the ordinary stressors that will test the strongest of bonds. And the publicity of the commitment means that the witnesses are given the moral right to hold the parties to the commitment when the going gets tough. This is not yet an argument for the state's blessing, of course.[4]

However, the idea of a marital commitment (state-approved or not) can be challenged for being irrational or even meaningless. Imagine that Alex and Jamie want to make a public commitment to each other in front of their family and friends. They are in love, they want to live together, and they publicly promise to keep loving each other as long as they both shall live.[5] But of course over time, Alex and Jamie will change, just as their relationship will change. And the younger they are at the outset, the more they will *be* changed by life events, especially events relating to their careers or other identity-conferring memberships. If they are lucky, they will change *towards* each other, and their relationship will deepen. But there are so many contingencies and unforeseeables involved, and they may well change *away* from each other, without either being to blame. Indeed, it might even be hard to speak of Alex and Jamie *consenting* to the original marriage, because they cannot know what they are consenting to until they are a few years into it and they have discovered what their mutual love amounts to in practice: the sacrifices and demands each is prepared to make for the other, the apologies and excuses each expects from the other, and all the practical joint decisions required to run a single household and co-ordinate their activities. Only at this later point will their consent become sufficiently informed during any renegotiations, without being bound by the earlier declaration of commitment. Neither partner can know whether one of them will be prematurely crippled by serious illness, or whether one of them will lose the job in which they have invested so much, or whether one of them wants her sick widowed mother to come and live with them, or whether their child will have a disability (Herring 2014). It might be argued that they consent to marriage in full knowledge that these things are possible – hence the promises made 'for richer, for poorer, in sickness and in health, for better or for worse' – but just as the events are ultimately unpredictable, so is the *effect* of the events on each of them, and on their relationship.

We might even say that relationships are Darwinian: we don't know how 'fit' they are until they 'survive'. Only after a few years together could an impartial observer confirm, retrospectively, that Alex and Jamie *have actually been* committed to each other, which might improve any predictions the observer would be tempted to make about their future. According to this sceptical picture, the only point of the original commitment might be to help preserve good faith on both sides. It might end up being no more than a matter of personal preference: some people prefer to hear the words of commitment, while other people are not bothered by vague statements about 'seeing how things go'.[6]

Back to Claudia Card, who raises a concern with the particular history of the institution of marriage, and the public understandings and norms of that institutions, reinforced by representations in the cultural discourse, in literature and film, and in media discussions of celebrity marriages.[7] When the state approves the commitment through the public ceremony called 'marriage', then Alex and Jamie's marriage will necessarily slot into the traditional institution, whether they like it or not: the public meaning will affect how Alex and Jamie see each other within the marriage (e.g. what each believes they can reasonably expect from the other), as well as how their friends and family and strangers will come to see the pair. There is *some* room for Alex and Jamie to redefine or sabotage the norms in their own way, but this will cost effort and might strain their relationship or the relationships to others. In short: the public meaning of marriage can only *distort* the private interpersonal meaning of this couple's relationship.

As one trivial example that reveals so much, consider the norm of the bride wearing white to the wedding. This was originally a symbol of virginity, and so it can easily become problematic for (i) anyone who thinks that the couple's sexual life is nobody else's business; for (ii) a non-virgin who would see it as hypocritical; for (iii) a feminist who resists the traditional sexual double-standard and the reduction of a complicated personality to the adjectives of 'innocent' and 'pure'; or for (iv) someone who cannot afford a wedding dress, and wants instead a formal suit that she can re-use on future occasions. And yet the public representations of bridal fashion seem to have stuck firmly with the white. So although the state is not directly involved in much of the day-to-day life of the particular marriage, the traditional institution pervades the most intimate spaces. Since one of the main components of the traditional marriage was patriarchal management and control of women and their fertility, Card doubts whether the institution can ever evolve beyond that shadow.

Internalizing oppressive norms

Card's other concern with the state's formal recognition of heterosexual marriage is that it reinforces oppressive norms associated with the concepts of a 'good wife' and 'good mother'. We have spoken about such norms before, but it is worth a more detailed examination of the risk to which Card alludes.

Norms are best understood as standards of behaviour that we have to learn as children, both at home and at school. Any particular society will only hold together with sufficient behavioural norms internalised by a sufficient number of members. Most norms are harmless, many are useful. If you want to ask a question in class, you put your hand up: that's a norm that has to be learnt. Often there is something arbitrary about a norm – why do I put one hand up rather than two? – but parents and teachers generally don't need to explain these norms, they just need to get the kids (i) to follow them, and (ii) to *want* to follow them (to 'internalise' them), to feel them as 'natural', and to exert pressure on others to follow and internalise the norm.[8] Norms include basic moral behaviour ('promises have to be kept') and self-protective behaviour ('look both ways before crossing'), and in such cases it will be possible to explain the point of the norm by pointing at the advantages of mass compliance. Behaviour is a central component of norms, but many norms also involve ways of looking and noticing (e.g. to look for moving cars on the road), and appropriate ways of thinking and feeling (e.g. to fear moving cars). If a norm is successfully internalised, the child will not think twice about adjusting her perception, deliberation, feeling and behaviour automatically, and this will usually allow her to navigate more and more of the adult world. Norms include norms of reasonableness, pervading the classroom, the workplace, the law – and the family. When an authority figure rules that my behaviour was unreasonable, I may bristle, I may rebel, but such bristling and rebellion only make sense *as* bristling and rebellion against the background of shared norms of reasonableness. Most of the time I successfully (and sometimes grudgingly) aim for behaviour I reliably know will be perceived as reasonable in the eyes both of the authority figure and of my peers.

But here's the point of this section: some norms are oppressive and unfair. They arbitrarily restrict the behaviour of a certain group of people rather than another group. Once the subject internalises these norms, then she starts to adjust her perception, deliberation, feeling and behaviour automatically, and loses her awareness of the norm as oppressive – they are (and always have been) 'natural'. This is the essence of social conservatism. We do not want to suggest that social conservatism is always a bad motivation for preserving a norm: some norms are important to the long-term structure and meaning of my life, especially my life as lived in my family: recall Brighouse and Swift's central example of reading bedtime stories.

But gender-specific norms are almost always restrictive and arbitrary. Dress norms are an obvious example. High-heeled shoes are uncomfortable and expensive. And yet women buy the shoes with their own money, and wear them, and complain about how uncomfortable they are. When challenged, a woman will usually say 'oh, but I have to wear them to be taken seriously' or 'oh, but they look great' – and these are internalised norms in action.[9] Whilst there are flat formal shoes for women, there are fewer designs available, and even these are often far less functional than men's formal shoes, with less arch support and thinner soles – here, the ballet flat is a prime culprit.[10] One has to be careful about postulating internalised oppressive norms. We seem to be advancing a feminist argument designed to liberate women, and at the same time we seem to be *telling* women what not to wear (i.e. the high heels), i.e. based on our conviction that we know better. Far better, the liberal feminist would argue, to let an adult woman buy what she wants to buy and wear what she wants to wear, without speculation about mysterious and malevolent norms undermining her freedom. The mere fact of her consent means it cannot be oppressive, by definition. However, women's consumer choices are shaped not only by their own free preferences but also by the range of choices available to buy; as far as norms in favour of high heels are reproduced by the market rather than (only) by women's free choices, criticism of those norms does not constitute condemnation of individual women's decisions. In one sense dress norms are trivial; far more damaging are norms of sexual behaviour and the connotations that go with them, norms of self-sacrificing associated with motherhood, norms of deference in the presence of men, norms of 'natural' maternal urges.[11]

Marriage contracts

For now, let's accept state-sanctioned marriage as one option for people. There is now a question of whether the state should make it a bit *harder* to get married. At the moment it's pretty easy, and each couple does so at their own risk. And certainly, that chimes with a lot of other big and risky decisions that competent adults are entitled to make about how they spend their money, for example, or what career they choose. However, insofar as the state is interested in promoting stability in caring relationships, then the state might be entitled to stipulate conditions to encourage seriousness and deter frivolity. As things stand, allowing any couple to marry without conditions results in a UK divorce rate of one in three (and even higher in other

Western countries), with all the damage that divorces do to the participants and to the children, not to mention the money wasted on expensive lawyers.[12]

In Chapter 1 we discussed Hugh Lafollette's proposal for parenting licences or tests. One clear practical problem for any parent licensing regime is that many people will go ahead and have children despite failing the parenting test. But a marriage test would face no such obstacle. The state would simply make an offer: 'if you want the formal recognition of the state, if you want all the marital advantages that the state offers, then you have to fulfil some conditions.' Some of the non-state marriage options already require something like a test. The Catholic Church, for example, requires couples to undertake a formal marriage preparation course or 'Pre-Cana' class prior to marriage, although what this looks like in practice varies widely (we return to this, below).

What might be some sensible conditions? Two potential options: the first might be a higher *minimum age*. Until very recently, this was sixteen in the UK; in some other countries, it is still that low. A sixteen-year-old is not considered mature enough to vote, to drive, to drink or to refuse life-saving medical treatment; these limits undoubtedly contributed to the legal reform raising the minimum age for marriage to eighteen as of February 2023.[13] Considering how much of an impact on one's life a marriage will have, and given how much people change between the ages of sixteen and twenty, it would surely not be very controversial to push even further and stipulate twenty or twenty-one as the minimum, say. (This age would allow for the great majority of young people to finish their secondary schooling and start to make decisions about their adult life.) As we mentioned earlier, there is a real question about how informed any consent can be for the very young, since they cannot know what they are consenting *to*, and they cannot know much about themselves as consenters; a twenty-year-old would surely have a better idea than an eighteen-year-old.

The second easy condition would be to insist on an *engagement period* of at least one year. During this year the couple could get to know one another better, and could 'try out' the marriage with much less risk if things go badly. One could even insist that the engagement would have to involve cohabitation, in order to reveal how compatible the parties are in a single household, making joint decisions. This requirement would not change much for many people: the average length of an engagement in the UK is nearly two years, and over 90 per cent of people cohabit with their partner prior to marriage.[14]

Prenuptial contracts

Another condition for a state-approved marriage could be the voluntary negotiation and conclusion of a prenuptial contract (henceforth 'prenup') between the fiancés.[15] Normally these contracts are limited to financial matters, and they determine (i) the use of the assets brought to and acquired during the marriage (including questions about whether and how a joint account will be used), and more importantly, (ii) the division of assets upon eventual divorce. The state could also offer free guidance and mediation in the formulation of the prenup, although ultimately the content would be up to the individuals (although egregiously one-sided contracts would be invalidated). They would of course not fix all financial disputes; but at least the prenup would generate a framework for resolving disputes within the marriage a bit less acrimoniously, and would simplify the post-divorce settlement.

At the moment, prenups are most used by wealthy people to protect their pre-marital assets when they marry a much less wealthy person; without a prenup, the divorce settlement might come closer to a 50–50 split of the combined assets. Prenups sound like very sensible insurance. If one out of three British marriages end in divorce, those are pretty big odds. If I saw a cheap house advertised with a one in three chance of being flooded, I would be sure to buy appropriate insurance; and if I couldn't, then I would walk away from the purchase.

A prenup in the UK will not be automatically legally binding; following a landmark precedent in 2010, however, they should be upheld by a court if they meet qualifying criteria.[16] Like any contract, the prenup requires the informed consent of both parties, and it requires full and honest disclosure. But there are additional criteria that distinguish it from other contracts. For a start, both parties must have received legal advice before signing. Second, the poorer party has to have her 'needs' met upon divorce, although there will be a question of how these needs are quantified; in addition, the needs of any children must also be met upon divorce. Finally, the court ruling on the divorce settlement can ignore the prenup if they consider it 'unfair'. The insistence on legal advice and on fairness helps to prevent bullying from one party and gold-digging from the other.

There remains something deeply paradoxical about prenups, however, something that distinguishes them from house insurance. When I contemplate the purchase of a house, I can easily hold two thoughts in my head at the same time: I can say (i) 'Wow, what a great house, I would love to live there!' together with (ii) 'I wonder what the risk of flooding is. I'd better enquire about insurance … ' In contrast, it is not clear that I can go in front of a registrar and *sincerely* declare a life-long commitment to my beloved (that's the first thought) whilst patting the reassuring prenup document in my back pocket (that's the second thought). The whole point of a sincere, whole-hearted commitment to one's beloved is that there is *no* room for the thought that 'this might fail'. Yes, one in three marriages fail, but failure is what happens to 'other people, not to us'. A sincere *life-long* commitment means the follow-up thought that 'whatever challenges we face, we'll make it work'.[17] Now of course a commitment might be foolish in lots of ways, and the one making the commitment might be ignorant about both the other person and about herself. And spectators at the wedding may well have good reason to say, with a smirk, 'I wonder how long this will last'. But the spectators necessarily have a spectatorial perspective, whereas the fiancés have the participatory perspective. They are looking at different objects: *their* wedding versus *our* wedding.

Could there be room for a more 'mature' approach to commitment and to the risk of failure, an approach between the naïve whole-hearted commitment and the 'objective' insurance-minded approach? Imagine I go to the altar with the thought 'I am fully committed to this person'. But the emphasis here is on '*this* person'. I am aware that this person might change, perhaps in bad ways (leading to abuse or adultery), and perhaps through no fault of her own. I also have to accept that *I* might change, perhaps in bad ways, and perhaps through no fault of my own. As such the possible failure could be understood not as *us* – 'you and I, here and now' – failing, but as failure coming from the outside, turning us into different people, with a different marriage, no longer bound by this vow we make today. And so it would be very sensible to insure oneself against such failure, and this would not undermine the commitment to *this* person here and now.

A more robust marital contract

Despite the above reasons for scepticism, we support prenups in a spirit of launching a conversation about important marital principles, launching a framework for dispute resolution, where such a launch is guided by good faith, fairness and legal advice, and aiming towards an ideal of full transparency. Even if the prenup cannot predict all future challenges, it is better than entering a marriage with nothing more than half-articulated hopes and assumptions and fears. Yes, there is something paradoxical about making the life-long wedding vows with the prenup in the back pocket, some of the paradox is reduced by seeing the prenup as part of a larger planning discussion that starts long before the wedding.

Could the prenup be expanded to include other things? Call this expanded version a comprehensive *marital contract*. This would include financial matters, but also the following:

- Who will do the housework, how clean will the house be?
- Where will the married parties live?
- Do both parties want children, and how many?
- Are the parties ready for assisted reproduction or adoption?[18]
- Who will do how much childcare, and how much care work will be outsourced (insofar as one can predict one's future earnings)?
- What status do careers have in the lives of each party?
- How ready is one individual to move to another city or country for the sake of the other's career?
- What role will each fiancé's own family have in the couple's married life?

Again, the state would not insist on a particular content; but it could insist on (and pay for) both a financial adviser and a family therapist, say, who can ensure fair negotiations and a fair outcome. Of course the marital contract will fail to predict a lot of things about the particular marriage as it evolves. But at least it would have launched the conversation about these topics, providing both parties with the concepts and the language with which to continue the conversation, and would reinforce the importance of transparency and trust into the future.

Perhaps the initial negotiations would be *destructively* transparent, by revealing more of each party's character to the other, to the point of calling off the wedding – but surely that's all for the good. Otherwise, if the original marital contract negotiations were successful and the marriage is now underway, then the contract could be renegotiated (perhaps again in the semi-formal presence of a financial adviser and family therapist) in response to new events, or to the new difficulties of one party. And if the marriage collapses and divorce proceedings begin, how much easier for the parties to wrap up a conversation that has a clear document trail describing the relationship's evolution over time.

There is a precedent that could be consulted when setting this up: the Catholic marriage preparation course.[19] The Church is in a position to insist: *if* you want a full Catholic wedding, in a church, officiated by a priest, then you have to undergo this course. The idea of the course is not only to discuss the theological status of the marriage and parenthood within Catholic doctrine, but also to talk about what marriage and parenthood involve in *non*-theological terms. The structure and content of the course can vary greatly; it is obviously ironic if the local priest leads the course, without any experience of either marriage or parenthood. But there are Catholic organizations offering courses taught by people who are both spouses and parents and who will know what they are talking about; the course need not even offer very much religion. At any rate, the course does not involve a test at the end, and is usually non-directive, so those forced to take the course can only benefit. We suggest this would be a good initial model on which to build a secular marriage preparation course, leading to a marriage contract.

Divorce, disorientation and remarriage

Given our assumption that people want a state-sanctioned wedding and marriage, and given that people divorce and want a second wedding and marriage, there are some new philosophical questions that we can ask. Let's start with another story. A woman named Ruth, who works contentedly as a GP, gets married at the age of thirty to another doctor. At the (civil) wedding she makes the serious, sincere vow to 'love and cherish' her husband 'as long as we both shall live'. After seven years (Ruth is now thirty-seven), the marriage is not going well. (Neither of them wanted children, so there are no additional complications there.) After several weeks in marital counselling, they agree to divorce. In sober moments she accepts that there was no clear trigger for the breakdown; she can't find serious fault in her husband, and accepts that they were both absorbed in their jobs, and just drifted apart. They both move out of their rental flat, and Ruth sets up her new life on her own. Through her work she eventually meets another man. Soon they begin an intimate relationship, and eventually move in together. After a year of living together, they decide to get married, ten years after Ruth made her first marital vow.[20]

Assumptions: Ruth's first vow is serious and sincere. This was not a marriage of convenience, for money, for immigration purposes, for tax advantages, for revenge; nor was it a purely conventional next step. She thought long about it, and was willing to accept the full implications of the life-long vow that she made to her first fiancé. She was old enough to know what she wanted, what she expected and what she'd settle for in a relationship. She knew her fiancé well enough (he was not hiding any 'deal-breakers'). We then assume that her divorce was morally and legally permissible, and not a matter of petulance or selfishness or whim. And we assume her second relationship is not a matter of rebound, of loneliness or of calculation.[21]

Our first question here is: does Ruth's divorce *breach* her first marriage vow? Elizabeth Brake begins her article on this question by acknowledging (i) the 'hard line' position (2011: 25), that would straightforwardly condemn divorce, whether this is supported by a religious conception of divinely sanctioned marriage or not. Like Brake, we want to exclude the hard-liners from the discussion of Ruth. Brake also considers the opposite extreme, (ii) a utilitarian position according to which the value of keeping the promise can simply be outweighed by the likely continuation of either or both parties' unhappiness in the marriage (27). We agree with Brake that this undermines the whole point of making the commitment in the first place.

Brake's account is essentially deflationary: what seemed like a promise was not actually a promise, and so there is no promise to be broken by divorce. If it is not a promise, then what is it? Brake first considers and rejects the possibility of the wedding vow being a mere intention, but the wedding vow *feels* a lot stronger than a mere intention. We can have lots of intentions (desires, plans) about the future, but marriage is supposed to be in a qualitatively higher plane. An intention, even when declared in public, is missing the element of commitment and resolve. The second deflationary possibility, and the one ultimately supported by Brake, is to re-describe the wedding vow as an *attempted* promise. The attempt might be successful or it might not, and it is possible for the promissor to fail without thereby breaking an actual promise. To illustrate this, Brake imagines herself (29) promising to take a visitor to a famous landmark that, unbeknownst to Brake, has been demolished and replaced by a new building. Brake and the visitor arrive, and are disappointed – but Brake has not broken a promise, since all along it had been impossible to fulfil. In the same way, Brake would say, Ruth-at-30 attempts to make a promise which Ruth-at-37 discovers to be impossible to keep. Ruth-at-40 is therefore not re-making the same promise she broke earlier, but is making a renewed attempt, presumably in the sincere belief that she can succeed this time.

We would argue that Brake's landmark example does not quite work as an analogy for marriage. At the time of promising to visit the landmark, there was in fact no reality to which the promise could refer; the promise was impossible to fulfil from the moment of its utterance. In contrast, at the time of the wedding vow, the future of Ruth-at-30's marriage is essentially indeterminate. It is not as if Ruth-at-37 can declare that the marriage was doomed right from the start (though she might be tempted to project the seeds of failure onto early marital disagreements). At the start, there was a very real possibility that the marriage might succeed in the future, partly as a result of her own sustained efforts, and that possibility is enough to give real content to the promise.[22]

Brake's visit of the non-existent landmark raises one interesting question for our purposes. After Brake and her visitor discover the error, even if Brake does not want to call it a breach of promise, she still owes her visitor an apology and a hasty alternative plan, based on her possible *negligence* in not verifying the existence of the landmark before making the promise. (In these days of the internet, there is no excuse for not checking every detail of one's itinerary!) Even if it had not occurred to her to check, it *should have* occurred to her, and this negligence is enough to generate the residual obligation to apologise and re-organise. However, the question of possible negligence is much more complicated for the fiancés. Although there will be many easy cases of ignorant, impetuous and superficial nuptials in Las Vegas, most cases of serious marriages are based on trust, not knowledge. It is not as if we expect Ruth to carry out due diligence and background checks and financial analyses of her future husband, to seek references or to await the results of stress-testing.

Change of identity

So we still have the problem that Ruth-at-37 seems to be breaking a solemn promise. We have already hinted at one way to resolve this: by speaking of Ruth being transformed: Ruth-at-37 is a sufficiently different person than Ruth-at-30 to be released from the promise that bound Ruth-at-30.

To see how this might work, consider a more extreme transformation. Tatjana marries a young professional soldier. Soon after their wedding, he is sent on his first combat mission to a war zone. He returns three months later, and it becomes clear to her that he has seen and done terrible things; he is brutalised, paranoid and angry. He is violent towards her and towards their marital possessions, he refuses to seek care, and drowns his pain in alcohol. Here it would make sense for Tatjana to declare, 'He's not the man I married.' Obviously he is the same man (i) in occupying the same body that traced a single spatiotemporal path, (ii) in being psychologically linked to earlier stages of himself (he remembers getting married to her), and (iii) in being treated by the law as the same person (he still has to pay the instalments on the mortgage contract he signed before he left). But there will be a real dilemma for her about whether to stay with him in order to look after him – as she promised to do – or whether to divorce him because he ('this *new* person') is just too difficult to be around. If he really was unbearable and she did divorce him, few would blame her. And it would not be hugely implausible for Tatjana to declare that her original husband had effectively 'died' in combat, leaving her with no residual wedding-vow obligations to this 'usurper'. He's not a *full* usurper, of course, because he still fulfils the other criteria for identity. So she is only partly released from her wedding vow, and ought to experience a moral residue upon divorce.

Although Tatjana the army wife will find the process leading up to the divorce traumatic, there is an important sense in which she can blame others: either the army, or the husband himself for joining the army, or cruel fate; in so doing she can keep her own self together through the trauma. This divorce situation contrasts with Ruth, where we have described the marriage and divorce as more or less faultless, despite minor grievances on both sides. Given the lack of fault, given the fact that Ruth's husband has not died, has not been radically transformed and has not forfeited his right to her commitment by his own abusive behaviour, how can she leave him without a breach of promise?

The answer, we suggest, lies not in the transformation of the husband but in the transformation of *Ruth herself*. This is important to understand something of the changes that are essential to families and marriages. Ruth is transformed, we will argue, into a sufficiently different person by the disillusion, disappointment and disorientation of the divorce process. ('Disorientation' is Ami Harbin's (2016) key term, and we will explore it in the next section.[23]) Notice we refer to a process. Divorce is not to be understood as the final decision to give up, and to initiate the legal steps; it is a slow (and slow-*burning*) process over weeks and months, perhaps over a year or two, as the reality of the irreversible decline sets in. It is not about Ruth's discovery of detached impersonal facts about the world; for the facts are about her husband, about her relationship and about her, and the discovery affects the discoverer deeply.

Instead, it is better to see Ruth's marriage as comprising an extension of her very self. She understood herself not as living 'in' the marriage in the way she and her husband lived contingently in a particularly flat; for she and her husband could have always moved – and could imagine themselves moving – to a new flat whilst remaining very much married. Nor did she herself as merely 'with' (or 'next to') this man, just as she negotiated a path between so many other people at work or in public, people who might help or hinder her in carrying out her projects. She took seriously the idea of overlapping selves; she never knew where she ended and he began. So when the divorce process begins, months and perhaps years before the concrete legal steps, it is not an exaggeration to see this as much more than the breakdown of a favourite *project*, but as the partial breakdown of her *self*. Not the complete breakdown – she does not suffer a nervous collapse, since she has always had other identity-conferring commitments, especially her job. She has a strong sense of duty to serve her patients, not just in the abstract, but particular patients who will need her in the coming weeks. And throughout the divorce process she is deeply grateful for her patients, her job and her professional identity; she also has close friends and siblings, people who know her well, and on whom she relies to make sense of the changes as she undergoes them.[24]

Disorientation and re-orientation

So it would not be accurate to say Ruth has been transformed in the way that the soldier has been transformed by war. She does not have PTSD, she has not become paranoid or brutalised, her deepest values and her basic humanity are not under threat. But it is enough of a transformation to disorient her. For the moment, she can continue holding down her job, indeed she needs the job more than ever right now. The disorientation is more than emotional sadness, or the loss of self-confidence; it is the loss of a stable 'platform' from where to survey the value-imbued world and plan her course into its future. She knows how to go on in the context of her professional life, but she does not know how to go on in her life as a whole.

Here is a strong intuition that underpins our discussion. Under Ruth's disorientation, it would be churlish in the extreme to remind her of her unconditional wedding vow, let alone to reproach her for breaking it. This is not just because it would be hurtful or discourteous; rather, it is because it would be almost irrelevant; not just *psychologically* almost irrelevant, but *morally* almost irrelevant too. Ruth is so hollowed out by the process of divorce that she loses touch with her earlier self, the one who made the wedding vow, the one who wholeheartedly embraced her new husband and her new life. With her head full of memories of her seven-year married life, the actual wedding vow is the furthest thing from her mind; and during the process of recovery and reorientation after the divorce, it recedes even further.

In her book, Harbin herself mentions divorce only briefly, but we think she would accept it as a paradigm case of disorientation. Harbin defines disorientation thus: 'temporally extended, major life experiences that make it difficult for individuals to know how to go on. They involve feeling deeply out of place, unfamiliar, or not at home' (2016: 2–3). She coins the term 'resolvism' to denote a widespread assumption in philosophy and among the general public that the essentially untouched subject can merely *resolve* to make the best of a bad situation.[25] Importantly, however, Harbin is not just interested in disorientation but also in reorientation: 'it is especially when experiences of disorientation exceed one's will that they stand to be morally beneficial in the senses that interest me' (2016: 2–3). Divorce can of course lead some to find it so difficult to go on that they fall apart entirely. But Ruth, in our example here, manages to recover and to discover something about herself in the process, and uses this new knowledge to generate a new momentum into the future. At the very least, she has learned that she will survive (if we may be allowed to quote the great Gloria Gaynor), but in so doing she has to partly re-invent herself to accommodate the permanent scars.[26]

It is worth remarking that two spouses' disorientation and reorientation can take place *without* divorce, that is, within a continuing marriage. Typically disorienting events include the birth of a child, diverging political allegiances, different responses to infirmity and ageing, different career success, etc. L.A. Paul (2014: 71) discusses the transformation brought about by childbirth. Such a transformation might even be enough to release them from their wedding vow in the sense we are arguing, even if they do not in fact seek divorce. Perhaps they might seek to 'renew' their vows. However, there remains an obvious but fundamental difference between in-marriage transformation and post-marriage transformation; in the former the couple remains together: it will make sense to speak of the transformation of each individual and of the *relationship* itself. In contrast, Ruth is alone, and her first marriage is no more.

So to take stock: we asked whether divorce marked the breach of an unconditional promise. Our answer is that Ruth-at-37 has become enough of a different person through the process of divorce to attenuate the hold of that promise on her. The corollary is that once Ruth is single again, she rebuilds and reorients herself over the coming years, and this process further distances her from the Ruth-at-30 who made the wedding vow.[27]

The role of luck and contingency

We have spoken in several places in this book about the constructive and destructive role of brute luck in people's lives, and we have to do so here as well. When we say that a certain event was necessary for epistemic improvement, we have to be careful to distinguish between greater and lesser degrees of contingency in the process. If I am struck down by a reckless driver and end up in hospital, Harbin could describe this as a disorienting experience. If I then meet a handsome nurse in that hospital and embark on a deep and passionate relationship with him, then it is probably true that I would not have met him without the traffic accident; but the relationship between the accident and the encounter remains deeply contingent and unpredictable. Although the accident may have been necessary for the encounter and therefore for the relationship, there is no sense that the accident *prepared* me for the relationship with *this man*.

On the other hand, Ruth's divorce has disoriented her in just such a way that she is now better prepared for marriage than she was the first time round: not only in terms of self-discovery, but also in terms of what Harbin calls 'epistemic humility'. We can say that her particular divorce was necessary for her to become *the particular person* who was ready to embark on the particular second marriage.

To put it another way, in contemplating my passionate relationship with the nurse after the accident, I can be grateful for the accident that brought us together. But I am not grateful for the accident itself, which I found deeply painful. There may well have been a way of meeting the same nurse in a different venue; let's say I met him again – and would have met him again – a couple of weeks later at an evening language class. In that sense I could wish the accident had never occurred. In contrast, Ruth had to undergo the divorce in order to undergo the disorientation and then to undergo the particular reorientation that led her to a position where she was ready to marry the second man – there is no possible world where she could have undergone the beneficial self-development without the divorce. As such *she cannot coherently regret the divorce*, because the very post-divorce perspective from within which she would regret it has been deeply shaped by the divorce itself.[28]

The words 'have to' suggest a kind of necessity, perhaps a kind of *fate*. Normally the concept of fate is taken by philosophers to imply a radical determinism, and so is quickly rejected. But when it comes to interpreting the past under the mode of necessity, it is less fanciful. Robert Solomon (2003) offers the example of a long-married couple who describe their first encounter, subsequent acquaintance, courtship and wedding as 'fated'. Of course all these events were contingent, the couple admits; but within their later perspective, looking back at their own lives, all the events *have become* a necessary condition for them to become who they are at this point. This is not just a matter of the couple 'affirming' or 'endorsing' the past events, for that is merely epistemic – fate is something stronger. Nor is it a banal point about the fixity of the past, since the vast majority of past events (e.g. whether he was wearing the red jumper or not) were certainly not necessary for the couple to reach their present perspective.

In Ruth's own marriage, of course she was free, and of course there were many other contingencies, of course each day offered new future pathways – and in the small hours she has gone through those contingencies again and again: her marriage might have been saved if X had happened, or if her husband had done Y, if she had said Z, etc. But now that she has reached the second marriage, now that her perspective has been irreversibly altered by these events, now she can plausibly describe the divorce as fated.

The second wedding vow

It is now time to bring all the strands together to tackle our main question: on the assumption that Ruth made a *first* unconditional vow in full moral seriousness, can she make a *second* one, in full moral seriousness, and can she expect to be taken morally seriously by observers – and indeed by her second fiancé? At first glance we would be tempted to say: surely not. She tried to make such a promise before, and we all know how that ended. She should learn from her failure and the accompanying disorientation and be more careful in what she promises ('let's just take one day at a time, shall we?').

In saying that she *is* entitled to make the second unconditional vow, there are two components to our response, flowing from the above discussion. The first concerns the double transformation arising from the processes of disorientation and re-orientation. Not only is disoriented Ruth-at-37 distant enough from Ruth-at-30 to be partly released (with moral residue) from her younger self's unconditional vow, but the reoriented Ruth-at-40 is even further away, and so it is even less appropriate to compare the two vows with the intention of discrediting the second. Under the second component of our response, Ruth is not only *changed* by the disorientation and reorientation process, but *improved*. That is, she is even more entitled to make the unconditional vow this second time round. Again, in the words of *Guardian* columnist Zoe Williams, there is nothing as deadly serious as a second marriage, *precisely because* one knows the sceptics are circling: both those watching the ceremony and those in one's head (see footnote 20).

In speaking of improvement, however, we have to avoid two simplistic interpretations. The first interpretation would see Ruth-at-30's wedding as ignorant, naïve and frivolous; this reduces the moral weight of the vow, reduces the first marriage to a dress rehearsal and allows her more room for the 'real thing' the second time round. This interpretation is too easy, however, and Ruth is not tempted by it. Given what she remembers believing and wanting at the time, marrying the first man was still a good and serious decision at the time, she still thinks.

The second simplistic interpretation takes Ruth as simply older and wiser, and better at a lot of things. She is a better GP, for starters. She has learned more about medicine, about patients (including particular patients) and about the healthcare bureaucracy, and this makes her more effective and efficient, and reduces the frustration of unreasonable expectations. Like many projects, medicine allows for never-ending improvement throughout one's career, guided by various perfectionist ideals, provided one does not become jaded or exhausted or bitter with experience. Is it possible to interpret Ruth's re-marriage in this perfectionistic sense? Not entirely, for the important reason that her first and second husbands are unique individuals, and the intimate relationships with each are also unique, to the point of incomparability. If Ruth stays with the second husband more than seven years, all she will be able to say is that she lasted longer with him than with the first, but that should not imply that he was a better man, or she a better wife, or that they had a better relationship.

Instead of these simplistic interpretations, Ruth has improved in the sense of having learned from the disorientation and reorientation process following the divorce, she has reached a position of greater epistemic humility and authenticity in her decisions about long-term relationships, and she is fully prepared to make a sincerely unconditional vow to her new fiancé.

9 Domestic abuse

At first glance, there might appear to be little philosophically interesting or controversial to say about domestic abuse – after all, most of us would think it's simply straightforwardly wrong. There are nonetheless important debates to be considered in this sphere: how to define and understand domestic abuse, how to characterise precisely the moral harms of domestic abuse, the moral blameworthiness of victims of abuse who fail to protect their children, the role of the state in addressing and prosecuting domestic abuse, and the place of parental rights in the context of custody battles between victims and perpetrators of domestic abuse.

Many use the terms 'domestic abuse' and 'domestic violence' interchangeably; we are taking the latter as a sub-set of the former. 'Abuse' is a much broader phenomenon, and may not involve physical violence at all. In what follows we will speak about the broader phenomenon of abuse, before speaking more narrowly about violence, and then returning to the broader context.[1]

The nature of domestic abuse

The first word that needs defining here is 'domestic', since we claim that necessarily colours the *meaning* of the abuse. It is one thing to abuse (in whatever way) a stranger in a bar; it is quite another to abuse one's intimate partner in the accommodation I share with her.[2] Domestic abuse carries the superficial denigrating insult, but at a deeper level it also constitutes a betrayal of the relationship and of the victim's hopes invested in that relationship. Moreover, the abuse is domestic in taking place *at home*, in the space which the victim normally considers a sanctuary against the vicissitudes of the world. In both senses of 'domestic' then, the victim is much more vulnerable and will find it much more difficult to get away. Finally, domestic abuse is the dark side of the liberal respect for family autonomy and privacy; for abuse takes place in a physical and semantic space which outsiders – be they concerned friends or social workers – find difficult to understand, and feel unauthorised to enter.

Many feminist philosophers, who have argued that both (a) the setting and its social status (not just the home, but the family home, and the 'private' home), and (b) the character of the intimate relationship within which such abuse occurs, shape the nature of this abuse rather than just its location. Michelle Madden Dempsey argues that we must therefore understand domestic violence by distinguishing three crucial elements: violence, domesticity and patriarchy (2009: 103). These (as noted above) cannot simply be added together; the effect of their interdependence is also important for a full understanding of the phenomenon. The domestic setting has a particular legal and social status: it is 'a "private" sphere, where people's conduct is protected from external scrutiny' (110). But the symbolic significance of the home ('as a place of comfort, safety, and protection') further means that domestic violence creates 'a moral opposition between "home as danger" and "home as protection"' (110–11). The intimate relationship between members of a shared household is part of this element of domesticity, and likewise carries both important connotations of privacy and 'the special symbolism of physical affection' (112). Battering stands in direct symbolic opposition to the hug or kiss.

The second word that needs defining is 'abuse'. In terms of the substance of abuse, physical assault comes to mind first for most people when they hear the term. However, domestic abuse has many faces: it may also be emotional and psychological in nature, involving manipulation, gaslighting, threats, humiliation, social isolation, spying, stalking and restricting access to finances (sometimes called 'financial abuse'). But further, when we talk about domestic abuse, it is essentially a *pattern* of behaviour. We can and do sometimes describe specific words or actions as abusive, but domestic abuse itself is sustained and systematic, within the context of a family relationship. (Indeed, it might become so habitual as to lose any initial malevolence.) Prima facie, this creates a dilemma for criminal prosecution, since the criminal law focuses on single instances instead of longer-term patterns, and the latter is that much harder to prove. The UK finally took an important step towards recognizing the patterned nature of domestic abuse by passing the *Serious Crime Act* 2016, in which Section 76 defines 'Controlling or coercive behaviour in an intimate or family relationship'. (We will discuss coercive control erelong.) For the moment, we're going to focus on childless adult couples, just to keep things simpler – we'll bring children back into the picture later on.

As we've discussed earlier in this book, we generally see family members as responsible for our wellbeing in crucial ways. Parental duties and spousal duties go far beyond the obligation *not to harm*. Of course, as a member of my society, I have a clear duty not to actively harm others; but as a member of a family, I am also supposed to be loving, nurturing and protective. Intimate relationships involve a great deal of vulnerability and, as a result, necessitate a great deal of trust, especially in the setting of a shared home. Our partner, spouse, parents or others with whom we live intertwined lives would have the greatest opportunity to hurt us *if* they choose to do so. They usually have access to our possessions (including crucial items like keys, wallets, passports) and to the food we eat; they know where we sleep, our daily routines and our deepest fears and anxieties. We could not live with people in this kind of intimate closeness without trust. All this amplifies the moral seriousness of any betrayal of such trust, let alone a systematic and sustained betrayal.

A further key difference between domestic abuse against family members and abuse carried out against strangers or acquaintances is that the former taints the (ideally safe and comforting) space of the family home and constrain opportunities for the victim to escape, or just for processing and moving on from the experience.

The victim of violence or rape carried out by a stranger must live with a traumatizing memory, but the victim of domestic assault has to live with her assailant. In many cases of domestic abuse, the victim is in some way dependent (most often, financially) upon their abuser, adding another layer to the moral seriousness of the abuse: it is not just victimization, but exploitation of vulnerability and a breach of one's duty of care to the dependent party. Emotional/psychological abuse and coercive control also often involve efforts to isolate the victim from other friends and family, reinforcing their dependence and vulnerability.

Defining domestic violence

Coercive control and emotional abuse are forms of abuse that, due to their nature, appear almost exclusively in intimate relationships. We can imagine exceptions – a supervisor who bullies or manipulates a subordinate – but generally, only those closest to us can 'get under our skin' in the relevant way. Domestic violence, on the other hand, is more directly comparable to assault in other contexts.[3] No special manipulative skill is required to punch, kick or strangle; the same physical damage can be inflicted by a stranger or a spouse. In comparison to non-violent forms of abuse, domestic violence is also easier to identify as harmful (by both victim and third parties), and easier to gather evidence in any informal or formal complaint against the aggressor. It does not follow, however, that we can treat any single incidence of violence equally, regardless of whether it happens inside the home or outside it, and regardless of whether it's carried out by a family member or by a complete stranger. We do not judge incidents of assault purely based on the weight of the physical blow or the damage incurred, but also by reference to the actor's intentions and their state of mind, and importantly, the meaning of the violence within the context of their relationship to the victim. How should we therefore define and understand domestic violence?

On some ('legitimist') understandings of violence, violence can only justifiably be performed by the state (through the police and military). For individuals, violence is only justifiable as the last resort in defence of oneself or another against a credible threat of severe imminent harm. All other uses of violence are illegitimate; indeed, on such a view, the very idea of violence already 'incorporates a reference to an illegal or illegitimate use of force' (Coady 1986: 4). We might therefore be inclined to try and define violence non-normatively, for example by some reference to the use of force to affect or influence a thing or person. There is nevertheless quite clearly a normative connotation embedded in the description of something as violent.

As noted at the beginning of this chapter, domestic violence is not simply as 'normal' violence carried out in private against a partner/family member; rather, it is widely understood as having a unique character and as deserving of a distinct kind of analysis. We may recall that Dempsey promotes an understanding of domestic violence by distinguishing a third element beyond violence and domesticity. Patriarchy, the final element Dempsey identifies, plays an important role in establishing the gendered power imbalances and inequalities highlighted by many as central to the nature of domestic abuse. In the words of Susan Moller Okin, 'There is now no doubt that family violence, as it affects both wives and children, is closely connected with differentials of power and dependency between the sexes' (1989: 129). Feminist theorists have emphasised, for the best part of a century, the important intertwinement between the institution of the family (as shaped by patriarchy) with the private home (and its relative freedom from state intrusion) with intimate violence, primarily of men against women. Domestic power is seen by the man as legitimate *against the background* of widespread patriarchal power in all areas of society. Indeed, men who are insecure about their position in society are all the more likely to assert their patriarchal 'right' at home.

Just as 'adding' domesticity and violence is inadequate for a full understanding of the nature of domestic violence, we likewise cannot simply add patriarchy to the mix. Rather we have to see patriarchy as essential to the *climate of permissibility* of domestic abuse; essential to the fact that abuse even *comes to the man's mind* as an option when he's not getting his way; essential to the man freely admitting to his male friends that he needs to 'teach the wife her place'. A study across fifteen EU countries found that men who knew a female victim of domestic violence were less likely to consider such violence acceptable, but that the probability of acceptance increased where men knew a male perpetrator (Gracia and Herrero 2006: 127). As Lundy Bancroft notes, partner abuse is not particularly self-destructive: 'A man can abuse a woman for twenty or thirty years and still have a stable job or a professional career, keep his finances in good order, and remain popular with his friends and relatives' (2003: 206).

Political analyses

When we look at wider society, we can see that some violence is about seeking political influence through instilling fear. In the worst cases, such political violence is called terrorism. It is precisely this aspect of domestic violence that have led some to call it also a form of terrorism (e.g. Bramer 2011; Pain 2014). Sometimes, the use of this terminology is more rhetorical, meant to draw greater attention to the problem of domestic abuse and to prompt governments and individuals alike to treat it more seriously. In other cases, the use of the term is the straightforward result of applying classical political analyses of terrorism to the case of domestic abuse and saying 'well, if the shoe fits …'

Whilst Madden Dempsey's definition (outlined above) purportedly allows for the possibility that some acts of violence can, all things considered, be morally justified, the characterization of domestic violence as terrorism does not come with this kind of normative wiggle room. Rachel Pain, for example, argues that 'terrorism is a form of violence that attempts political influence or control through instilling fear […]. Domestic violence stands out from other everyday crimes in this respect' (2014: 533). Her analysis distinguishes domestic violence on the one hand (or 'everyday terrorism') as an on-going pattern of controlling one's partner through violence and the threat of violence, from one-off incidents of physical assault, be it against loved ones, acquaintances or strangers, on the other hand. Rhonda Hammer similarly argues that the term 'family terrorism' – as compared with 'domestic violence' – 'better represents the contextual and systemic nature of relations of subordination, domination, and violence through which those in hierarchical positions of power control others' (2003: 237).

Karen Boyle expresses wariness of descriptions of rape and domestic abuse as torture on the grounds that such an approach does not give *enough* emphasis to the systematically gendered nature of domestic abuse. She argues that this runs the risk of suggesting that women's victimization by men can only be recognised when described relative to types of violence that may be inflicted on men: 'There is a curious paradox here: men's violence against women is most visible when its gendered dimension is denied and when it looks most like men's own experiences of extreme violence' (2019: 23). This criticism finds parallels in Catherine Mackinnon's famous declaration that women's rights are not (treated as) human rights: 'When a woman is tortured in an Argentine prison cell, even as it is forgotten that she is a woman, it is seen that her human rights are violated because what is done to her is also done to men [...] But when a woman is tortured by her husband in her home, humanity is not violated' (2018: 43).

Jay Sloan-Lynch observes that there might be other problems for a characterization of domestic violence as terrorism. One of these is the fact that terrorists are defined as being motivated by clear political goals, and 'domestic abuse does not, at least on its face, appear to involve any straightforward political motivations' (2012: 777). Quite the opposite, in fact: we generally reduce it to an entirely personal matter. But of course, terrorist acts are defined as such according to a much broader understanding of 'political' motivation than we might think, such as when (for example) a terrorist act is motivated primarily by religious zeal, or a personal vendetta. Furthermore, as Sloan-Lynch points out (and as the analyses above make clear) the family clearly has a political nature and status within patriarchal societies; it is 'the central source of a society's power structure and is thus integral to sustaining the power relations that exist in the public, and correspondingly, political world' (779). As such, domestic violence can be properly characterised as a political act, designed to maintain the power of one man within the family, but also symbolically, to maintain power of men in society, even if the one man does not actively co-ordinate the exercise of political power with other men.

Both society at large and the institution of the family are shaped by gender roles defined not just in opposition to one another by in a hierarchal relationship to one another (e.g. Okin 1989; Connell 2002; Haslanger 2012). The abstract association between masculinity and dominance, aggression and control has been examined at length. The practical association is made clear in sociological and psychological research. One example of such research is Anderson and Umberson's in-depth interviews with batterers; their study suggests that violence is (at least temporarily) an effective means by which batterers reconstruct men as masculine and women as feminine. Participants reported that they were able to control their partners through exertions of physical dominance and through their interpretive efforts to hold partners responsible for the violence in their relationships. (2001: 375)

These interpretive efforts included, for example, depictions of violent behaviour by female partners as irrational and hysterical, which 'helped respondents to justify their own violence and present themselves as calm, cool, rational men' (365). On other occasions, however: 'Although female partners were represented as dangerous only to themselves, the participants depicted their own violence as primal, explosive, and damaging to others' (366). Even when violence is interpreted using a different set of stereotypes, the stereotypes applied for male and female partners are fixed in opposition to one another: if women are seen as hysterical, then men are calm; if women are ineffectual, then men are explosive.

Two kinds of moral harm

Alongside physical and psychological harms, Macy Salzberger (2022) argues that we can understand victims of domestic violence as suffering two kinds of distinctively moral harms, which she calls *moral damage* and *moral injury.* Moral damage occurs 'when the ability to develop or sustain good moral character has been compromised by an agent's circumstances' – for example, when violence is used to enforce the expectation that a woman acts servilely and deferentially towards her assailant in a way that she otherwise would not. This argument is based on the belief that to act in this way undermines desirable moral characteristics, such as autonomy, dignity and self-respect.

Thomas Hill, for whom extremely servile behaviour is a sign of moral failure, describes a 'deferential wife' who illustrates this problem. The deferential wife, who either undervalues or is ignorant of her own rights, and caters to her husband's every whim, 'betrays the absence of a certain kind of self-respect' (Hill 1973: 89). Her 'moral defect' is 'a failure to understand and acknowledge [her] own moral rights' (93). Importantly, Hill's deferential wife is *not* abused by her husband, or pressured by him in any way. She is perfectly autonomous; she just believes that it is appropriate for her to defer to him. Hill was making a point about the limits of autonomy; that we would speculate about the wife having internalised oppressive norms that would have undermined her autonomy. The wife who tolerates her husband's abuse and responds to his demands because (e.g.) she is protecting her only means of survival or is afraid for her life is not *servile* on this account.

We may then consider the differences between these three women:

- Abigail, a model of Hill's 'deferential wife', who is not abused but autonomously chooses to defer. She is servile and therefore morally blameworthy, says Hill.[4]

- Beatrice, a woman who is abused and trapped by circumstances, and who calculates that succumbing to her husband's demands for obedience is the lesser evil for the moment. She is not servile.
- Claire, a woman who has been abused for so long as to wear down her autonomy, to the point where she accepts the abuse as her fate. She is not servile, because servility (on Hill's account) requires autonomy.

When she is aware of her rights and willingly degrades them, the deferential wife is both servile and morally blameworthy. However, when her servility is the result of manipulation or coercion by her abuser then, whilst this is morally objectionable, she is not blameworthy. This is the *moral damage* of domestic abuse that Salzberger identifies.

The second kind of moral harm Salzberger describes, moral injury, is the psychological anguish that occurs when a victim of domestic violence is causally implicated or enlisted in some morally grievous offence, and suffers 'from the guilt, shame, or regret that follows from being implicated in seriously wrongful actions' (Salzberger 2022). One example of implication in grievous wrongs that Salzberger considers here is implication in child abuse: either when a mother, herself a victim of domestic violence, is enlisted in the father's mistreatment of their children, or 'fails to protect' those children from abuse. Under UK law, she is guilty of an offence if the child is physically harmed by the abuser and she 'was, or ought to have been, aware of the risk'; 'failed to take such steps as [she] could reasonably have been expected to take to protect [the child] from the risk'; and the harm 'occurred in circumstances of the kind that [she] foresaw or ought to have foreseen'.[5] This may capture various kinds of complicity in the abuser's partner, including self-deception and wilful blindness; however, it has been criticised for failing to attend to the situation in which mother and child are both victims of a single abuser. Herring (2007) argues for a defence to this provision for victims of domestic violence, for whom the fact of their own abuse has been treated by some prosecutors as proof of their awareness of the risk of harm.[6] It might be argued that such an exemption is not necessary, as the 'reasonableness' of the steps the victim could have taken to prevent harm to the child must be understood by reference to the victim's capacities as constrained by fear of violence or coercive control.[7] Nonetheless, gendered stereotypes of parenthood continue to shape judicial assessments of what can reasonably be expected. As Sarah Singh argues,

> Archaic associations between femininity and suffering mean that the good mother is required to be self-sacrificing to the point where she will die for her child […] It follows that, even where domestic abuse is disclosed, gendered expectations of mothers mean abused mothers are not exonerated from responsibility for their child's death. (Singh 2021: 194)

Even if the complicit mother is not held *legally* responsible for failing to protect the child, Salzberger affirms that, in some cases, 'inner conflict or anguish of moral injury not only seems appropriate [...] but even morally praiseworthy' (2022: 176). Although the victim of abuse may not be morally blameworthy for the wrongdoing they are implicated in by their abuser, that causal implication constitutes moral injury precisely because it gives rise to appropriate occasion for moral anguish.

Justifications and excuses

Madden Dempsey, as we saw above, conceives violence narrowly as 'the direct, physical use of force'. However, she still includes a normative element: 'violence is merely a pro tanto wrong, the doing of which can be morally justified, all things considered' (2009: 108). The most obvious context of justified violence is in self-defence. It would follow from this that domestic violence, whilst also a *pro tanto* wrong, might be morally justified in certain situations. However, when domestic violence is an on-going pattern of abusive behaviour, it is both unjustifiable and inexcusable by definition.

Nonetheless, perpetrators of domestic violence will often consider their actions justified, and/or attempt to excuse them.[8] Lundy Bancroft is a counsellor who has worked for many years with male domestic abusers; he observes that the abusive individual is generally under no illusion that their behaviour is justified in the eyes of *society*. They will put on a different face to the outside world than that seen by their partner, and will present excuses for their behaviour when caught or reported (rather than trying to persuade others that the behaviour was justified). However, they have an *internal* justification for their actions, tied to the relationship itself and their beliefs about how their partner should behave: 'An abuser almost never does anything that he himself considers morally unacceptable. He may hide what he does because he thinks other people would disagree with it, but he feels justified inside' (Bancroft 2003: 199). The internal moral line becomes clear when Bancroft asks whether the abusive men he works with behave in the same manner with other people as they do with their female partners. For example, he asks them: they have called their girlfriend or wife 'bitch' – have they ever acted on the same urge when speaking to their own mothers?

> The same answer shoots out from the men each time I do this exercise: "But you can't treat your mother like that, no matter how angry you are! You just don't do that!"
> The unspoken remainder of this statement, which we can fill in for my clients, is: "But you can treat your wife or girlfriend like that, as long as you have a good enough reason. That's different." In other words, the abuser's problem lies above all in his belief that controlling or abusing his female partner is justifiable. (Bancroft 2003: 199–200)

Patriarchal culture, rather than the letter of the law, shapes the internal moral standards by which abusers moderate and justify their behaviour to themselves. The abuser may show his true colours among peers who share his moral standards.

At the same time, he will usually be aware that his actions may be judged as morally wrong by others, or could land him in legal hot water. He will therefore either hide his actions behind closed doors, or (if caught) produce excuses for his behaviour, often redirecting blame to his victim. For example, in one batterer's words: 'I've never hit another woman in my life besides the one that I'm with. She just has a knack for bringing out the worst in me' (Anderson and Umberson 2001: 367). Men who kill their female partners sometimes attempt to rationalise or excuse their behaviour by placing blame on their own experiences of adversity and victimization earlier in life, or by blaming the victim herself. They sometimes characterise her as 'at fault because of her "flaws" as an intimate partner, mother and/or housekeeper' and sometimes refer to provocations that caused them to 'snap'. (We discuss 'loss of control' below.)

Men – far more often than women – are also motivated to violent measures by a partner's attempt to leave the relationship. One study of risk factors for femicide found that leaving a physically abusive male partner for someone else was associated with a nearly five-fold increase in the woman's risk of being murdered, whilst leaving him for any other reason was associated in a four-fold risk (J. C. Campbell et al. 2003: 1097). In contrast, most women who kill male intimate partners cite self-defence as their motivation (Swan et al. 2008), and intimate homicide of a partner of either gender is preceded in the vast majority of cases by abuse of the female partner by the male (J. C. Campbell et al. 2003). This trend is further evidenced by the strong negative correlation between homicide of male domestic partners by women and state provisions to help battered women leave abusive relationships: 'efforts to protect women in the United States have had the effect of reducing the homicide rate of men by their partners by almost 70% over the past 24 years' (Kimmel 2005: 214). When women are supported in their attempts to leave abusive relationships, it seems that they have far less 'need' for violence. Motivations and justifications for domestic violence below the level of homicide also (generally speaking) diverge along gender lines:

> Family violence researcher Kersti Yllo argues that men tend to use domestic violence instrumentally, for the specific purpose of striking fear and terror in their wives' hearts, to insure compliance, obedience, and passive acceptance of his rule in the home. Women, by contrast, tend to use violence expressively, to express frustration or immediate anger, or, of course defensively, to prevent further injury. (Kimmel 2005: 194)

This characterization seems to lend support to understandings of domestic violence as a phenomenon distinct from the mere 'mix' of violence and the domestic setting. It also underlines the need to differentiate between different forms of violence in the home and in intimate relationships, by using more specific language – for example, as Johnson and Ferraro distinguish between 'intimate terrorism', 'common couple violence' and 'violent resistance' (2000: 950).[9] This enables us to identify and analyse the particular moral and political wrongs of specific forms of violence within the institution of the family and to trace the influence of different patriarchal contexts. Even if a perpetrator has no explicit intention to inspire terror in his victim, the institution of domestic abuse can 'be seen to embody a social activity and system of rules that seeks to terrorize women into accepting male dominance and female dependence through violence and the threat of violence' (Sloan-Lynch 2012: 783).

The state and domestic abuse

As suggested above, domestic abuse is characterised by moral wrongs going far beyond a 'mere' violation of the basic obligation not to harm others; its systemic nature and the intimacy with which a victim lives with the perpetrator makes domestic abuse a violation of trust and an exploitation of vulnerability. But when we examine the ways in which our judicial system currently treats domestic abuse, it becomes clear that we generally treat the domestic setting and intimate relationships as a mitigating factor, rather than an aggravating factor.

There are a number of reasons for this. One is the need for police and barristers to make sense of a complicated relationship in order to determine guilt precisely. It's easier to say 'it takes two to tango' than it is to judge, from the personal reports of both parties, who bears the greater responsibility. A significant role here is played by gendered expectations, bias and social norms – for example, the widespread belief (held by well over 50 per cent of both men *and* women) that 'provocative behaviour' by women is a cause of domestic violence against them (Gracia and Herrero 2006: 126).

A further reason is the difficulty of gathering evidence for prosecution 'beyond reasonable doubt', especially when non-physical abuse leaves no marks. An assault in a bar or a verbal altercation on the street usually has plenty of witnesses. In contrast, even if a neighbour hears raised voices in the home, they are unlikely to hear details; bruises and cuts caused at home may be explained away as the result of accidents. Evidence of premeditation is also harder to gather when the perpetrator, victim and weapon were all in the same place to begin with. The use of sentencing guidelines referring to premeditation, as evidenced in specific ways, may thus result automatically in more lenient punishment of violence in intimate relationships and domestic settings. UK Member for Parliament Rachel Maclean raised this problem during the debate over the 2022 Domestic Homicide Sentencing Review,[10] referring to two recent cases of domestic homicide:

> The families point out that had the killers taken a knife out of the home and gone to the local park to stab their daughters, they would have received a much higher sentence, with a 25-year starting point, but most domestic homicides take place in the home, meaning that a knife is not taken to the scene; it is already there in the home. That automatically reduces the available sentence starting point to a minimum tariff of only 15 years.

The claim that an attack was carried out spontaneously in a fit of rage is less plausible if it's carried out in some time and place other than the site of provocation. But when both the victim and weapon are with you at home, premeditation is harder to prove, and claims of provocation easier to make. As MP Ellie Reeves pointed out in the same debate, if domestic murder tariffs reflected the severity of the crime rather than its location, 'the fact that a knife was used would be the aggravating factor, rather than the act of bringing it to the scene'.[11] However, *this* approach might predispose courts to treat women more harshly than men in domestic homicide cases. Women, being generally physically smaller and weaker than their partners, use a weapon in nearly 80 per cent of such cases, whereas men frequently use their bare hands; strangulation is the second most common method employed in femicide cases.[12] Furthermore, most people would think that factors like planning and provocation *should* be relevant to sentencing. Our approach to judging the 'badness' of violence in both law and in everyday morality is shaped by widespread beliefs about the significance of factors like premeditation, means and the emotional state of the perpetrator. We judge violence as morally *worse* (and more deserving of heavy legal penalty) when it is planned, cruel and calculated, than when it is spontaneous, blunt and carried out under the influence of passion or fury or fear.

Loss of control and diminished responsibility

UK courts recognise a number of mitigating factors as constituting a partial defence against murder charges. A successful appeal to self-defence would be a *complete* defence against murder charges, resulting in acquittal. Partial defences such as diminished responsibility and loss of control (previously called 'provocation') will, if successful, reduce the charges from murder to voluntary manslaughter, though the offender will still go to prison.[13] Domestic homicide is more likely to be prosecuted as manslaughter, resulting in a shorter sentence, than homicide of a non-partner. For example, in Ireland, men charged with manslaughter serve an average of 2.8 years less in prison when they kill their current or former wife/girlfriend, than when they kill women with whom they did not have a relationship.[14] The UK *Coroners and Justice Act* (CJA) 2009 s. 54–56 defines the new defence to murder of 'loss of control'. The relabelling of the traditional 'provocation' defence was more than merely cosmetic: the Act aims to shift attention away from the alleged provocateur to the killer. In addition, the Act resists the traditional use of the defence by jealous, possessive men: s. 55(6)(c) states that 'the fact that a thing done or said constituted sexual infidelity is to be disregarded'. Finally, one of the problems of the traditional defence was that it required a spontaneous loss of control, and did not recognise 'slow burn' or 'last straw' events that led to the killing. As such it 'revealed a gender bias in the law, in that it reflected a typically male reaction to provocation, but one that women were very unlikely to display' (Mitchell 2011: 42). The CJA s. 54(2) now states that ' … it does not matter whether or not the loss of control was sudden'.

Similar problems have historically arisen for women who claim self-defence when killing an abusive spouse or partner. To claim self-defence, the defendant must prove that she faced a credible and threat of imminent serious violence, and had no other way to respond; however, if the abuse victim kills her abuser in his sleep, it is hard to accept that he was threatening *imminent* violence. This is partly down to expectations regarding violent crime and legitimate responses based on predominantly male standards, and partly due to the failure to understand the difficulty many abuse victims face in leaving a relationship: 'from the perspective of the average judge or juror, uninformed about the dynamics and effects of domestic violence, the killing may appear entirely unreasonable; as either irrational or retaliatory' (Hopkins and Easteal 2010: 132). However, traditional definitions of self-defence also present a practical problem. The woman whose violent husband is stronger and heavier cannot make use of 'proportionate' force to protect herself in the moment of attack. In most cases, she will not have the strength to subdue him, and a 'proportionate' blow in self-defence might have serious – even fatal – repercussions for her. The only way to stop the violence, if escape is not a viable option, is therefore to use seemingly disproportionate measures, and to use them pre-emptively when he is in a position of vulnerability (e.g. sleeping).

The famous English case *R v Ahluwalia* 1992 deals with the situation of an appellant who was violently abused by her husband for many years, leading to a breaking point. Unable to sleep after one such bout of violence, she mixed petrol with caustic soda in a bucket, poured the mixture over her sleeping husband and set him alight. Kiranjit Ahluwalia was convicted of murder in 1989, receiving a sentence of life in prison.[15] Ahluwalia's original defence – that her husband's abuse had provoked her reaction – failed, since precedent indicated that a response to provocation should be immediate; any attempt to claim self-defence would have failed for the same reason. The conviction was overturned on appeal, and she was convicted instead of voluntary manslaughter on the basis of diminished responsibility. Although we should welcome the availability of the excuse of diminished responsibility in the *Ahluwalia* scenario, we should recognise the unfortunate underlying message: that there was 'something wrong' with the abuse victim. The excuse of 'loss of control' is the same. In contrast, a successful justification of self-defence would send the message that there was 'something wrong' with the abusive partner.

The problem with an appeal to self-defence is that killing as a mode of self-defence must be a last resort; the jury will tend to ask why a victim did not leave instead, particularly in the case of women who have been victims of on-going abuse for substantial periods prior to the killing. This is part of a larger problem for the public's understanding of, and ability to sympathise with, domestic violence victims. The phrase 'why doesn't she leave?' is a common reaction among those who withhold sympathy for the abuse victim who lashes back. However, it represents a misunderstanding on multiple levels, one being the increased risk of violence or death for women who leave their abusers (noted earlier in this chapter). Other factors include a woman's lack of financial resources, or a lack of friends or family nearby, or (as in Ahluwalia's case) a minority ethnic community that helped her husband find her when she tried to run away on earlier occasions. The difficulty of leaving her abuser – and, even more so, the difficulty of disappearing, such that he cannot find her – is exacerbated when the victim is a mother attempting to leave with her children.

The privacy of the home

A key problem for the policing and prosecution of domestic abuse (even in the case of physical violence, which can be more easily documented and proven than emotional abuse or coercive control) is that it happens in private, and in the context of an intimate relationship. As we've discussed in other chapters, non-intervention in the family home and in personal relationships is a central feature of liberal societies; family privacy is supposed to be respected by the State up to a certain boundary, often described in terms of Mill's Harm Principle. As David Archard puts it:

> Only when an individual's acts harmfully intrude upon others is the State permitted to intervene. Mill believed that such a guaranteed private space was necessary to the flourishing of individuality, and thereby to the improvement of society as a whole. Similarly, the liberal ideal of family policy guarantees a space for the life of an individual family within which what is done is both unsupervised by State and freely chosen. The flourishing of the family, and its members, is argued to be secured by such a guarantee of non-interference. (Archard 1990: 185)

Whilst the traditional liberal state can protect one individual against harm from another individual, and protect one family against harm from another family, it thus hesitates to protect one individual from another individual *within* a single family.

However, Archard argues that the private nuclear family is 'a peculiarly late twentieth century Western phenomenon, a compound of various changes in society' (1990: 191). Familial privacy understood in this way has 'dubious value' and is challenged by the kind of state monitoring and intervention that may be justified by the interests of children in protection from abuse.[16] The sharp boundary between private and public that many of us take for granted is a relatively recent invention, and may not be underpinned by any genuine moral claim to domestic privacy. Non-interference by the state in familial relationships has been defended as crucial for the goods of intimacy to be reaped (see e.g. Schoeman 1980; Brighouse and Swift 2006) there are also clear downsides to the state taking a wide berth around the private family home. The state's greatest intervention in family privacy is compulsory education. (And it's no accident that teachers have a duty to report any suspicions of child abuse to social services.) However, there is again the question of *location*. It is one thing for the state to insist that children come from the home to the school for their education; it is much more difficult for the state to enter the home.

Archard notes that 'whilst privacy may serve as the precondition for a healthy and loving intimacy, it can equally function as a cloak for abuse and neglect' (192). The view that the State should respect the privacy of the home and the autonomy of the family has similarly been a longstanding subject of criticism by feminist philosophers and legal scholars. For Catherine MacKinnon, for example:

> The law of privacy treats the private sphere as a sphere of personal freedom. For men, it is. For women, the private is the distinctive sphere of intimate violation and abuse, neither free nor particularly personal. Men's realm of private freedom is women's realm of collective subordination. (MacKinnon 1989: 168)

There are two ways in which we might look at this problem: we might see the greater opportunities afforded to abusers by state non-interference in the family as an unfortunate side-effect of those social structures necessary to preserve and respect privacy for families and intimate relationships. One key argument against mandatory arrest/prosecution policies appeals precisely to this need for respect; if the victim of domestic abuse does not wish to proceed, then prosecution would require interference in the couple's private life. Herring et al. suggest, 'Where the couple have resolved their differences and are keen to move on the state should not in a ham-fisted way seek to intervene' (2012: 217). But of course, this presupposes that a victim's withdrawal of a complaint (or declining to report the incident in the first place, in cases where the police are called by neighbours or other witnesses) reflects a genuine resolution of the incident. The two may well be keen to move on, but 'in most cases where the victim is withdrawing the complaint she has two contradictory wishes: she wants the violence to stop and she wants the relationship to continue' (Herring et al 2012: 213).

If family privacy is itself justified as necessary for autonomy, there may be a conflict between respecting the victim's autonomy with regard to prosecution, and (given the rates of recidivism in domestic abuse) protecting the victim's future autonomy by removing the abuser. A fear of partner revenge, family disapproval, the logistical and financial difficulties of starting out on her own, and many other factors besides may present barriers to autonomous consent; any policy of mandatory arrest must therefore be accompanied by robust state support for victims, especially where there is a risk to children.[17] Such support does not, however, guarantee that a policy of mandatory arrest will always be welcomed by victims or that rates of prosecution will increase; such a policy will also have different consequences for communities which (understandably) have less trust in police intervention. As Forelit observes, 'The root causes of the violence that women of color and poor women suffer and the impact of mandatory arrest's removal of the batterer from the home are likely to be different than for white middle class women' (1990: 222). The privacy of the family home carries additional meanings for members of oppressed groups, for whom the home is often a haven from societal prejudice, restriction and the heightened risk of violence. However, this still does not justify an uncritical acceptance of the traditional and idealised public/private dichotomy, which 'fails to consider that many men treat the other occupants of their refuge harshly, turning their private haven into some women's private hell' (Forelit 1990: 225).

As long as we deem respect for privacy to be fundamentally valuable, we will have to accept greater difficulties in monitoring, preventing or prosecuting crimes carried out behind those closed doors. Trade-offs of this kind are a regular feature of social life: greater individual freedoms in one sphere will often allow for more opportunities to cause harm to others, and social workers will have to wait for the harm to occur before intervening (and even then there will be problems of gathering sufficient evidence). Liberal societies, we might argue, simply accept that this risk is the cost of freedom, and chooses to *punish* those who use their liberties to harm, rather than to impose restrictions for the sake of *prevention*.

Alternatively, we might critically interrogate the supposed value of family privacy – has it been defended because this was in the interests of the powerful? Has state non-intervention in the family home been defended because this enabled a patriarchal status quo to be maintained? Focusing on the US legal system, Brian Decker argues that this system 'has historically been unwilling to heavily penalize domestic violence – private violence – because [...] it has tacitly viewed victims of such violence as sacrifices providing an outlet against public violence' (2008: 114). The public/private dichotomy staves off chaos and allows a social order to be maintained. He argues that:

> society opts to tolerate ordered violence because of the belief that it might mitigate disordered violence. In this model, the private sphere provides the needed order: private violence is ideally limited geographically (to within or around the home) and temporally (to those times at which the abuser and victim are together), and it selects its victims from a limited pool (sometimes children, usually wives or partners, and almost always women). (Decker 2008: 114–15)

Partner abuse and parental rights

Abusive individuals often inflict abuse on their partner and children alike. A literature assay by Jeffrey Edelson found that the majority of the studies reviewed 'indicate that in 30% to 60% of families where either child maltreatment or adult domestic violence is occurring one will find that the other form of violence is also being perpetrated' (1999: 136). Children also suffer indirectly from the abuse of one of their parents at the hands of the other, regardless of whether this is violence or non-physical abuse. In a fact-finding hearing for a 2021 domestic abuse case, the court noted that:

> the circumstances encompassed by the definition of 'domestic abuse' in PD12J fully recognise that coercive and/or controlling behaviour by one party may cause serious emotional and psychological harm to the other members of the family unit, whether or not there has been any actual episode of violence or sexual abuse. In short, a pattern of coercive and/or controlling behaviour can be as abusive as or more abusive than any particular factual incident that might be written down and included in a schedule in court proceedings.[18]

It is uncontroversial that parents who abuse their children, or whose abuse of their partner is such as to directly cause their children to suffer, undermine their own claim to moral parental rights. Many philosophical accounts of parental rights ground these rights in parental duties to children, or otherwise make those rights conditional on the child's needs and interests. But there is still a gap in our account: parents who, despite perpetrating partner abuse, do not abuse their children (directly or indirectly). Should their parental rights still be protected?

Here, it should be clarified that we are speaking about *moral* rights. Legal rights, visitation orders and custody decisions might well diverge from the moral rights parents have to custody and control of their children, depending on the account of moral parenthood one adheres to. When speaking of legal rights, an immediate answer to this question is to appeal to the potential harm to a child whose parent abuses, or used to abuse, their other parent. It would certainly seem logical to argue that individuals who commit violence against their intimate partners are demonstrably abusive, and that their custody therefore poses an increased risk of harm to the child:

> Advocates for laws requiring courts to consider domestic violence had to overcome the argument that domestic violence directed at an adult is irrelevant to a determination of the child's best interests. They relied on empirical studies showing that men who abuse their mates harm or create risks of harm to children. (Harris 2010: 177)

But in the absence of actual child abuse or harm to child welfare, is the mere statistical pattern a reason to think that the abuser loses their *moral* parental rights? A parent with the 'full complement' of moral parental rights and obligations will, on some accounts of moral parenthood, only have the right to *continue* the parent-child relationship as long as this is in the best interests of the child (e.g. Brennan and Noggle 1997; Vallentyne 2003). Other philosophers, however, argue that parental rights are at least partly based in the parent's interests in the goods of the parent-child relationship, and their rights to maintain existing relationships more generally (Brighouse and Swift 2014; Gheaus 2018b). If this person then commits a moral wrong against *someone other than the child*, whilst remaining a devoted and capable parent, it is less plausible that one's moral rights to rear the child disappear by default.

Take an example: a man with a plentiful resources (and thus no financial need) fiddles his dying father's paperwork to ensure for himself a greater share of the inheritance. This violation of his father's trust and betrayal of other family members is a clear moral wrong. However, few would believe that this individual loses his moral parental rights as a result. To think so would be to see childrearing rights as conditional on untainted moral character, or to see the loss of these rights as the punishment demanded as a matter of justice. Neither option seems consistent with common understandings of moral parenthood. Moral parental rights aren't generally framed as conditional upon being a good person *per se*. Rather, they are originally determined by one's relationship to the child, one's capacity and willingness to meet the child's needs, etc. They are then further reinforced down the line by the existence of the parent-child relationship and both parties' interests in maintaining it. Going back to those philosophers who argue that rights of child-rearing are held only by those for whom it's in the *child's* best interests that they parent them: we must admit that one need not be a moral saint for this to be the case.

The question, then, is whether abusive behaviour towards one's intimate partner is a form of behaviour that undermines parental rights, as long as one continues to fulfil one's obligations to the *child*, and if the child still benefits from the parental relationship. In the (admittedly extremely rare) case in which a child is not negatively affected by one parent's abuse of the other, it is not straightforwardly clear that the abuser would lose all moral right he previously had to maintain a relationship with his children.[19]

Parental alienation

As we saw in Chapter 6, courts are generally loath to terminate an individual's *legal* parental rights without strong evidence of unfitness and/or child abuse. Unwillingness to terminate parental rights can leave children lingering in the foster care system for years, or in the care of parents whose behaviour falls just shy of outright abuse.[20] Violence against the child's other parent is not seen as grounds for rights of custody and control to be removed entirely. This is especially so when this violence has not been witnessed by the child or hasn't been shown to have a significant impact on the child's welfare or relationship with the abusive parent. If these parents separate, it is often the case that a shared custody plan or visitation rights will be required, an on-going relationship with both parents being considered in the child's best interests. In one 2017 case, the court put it thus: 'Contact between parent and child is to be terminated only in exceptional circumstances, where there are cogent reasons for doing so and when there is no alternative. Contact is to be terminated only if it will be detrimental to the child's welfare.'[21] However, the expectation that such arrangements will be mediated by the parents with civility and mutual respect – with courts responding punitively to parents who do not meet this expectation – gives rise to a serious problem for victims of abuse:

> [T]he friendly parent construct has been widely adopted by judges, family law lawyers, mediators, and evaluators to reward the parent who is most likely to promote contact and a positive relationship with the other parent. In partner violence cases, a victim who attempts to limit contact with an abuser may be deemed hostile and unfriendly and be punished for her or his protestations and hypervigilance. (Jaffe and Crooks 2004: 918)

In the light of the above, and our other discussions regarding parental duty, we might think that separated parents have an obligation to respect custody arrangements determined to be in the best interests of the child, regardless of their own feelings towards each other. However, a victim of abuse instructed by the court to arrange child visitation for the perpetrator of this abuse might reasonably have concerns about the child's safety. If the abuse has not been recognised by the court, their concerns may be overlooked or even held against them as an indication of hostility.

We saw earlier that abuse victims may themselves be held morally and legally responsible for their partner's abuse of the child. It therefore seems that such victims may find themselves between a rock and a hard place: between accusations of 'failure to protect' and accusations of 'parental alienation'. Parental alienation has been defined recently by the Children and Family Court Advisory and Support Service as occurring 'when a child's resistance/hostility towards one parent is not justified and is the result of psychological manipulation by the other parent'.[22] A parent who, during custody determination proceedings, reports abuse (of themself or the child) by the other parent may face accusations of alienation. The same may happen if the child expresses a preference to stay with their custodial parent or resists contact with the non-custodial parent.[23]

This is not to say that parental alienation is always or exclusively concomitant with abuse – far from it, since abuse would seem to be a factor justifying a child's resistance or hostility towards their parent.

Appeals to parental alienation (even without the scientific moniker 'syndrome'[24]) have held significant on-going power in custody disputes, helped along by the popularization of the idea in mass media. Recent studies show that courts remain sceptical of abuse allegations made in the course of custody hearings, and especially so when the accused parent makes a cross-claim of alienation. When fathers cross-claim alienation, courts 'are almost 4 (3.9) times more likely to disbelieve mothers' claims of child abuse than if fathers made no alienation claim' (Meier 2020: 98). This study's authors observe:

> [T]he impact of credited alienation is apparent in cases where both abuse and alienation were credited by the court. Even when courts believe a father has abused a mother, if they also believe the mother is alienating, some mothers still lose custody to the abusive fathers. In other words, in these cases alienation trumps abuse. (Meier et al. 2020: 99)

Parents (particularly mothers) sometimes lose custody to an abusive parent even when their allegations are credited: 'Even when courts find that fathers have abused the children or the mother, they award them custody 13% of the time. And in cases with credited child physical abuse claims, abusers still win custody 20% of the time' (97). This statistic shines a damning light on the understanding of parental rights that such court decisions seem to reflect: as possessive and unconditional, rather than as grounded in the parent-child relationship and in the needs and rights of the child. In the words of Meier et al.: 'courts' persistent focus on *mothers*' responsibility for *fathers*' relationships with their children smacks of patriarchy, and the beliefs that fathers should not be criticized and that mothers and children must respect their paternal rights regardless of their behavior' (102).

Closing remarks

As a topic of study, the family is an endlessly fascinating one, and the sources from which we can draw inspiration and explanation are likewise unlimited. We accept that any two others would have written a very different book, just as we accept that we might well be accused by sociologists and political scientists and social workers and lawyers of having omitted some key topics, and just as we anticipate criticisms from both the left wing and the right wing on the political spectrum. For a book of this length, we simply had to be selective. But at least we can agree with our critics that the family is an exceptionally important topic for discussion from any disciplinary background. The idea of the family unit, the moral rights and duties of its members, and the status of the family in society have significant impacts on our daily lives as individuals, families and as a whole society.

Far from a comprehensive summary of the field of philosophy of the family, this book can claim only to offer a constrained – but hopefully tantalizing – overview of some of the foundational themes and debates in this area. The astute reader will have noticed our asides, every so often, to the tune of 'We assume X for our purposes, but there is more to say' or 'We don't have the space to address Y here.' In many cases, this was in deference to our goal of providing a (relatively) concise starting point for those new to philosophy of the family, focusing on those topics most central to the notion of 'the family' and/or relevant to the lives of the majority of families in the UK. In other cases, our choice not to dive into particular discussions and disagreements was (as we noted in the introduction) based on the belief that those disagreements were more cultural than philosophical – at least in their main expression. Where we have touched on law or on sociological data, we've drawn mainly from the UK context, or from the West more broadly – our analyses are far from globally applicable. (To make them so would have required us to expand each chapter tenfold, for which neither the publisher nor our readership would have thanked us!)

At its core the philosophical approach looks at concepts: what they mean, what they assume, how they are used, how people disagree in their use. At the very least, therefore, we hope that people from any disciplinary background can take the conceptual distinctions from this book back to their 'home' discussions to improve them. In addition, we have argued in favour of a number of family policies, and we hope that some of our argumentation might find its way up to the decision-makers in government. But most of all we wanted to inspire readers to examine their own families and the decisions and assumptions they make, consciously or unconsciously, in order to build and sustain them.

Notes

Chapter 1

1. The title is unfortunate, for it misleadingly suggests social conservatism, whereas the book is socially liberal to the core. As we explained in the Introduction, we are starting our discussions from the same social liberal position.
2. However, B&S are quick to reject (p. 101 ff.) two kinds of 'benefit to the parent' as morally irrelevant and possibly pernicious. The first benefit involves 'creative self-extension', whereby the parent is motivated primarily by the vanity project of creating a 'mini-me', as opposed to recognizing and respecting the child's developing autonomous interests and needs. The second benefit involves some *biological* family project, whereby children are only a means of promoting the long-term success of the 'blood' to which the parents are committed, possibly at the expense of the autonomous child's own legitimate interests and plans.
3. In fact, the mere presence of books in the family home has a greater impact on children's academic success, vocabulary and later employment than their parents' level of education (Sikora, Evans and Kelley 2019).
4. See Millar F. 'Last year one Oxford college admitted 96% of its students from state schools. How did they do it?'. *The Guardian,* 24 March 2020. Although private school students are no more than 7 per cent of the population, 30–40 per cent of successful Oxford applicants are from private schools. https://www.theguardian.com/education/2020/mar/24/one-oxford-college-has-96-of-students-from-state-schools-how-did-they-do-it
5. Sixty-five per cent of senior judges, 59 per cent of civil service permanent secretaries, 52 per cent of diplomats ... See Weale, S. 'Britain's top jobs still in hands of private school elite, study finds' *The Guardian* 25 June 2019. https://www.theguardian.com/society/2019/jun/25/britains-top-jobs-still-in-hands-of-private-school-elite-study-finds.
6. Of course, such schools might still remain elitist even without charging fees, since their reputation would attract wealthy parents to move into the catchment area, thereby pushing up real estate prices.
7. The Irish state has taken this approach. The result is that private schools, even the 'poshest', charge between €4000 and €9000 a year. In comparison British private schools charge £13000 to £21000. In theory, a lower-middle-class Irish family can therefore afford to send one child to a subsidised private school. In practice, very few lower-middle-class parents do this, and so the policy effectively amounts to a subsidy of the middle and upper-middle classes, making it less egalitarian than might first appear. Adam Swift already discussed the question of whether left-wing parents can morally justify sending

their children to private schools in his book *How Not to Be a Hypocrite: School Choice for the Morally Perplexed Parent* (London and New York: Routledge 2003).

8. We are over-simplifying. All schools need to be recognised by the Department of Education, need to conform to the national curriculum, need to abide by health and safety laws, employment laws, etc. – so there is no such thing as a *purely* private school. In addition, British private schools have charitable status, and this exempts them from paying taxes; so the lack of tax revenue could be described as depriving third parties from redistributed benefits.
9. Even if she is resurrected in heaven, she cannot own and manage the earth-based X *from heaven*!
10. The same logic would justify compulsory removal of organs for transplant or for research: if X is Margaret's organ, then the state should take it and allocate it in accordance with some utilitarian procedure, regardless of Margaret's ante-mortem wishes.
11. 'How Inheritance Tax works: Thresholds, rules and allowances': https://www.gov.uk/inheritance-tax.
12. Office for National Statistics, 'UK House Price Index: April 2022': https://www.ons.gov.uk/economy/inflationandpriceindices/bulletins/housepriceindex/april2022.
13. There are different situations here. If the child is under fifteen, then parental consent is always required. If the child is fifteen *and* a doctor assesses them to be 'Gillick competent', then the doctor can offer them treatment, even without parental knowledge or consent. When the child is sixteen, parental consent or knowledge is no longer required. Note, however, that a seventeen-year-old child cannot *refuse* a treatment recommended by their doctors once the parents have already agreed on the seventeen-year-old's behalf. And no child (regardless of age) can refuse life-saving treatment (regardless of the parents' views). For a recent discussion, see Dominic Wilkinson (25 November 2020). 'Refusal redux: Revisiting debate about adolescent refusal of treatment', *Journal of Medical Ethics blog*. https://blogs.bmj.com/medical-ethics/2020/11/25/refusal-redux-revisiting-debate-about-adolescent-refusal-of-treatment/.
14. See also a recent case from mid-2019: https://www.independent.co.uk/news/uk/home-news/jehovahs-witness-blood-transfusion-doctor-judge-ruling-girl-leeds-nhs-trust-religion-a8977066.html. Ian McEwan's 2014 novel *The Children Act* concerns a judge who rules in favour of a hospital transfusing a seventeen-year-old JW boy with leukaemia, against the wishes of both the boy and his parents. After the transfusion, the boy is personally grateful to the judge, and becomes disillusioned with his religion. After various twists, however, he returns to the religion, develops leukaemia anew, and this time, as a competent adult, refuses the transfusion and dies.
15. Some version of Lafollette's 'ex ante' (before the fact) parenting licence would certainly reduce the incidence of child abuse. However, those who resist the intrusiveness of any ex ante solution might favour tightening up the current 'ex post' (after the fact) investigations and interventions by social workers in order to remove at-risk children earlier. Child protection policies are very complicated, and we do not have space to describe them in detail. Suffice to mention the recent Berrick et al. (eds.) (2023). *Oxford Handbook of Child Protection Systems*, Oxford University Press.

16. Office for National Statistics. 'Abuse during childhood: Findings from the Crime Survey for England and Wales, year ending March 2016', available at: https://www.ons.gov.uk/peoplepopulationandcommunity/crimeandjustice/articles/abuseduringchildhood/findingsfromtheyearendingmarch2016crimesurveyforenglandandwales.
17. For the moment we're not going to try to define abuse and neglect, since we discuss that in Chapter 9. But see the definitions available at the Crown Prosecution Service (updated 2020). 'Child Abuse (non-sexual) – prosecution guidance', available at: https://www.cps.gov.uk/legal-guidance/child-abuse-non-sexual-prosecution-guidance.
18. In practice, however, as we discuss further in Chapter 9, even credited claims of abuse are far too often not considered grounds for terminating the parental rights of the abuser.
19. There is a concern here. If the baseline support for new parents (who have passed the test) is not very generous, then many parents-to-be would deliberately fail the test in order to be granted the extra support.
20. 'Currently, 45% of pregnancies and one third of births in England are unplanned or associated with feelings of ambivalence.' Source: Public Health England (2018). 'Health matters: reproductive health and pregnancy planning'. https://www.gov.uk/government/publications/health-matters-reproductive-health-and-pregnancy-planning/health-matters-reproductive-health-and-pregnancy-planning.
21. The problem here is that abusive partners tend not to be actually abusive until their partner is 'locked in' (generally after marriage or pregnancy), and will be careful not to expose themselves at the testing stage. For further discussion, see Baron (2023: 101–4).
22. There are some adoptions that lie at the border with natural reproduction: if the child's parents die, and a *relative* applies to formally adopt it, then there may be a presumption that the child already belongs to the family and ought to remain there.
23. In addition, given that there are many 'looked after' children up for adoption, the social workers can match the child better to the particular applicants.
24. See Freiman (2021) for detailed arguments against such a testing regime.
25. Singapore passed the Maintenance of Parents Act in 1995. https://sso.agc.gov.sg/Act/MPA1995. For more general discussion, see Serrano 2017.
26. Indeed, filial duties can be said to last beyond my parents' death, in the sense that I have a duty to protect their reputation and perhaps also the interests of the projects with which they identified; children who take over their parents' business, for example, may feel duty-bound to honour their parents' vision.
27. In addition, speaking of a filial duty invokes strong sexist norms, since daughters are expected to sacrifice their own interests more than sons. The expectations on the daughter will be even greater if she is childless, since she therefore has more 'care capacity' to expend on her parents. See our discussion of distributions of caring labour in Chapter 3. There are other issues in the adult children's life situation that might affect their perceived filial duty unfairly: if two sisters work as a doctor and a novelist respectively, the doctor can more plausibly point to a rigid schedule and the urgent needs of suffering patients when 'bowing out' of filial care; if two brothers both pursued their career dreams, but by pure coincidence one ends up working in the neighbouring

town whilst the other lives in another continent, then the geographically close one would seem to have incurred a greater filial duty.

28. See Chapter 7 for a more detailed discussion of the difference between saving life and creating life, and the place of gratitude and regret in this equation.

Chapter 2

1. In this chapter, we will be mainly concerned with parental obligations; see Chapter 3 for familial duties more broadly, and discussions of filial duties to parents in Chapters 1 and 3.
2. The only exception would be where a person or couple are given permission to formally adopt a known, specific child, for example, an orphan of another family member.
3. See Chapter 6 for a discussion of both adoption in general and of the 'giving up' of a child for adoption.
4. As we will discuss in more detail later in this chapter, and further in Chapter 6, some causal accounts include people like sperm/egg donors as causes of the child's existence, giving rise to the uncomfortable conclusion that these donors actually have parental duties to the child. Others attempt to construct their account in a way that accommodates the widespread practice of gamete donation, creating further rules to delineate *which* causes count as producing parental obligations.
5. Some might read the 'Hazmat' account as implying that abortion isn't morally permissible, but Weinberg does not commit to this conclusion. She states, 'It is the fact that the risks we take with our gametes sometimes result in needy *persons* that makes us responsible for the care of those persons' (2008: 178). Whether abortion is permissible simply depends on the boundaries of personhood (i.e. when we believe that a foetus or infant attains full moral status). It is at that point that our parental responsibilities kick in. But this leads to a potential problem. We could argue that if Weinberg allows that abortion can be morally permissible, then the key causal step for this theory isn't conception, but the decision not to have the abortion. *That*'s what would make me responsible for the resulting child. However, Weinberg might respond that access to abortion in many places is sufficiently insecure that the decision to abort if I become pregnant is analogous to the decision to take someone to the hospital if my lion mauls them – that is, a risk mitigation strategy, as opposed to the key moment of risk.
6. Here, we may note that the causal account applies to *initial* parental obligations. One may transfer these to others by giving the child up for adoption, but the causal account still allocates these obligations to the biological parents in the first instance.
7. That is, whilst he *can* claim to be unwilling to accept the child, he cannot claim to have been unwilling to take the risk of creating the child. Of course, some men can and do deny *all* responsibility, and declare sex, birth, child-raising and child maintenance to be the 'woman's problem'. We are taking such men to be straightforwardly blameworthy, and we are amazed that the UK Child Maintenance Service is not given more effective powers to enforce its decisions. See the blog post by Stowe Family Law (2017). 'Why do some fathers think they shouldn't pay child maintenance?' https://www.

stowefamilylaw.co.uk/blog/2017/07/05/why-do-some-fathers-think-they-shouldnt-pay-child-maintenance/?utm_content=defaultcallback_control-cro–9.

8. Marsh S. '"It's the breaking of a taboo": the parents who regret having children'. *The Guardian*, 11 February 2017. https://www.theguardian.com/lifeandstyle/2017/feb/11/breaking-taboo-parents-who-regret-having-children. We are reminded of a discussion by Ronald Dworkin (1993: 201). Dworkin describes his love for his children as one of his 'critical interests', that is, one of the interests that are central to the meaning of his life. If he were to lose his preference for Chinese cooking, say, this would not affect his life much. It would result in a mere change, not a loss. In contrast, if he were to lose his love for this children, this would significantly undermine the meaning of his life. We disagree. Imagine that, twenty years after writing about his children, Dworkin has lost all interest in them; maybe because the children are boring, maybe because he has discovered much more interesting identity-conferring commitments. Although we would still hold Dworkin to his parental responsibilities, we would call that a mere change rather than a deterioration. It would be *sad* that Dworkin and his children no longer enjoy each other's company as they used to; but people change, relationships change, often at no fault to the participants.
9. It depends on how one defines love. Some people will say they have a duty to love their spouse, where such love is closer to the love and respect between intimate friends (something that is subject to some control), than to the romantic love with which the marriage began. See Chapter 8 for a discussion of obligations in marriage and divorce.
10. Also note the right-wing inclination to blame the parents for teenage criminality, as expressed in s. 444 of the *Education Act* 1996, which reads: 'If a child of compulsory school age who is a registered pupil at a school fails to attend regularly at the school, his parent is guilty of an offence.' The glaring and unfair assumption behind such a provision is that parents can still *control* their fifteen-year-old's extra-curricular activities. At the same time, the criminal law holds children responsible from the age of ten for their criminal acts. We would suggest that the criminal justice system is a particularly blunt instrument to deal with teenagers, and better-funded interventions and support from Social Services would be a better way to tackle teenage truancy and criminality.

. Another way of interpreting such legislation is not as penalizing parents for their *present* lack of control, but part of a much stronger right-wing agenda to penalise parents for their *past* failure in morally educating their children. This interpretation is explored by Le Sage and De Ruyter (2008).

11. We discuss the relationship between familial duty, love and behaviour in the next chapter.
12. We have to note here the difficulty of admitting that you do not love a child, as we discuss further in Section C; it is more common to suppress this knowledge and (perhaps clumsily) over-compensate through action. We should also distinguish between *loving* and *liking* one's child: it's perfectly possibly to love them without liking them, for example, not liking the sort of person they have turned into, their interests, values, their friends.
13. Pre-implantation genetic diagnosis. At present PGD can detect the presence of certain genetic anomalies. But in the future it may be able to detect much more. We discuss this further in Chapter 6.

14. Following the discussion in the last section, any question of whether parental love is/should be unconditional does, of course, have to presuppose that parental love is present to begin with.
15. See Chapter 3 for further discussion of the relationship between gender role dynamics and the distribution of childcare (as well as housework) in LGBTQ+ families.
16. In Chapter 3, we explore this more when we look at sibling care and 'parentification'.
17. There are tricky situations in between. At one end, I can endorse my daughter's sexuality (part of her deep identity), but I won't let her smoke in the house (only a shallow pastime). We discuss this below.
18. We may also note that some may in fact have very clear and deep self-knowledge regarding their capacity: if somebody knows that they do not have the temperament to parent a severely disabled child, it's not clear whether – if such a person *has not yet conceived* – Vehmas would suggest that they commit to overcoming their temperament or abstain from parenthood entirely. In the case that somebody has already conceived, Vehmas argues that they have morally sufficient grounds for termination due to foetal impairment *only* 'where the combination of certain impairment and environmental conditions is such that parents would be required to make the kind of sacrifices where their own, as well as their child's well-being would be endangered' (2002: 481).
19. There are currently over 600 genetic conditions that have been approved by the Human Fertilisation and Embryology Authority for PGD. We discuss PGD further in Chapter 6.
20. HFEA 2008, 1ZB(1) and 1ZB(3).
21. Note that procreative beneficence could commit Savulescu to choosing the embryo with the race, gender and sexuality that would maximise the child's opportunities in a given society. To many ears, this sounds prejudicial enough to reject Savulescu's proposal out of hand.
22. For the purposes of this book, we do not want to stray much further into the abortion debate. Suffice to say that in most Western countries, abortion is legal and most of the populations are satisfied with that situation. Certainly in the UK, there has been no substantial political movement that would repeal the *Abortion Act* 1967. So we are inclined to take that situation as given. Even if we reject the presupposition that unconditional love can or should predate a parent-child relationship, we may sympathise with certain parts of their arguments. For example, we might be concerned that some uses of PGD are symptomatic of perfectionism in family-making, which may then seep into the expectations a parent places on their child. We explore this debate further in Chapter 6.
23. Loving a person whilst not liking them is, of course, not a tension unique to parenthood. Iranian-American novelist Dina Nayeri expresses a similar internal struggle in her relationship with her own mother, describing her resentment of the older woman's moral judgements and intrusions into her privacy and her discomfort with the fantasies that 'good Asian daughters' are supposed to perform for their mothers. The loving closeness Nayeri felt with her mother as a child is now a relic of their shared past. Reflecting on this, Nayeri worries about the day when her own young daughter may push away from her, enforcing new boundaries and leaving behind their shared 'private space'. She writes:

Many grown children understand that you can love someone deeply and not like them at all. And we prepare ourselves to survive the painful moment when our own child struggles with this distinction – we hope they'll like us and love us, too, but the frightening possibility remains: maybe it won't be a struggle for them; maybe they'll just decide that loving us is enough.

Nayeri, D. (2023, March 9). 'Foreign mothers, foreign tongues: "In another universe, she could have been my friend"'. *The Guardian*. https://www.theguardian.com/news/2023/mar/09/foreign-mothers-foreign-tongues-in-another-universe-she-could-have-been-my-friend.

24. The anonymity enabled by online spaces (e.g. the Reddit forums r/regretful parents and r/parenting) produces significantly more honest accounts of this kind of conflict than might be achieved by formal studies and interviews.
25. Finn, Suki. 2018. 'Beyond reason: The mathematical equation for unconditional love | Aeon Ideas'. Aeon, 2018. https://aeon.co/ideas/beyond-reason-the-mathematical-equation-for-unconditional-love.
26. And indeed, whilst Vehmas suggests that parents can attempt to 'reform their criteria for an acceptable child and a happy family life' (2002: 480), something we might think could plausibly be achieved through serious critical engagement with one's beliefs, he does not address the practical problem of how to cultivate unconditional love.
27. The concept of a 'duty' is problematic because it can get 'in the way' between the dutiful provider and the intended beneficiary. The provider might be so concerned about doing her duty (and being seen to do her duty) that she might not notice what the beneficiary needs or wants. In that sense it might be better to speak of the provider's *responsibility* to the beneficiary, where the etymology suggests the importance of a disposition to *respond* to the beneficiary.

Chapter 3

1. Such stereotypes nevertheless affect the distribution of care, and sometimes in a multitude of ways. Consider, for example: in step-families (where one partner has children already prior to forming a couple), the biological parent of the child will generally be the primary caregiver. However, Moore's (2008) study of Black lesbian step-families suggests that the maintenance of this division is not just about parental privilege, but about gendered self-identity within the partnership itself: 'In an environment where one's identity as a mother becomes less salient to others since both partners are female, some women may feel compelled to show, both to others and to themselves, that they are good mothers and homemakers in ways that reflect "gendered norms of accountability"' (2008: 348).
2. We describe this as a *middle*-class paradigm because working-class men and women did not generally have the luxury of supporting a family on one salary, and so childcare often fell to grandparents, older siblings or group childminders. Upper-class households, on the other hand, departed from that paradigm in the other direction: domestic and caring work were often carried out by paid staff like maids, cleaners and nannies, and so re-entered the economic sphere.

3. Some families also make use of 'au pair' schemes for affordable childcare. These are schemes through which young people (usually female students) make a little money whilst experiencing a foreign culture, learning a new language or taking training courses whilst 'helping out' at home with their host family's children and domestic chores. Whilst some countries, such as Austria, subject au pair arrangements to specific regulations, there is still room for exploitation (and all the more so in countries where such schemes are not regulated). See Busch 2015.
4. Here is an article comparing childcare costs in the UK and Sweden: Ferguson, D. 'The costs of childcare: how Britain compares with Sweden'. *The Guardian*, 31 May 2014. https://www.theguardian.com/money/2014/may/31/costs-childcare-britain-sweden-compare
5. From the Euro-Carers country profile for Sweden: https://eurocarers.org/country-profiles/sweden/.
6. A related debate concerns the provision of Basic Income, an idea which has likewise met with both support and criticism from feminist philosophers, on the grounds that this might (a) provide financial support to women whose caring obligations make them dependent on others and therefore vulnerable to abuse, and (b) provide further incentives to women to exit the labour market in favour of caring work at home (to which gendered socialization already predisposes them in many cases) and thus reproducing a gendered division of labour and the associated forms of discrimination (see e.g. Robeyns 2001; Baker 2008; Gheaus 2020).
7. The exception being demands for financial support in those areas in which we are simply used to collective responsibility, such as (as noted above) state provision for children's education.
8. However, in some situations of developing personal trust it might be more beneficial to the caregiver to switch to an informal relationship. If a householder pays an agency £20 per hour for a single caregiver employee to come regularly to the house, then chances are the caregiver is only getting £10 of that, and might have to pay tax as well. Once the householder and the caregiver and client develop a good relationship, the householder might prefer to give the same £20 in cash directly to the caregiver. For some costs associated with homecare, see: https://ukcareguide.co.uk/home-care-costs/.
9. In itself, subordination by itself might not be unusual or unhealthy. If the parents hire a plumber to come and fix the pipes, there is subordination; but there is also the plumber's expertise, and the high price that she charges for that expertise. In addition, the plumber only visits for an hour or two. Not only does the nanny seem (to the children) to have no more expertise than the parents, but she is also there for so much more of the day, all the whilst taking orders.
10. Their own children must generally remain 'back home' precisely because the wages they can earn as a nanny or au pair are insufficient to support their family in the country they have migrated to. Instead, these wages are sent home, where they can easily pay the salary of a domestic worker or nanny to look after the migrant's own children. Parreñas notes, for example, that a nanny from the Philippines can earn $1000 a month working in Italy, whilst a nanny working *in* the Philippines earns an average of $40 a month. Whilst these figures are now over two decades old, we can reasonably expect

a similar ratio to persist when we compare wages for domestic labour between Global North and Global South (2000: 571).

11. A paradigmatic form of role reversal in care for older parents by children arises when the cared-for parent no longer has decision-making capacity. At this point, they are dependent on their child to make decisions and give consent (e.g. to medical treatments) on their behalf. This is not a complete mirror to the child's own dependence on the parent earlier in life, however, as the adult child will usually have an understanding of the values and preferences the parent held previously, and can use these to guide decision-making. See National Institute of Health and Care Excellence guidelines on 'Decision-making and mental capacity' at https://www.nice.org.uk/guidance/ng108.
12. Civil Code, Article 207.
13. Chandra, Nivida. 'Were you a "Parentified Child"? What happens when children have to behave like adults'. *The Guardian*, 20 September 2022, sec. Life and style. https://www.theguardian.com/lifeandstyle/2022/sep/20/parentified-child-behave-like-adult.
14. Nuffield Trust (2023). 'Teenage pregnancy: We look at the under-18 conception rate in England and how it has changed over time'. https://www.nuffieldtrust.org.uk/resource/teenage-pregnancy. The UK teenage pregnancy rates, though declining, were still the highest in Europe. See the Guttmacher Institute (2015). 'Adolescent Pregnancy and Its Outcomes across Countries'. https://www.guttmacher.org/fact-sheet/adolescent-pregnancy-and-its-outcomes-across-countries.

Chapter 4

1. The word 'indoctrination' has come to have pejorative associations, so we will not use it. Strictly speaking, though, the inculcation of a religion involves the child learning about and believing the religion's doctrines. But inculcating or indoctrinating is not automatically suspicious: most training in pro-social behaviour has to be inculcated or indoctrinated: 'if you want to ask a question, put up your hand' – the child simply has to learn to do this, whether she likes it or not.
2. There is, however, a clear extent to which sincere expressions of religious belief (or indeed other kinds of belief) may blur the line between information and inculcation. The parents who tell their child 'As Catholics, we believe that lying is a sin and that God has forbidden it' are technically informing the child *about* their beliefs. But children – especially young children – identify strongly with their parents, and will not usually draw a fine-grained distinction between their parents saying 'We believe that X' and 'X is the case'.
3. Feinberg was focusing mainly on the *community* of the Amish. Matthew Clayton deploys a similar argument in his focus on the *parents* (2014). Clayton argues that parents should not 'enrol' their children in a particular 'comprehensive practice' such as an organised religion. A religion is 'comprehensive' in offering a unified way to think about everything in the world. Instead, Clayton argues, children should be taught to navigate and respect the irreducible plurality of practices that they will encounter in their lives.
4. *Re G (Children)* [2012] EWCA Civ 1233.
5. For an excellent discussion of this case and others, see Taylor (2015).

6. Among other things, the Convention protects children from forced labour, child marriage, deprivation of identity, and grants them the right to healthcare, education and freedom of expression. As of 2023, all members of the United Nations, 196 nations in all, are party to it, with one striking exception – the United States.
7. Of course, there is a substantial literature within the legal rights discourse that addresses these two defects, but it would take us too far afield to consider it in detail.
8. Perhaps some of the ancillary attitudes might be more difficult to drop. Many religious cultures promote notions of 'purity' or 'guilt' in their believers, and these can remain even if the metaphysical and doctrinal principles lose their hold.
9. Andre Agassi is the classic case of a child who benefitted enormously from hot-housing, rising to be the no. 1 male tennis player in the world in 1995. At the same time, he had recurring problems with drugs and depression. In his 2009 Autobiography *Open*, he described his hatred for his father, who was his first trainer.
10. See also Lotz (2006), who discusses the disagreement between Feinberg and Mills.
11. See Teather, D. 'Lesbian couple have deaf baby by choice'. *The Guardian* 8 April 2002. [https://www.theguardian.com/world/2002/apr/08/davidteather]. We use the capital 'D' here in accordance with its widespread use by the Deaf community, signifying Deafness as a culture and not merely as a physiological state.
12. Note the important difference here, however: Feinberg complains that the Amish are irreversibly harming *already existing* children by removing them from the state curriculum, but the Deaf lesbians are not planning to deafen already existing children. We discuss this difference in more detail below.
13. For the science of screening for the genes causing deafness, see McDermott et al. (2019). 'Diagnosing and preventing hearing loss in the genomic age'. https://www.ncbi.nlm.nih.gov/pmc/articles/PMC6798159/.
14. See, for example, Glover (1977: 162–3).
15. We also discuss moral and legal restrictions on the use of prenatal genetic diagnosis in Chapter 5.
16. It may appear that there's a kind of double-think required of good parents. On the one hand, they have to be prepared to unconditionally love whatever comes out of the womb; on the other they have to give the message to *this* child that she is exactly what they wanted. When it comes to the desired sex, the required double-think is reflected in the prohibition against sex-selection in PIGD (except for sex-linked genetic disorders).
17. Overall questions whether we would think this (as) acceptable if the saviour child was created not for a sibling's benefit, but for the benefit of their own sick *parent*. Alternatively, she imagines a scenario in which a couple give away their child's life-saving bone marrow, blood or a kidney to another couple's sick child. These scenarios, she suggests, 'may provoke a visceral reaction of distaste and rejection' (2012: 91). But if – as the consequentialist would claim – saving a life outweighs the cost to the child whose donations are taken without consent, why should it matter whether the life saved is their sibling, their parent or someone else's child? However, despite Peter Singer's pleas, it is generally accepted (and recognised in common law jurisdictions) that we do not have a duty of costly rescue to strangers.

18. Then again, when the older sibling relapsed, the parents could pretend to 'discover' that the younger sibling 'happened' to be tissue-compatible. That might still create an uncomfortable moral pressure, but without the ugly message behind instrumental creation. By 'moral pressure', we have in mind a situation where, for example, someone requires a kidney transplant, and could go on the general population waiting list for months, unless a family member (sibling or parent) with matched tissue can be 'urged' to donate their own kidney.

Chapter 5

1. With pun intended, we might call Velleman's article seminal. It launched a fairly large discussion about the role of biological connectedness in identity formation. The most recent book-length account is Groll (2021), and we shall be referring to him again. Below we consider Haslanger's (2009) critique of Velleman. Despite all the recent literature, we decided to remain with Velleman because it is a great article, and strikingly original in its style.
2. See Velleman (2005: 359), footnote 1. He cites the work of Muller and Perry (2001).
3. In the next chapter, we discuss reasons for giving up children and the relationship between this question and parental obligation.
4. Wikipedia even has a page of fictional and real examples: https://en.wikipedia.org/wiki/Babies_switched_at_birth.
5. There is a question of whether parents might distinguish between natural and adopted children in a single family. Even in a harmonious loving family, one can imagine good-natured teasing going in either direction: the natural children might claim that the adoptees do not really 'belong' to the family; the adoptees might respond by calling themselves 'chosen', as opposed to the natural children, who were 'accidents'.
6. As Daniel Groll puts it, some people who are the products of natural reproduction 'will see it as significant that, metaphysically speaking, there is at least one point in history leading to them that could not have gone differently. As a result, building an answer to the question "How am I?" largely around that point might well be very important to them' (Groll 2021: 93). Of course, your mother could have chosen not to have sex on a particular day roughly nine months before your birth – in that sense everyone's identity remains contingent. But *given* that she did have sex, that the particular sperm joined the particular ovum, then you were the product and had to be the product; no other product was possible, and no other producers were possible.
7. Support for Velleman's argument can be gleaned from the English case of *Rose & Anor v. Secretary of State for Health (Human Fertilization and Embryology Authority)* [2002] EWHC 1593. Joanna Rose was conceived in 1972 through anonymously donated sperm that was used for artificial insemination. She successfully claimed that Article 8 of the ECHR was engaged: in virtue of her right to private and family life, she was seeking information (ideally identifying, but at least non-identifying) about the donor. Partly as a response to this case, the UK banned all anonymous sperm donation in 2005.

8. Most websites of fertility clinics emphasise the relief offered to the couple or the woman, and barely mention the child – see Velleman's footnote 9 on p. 373.
9. Morin, Roc. 'An interview with Nazi leader Hermann Goering's great-niece; How do you cope with evil ancestry?'. *The Atlantic*, 16 October 2013: https://www.theatlantic.com/international/archive/2013/10/an-interview-with-nazi-leader-hermann-goerings-great-niece/280579/. There is a whole genre called *Väterliteratur* ['Fathers Literature'], where the children or more distantly removed descendants of notorious Nazis grapple with the effect on their identity (see Pearce 2018). Whilst some, such as Bettina Goering, distance themselves strongly from these ancestors, others, such as Horst Wächter, come to opposing conclusions regarding their ancestors; Wächter refuses to believe that his father might not be a decent man, despite the mountain of evidence of his activities as the Nazi Governor of Krakow. The paradox is explored by Phillippe Sands in Sands 2019.
10. As Groll puts it: 'I think there is a tendency – and I would say that it is on display in Velleman's piece – to oversimplify the genetic story so that people are inclined to explain a complex personality trait, for example, fretting in the face of simple challenges, in terms of a simple genetic story ("My [genetic] mother is like that too! Genetics!"). This is a form of genetic essentialism according to which what I am like is almost entirely a function of, or at least is very tightly constrained by, my genetics' (Groll 2021: 99).
11. We will be discussing Haslanger (2009). For completeness, we should mention that she co-edited a philosophical book (Witt and Haslanger 2004) on adoption.
12. Charlotte Witt (2014) develops the critique of the 'bionormative' further. See also Groll's criticism of bionormativity in (2021) Ch. 5.
13. There is a separate argument about adoption that neither Velleman nor Haslanger raises: whether or not I am physically able to have a child, I should give priority to adoption for *moral reasons*. Those reasons centre on the assumption that there is some child in the world who could definitely benefit from my adopting it, whereas there is no child who will lose out from not coming into existence. We consider this argument in more detail in the next chapter.
14. See the interview with Sue Klebold in *The Guardian* on 14 February 2016: https://www.theguardian.com/us-news/2016/feb/14/mother-supposed-know-son-columbine-sue-klebold.
15. Importantly, she claims to have always loved him, and indeed she still loves him. Recalling our discussion (in Chapter 2) of the three kinds of unconditional love, Sue Klebold was prepared to love Dylan whatever he did or turned into. However, when Dylan's deeds are so pointlessly horrific, one may really struggle to understand such parental love can mean, even if we accord her a grudging admiration.
16. In fact, David was worried that he may have unwittingly causally contributed to the bombings – on occasions during Ted's long period of activity he lent Ted some money and David feared that the money might have been used to source the bombing materials. This would not be enough for legal complicity, it would add to David's moral taint.
17. Brake and Millum, 'Parenthood and procreation'. https://plato.stanford.edu/entries/parenthood/.

18. There is some irony here in that the initial process of changing one's surname is far from bureaucratic simplicity.
19. *Dawson v Wearmouth* [1999] UKHL 18.
20. See, for example, Kingma, E. (2019). 'Were you a part of your mother?' *Mind*, *128*(511), 609–46.
21. See Hall, M.C. (2019) 'Critical disability theory'. *Stanford Encyclopedia of Philosophy*.
22. Although it's not *entirely* true, we now also know that mitochondrial DNA is only passed down from mother to child, challenging the idea that it's a precise 50:50 split. But what's a few per cent among friends?
23. And indeed, we also know that the genetic data provided by the mother and father together fall significantly short of a blueprint; genes are expressed in relation to the uterine environment, such that gestation itself contributes to that 'design'.
24. Spain has always been interesting because each child inherits two surnames, one from each parent. However, the paternal name usually goes first, and is usually the one passed on to the child's future child.
25. EWCA Civ 1344.
26. *R v P* (no. 2) [2019] EWHC 2175 (Fam).
27. There would presumably need to be some limit, though. We don't want to support parents' rights to change their children's names as often and however they choose – that detracts from the child's name as important to their developing sense of self, and would suggest that the child is the parents' property and can be renamed the same way one decides to redecorate the kitchen.

Chapter 6

1. Adoption and Children Act 2002, s 67(2).
2. In the same year, around 70 per cent were living in foster placements, whilst 14 per cent were living in institutions such as children's homes or semi-independent living units. Data taken from https://corambaaf.org.uk/resources/statistics/statistics-england, accessed 28/11/2022.
3. Of course, these might overlap – individuals who might otherwise register as prospective adoptive parents are often put off by the waiting times and the (often arduous and invasive) screening and placement processes involved in adoption.
4. Some countries have responded to falling fertility rates and the problem of an ageing population by appealing to narratives of national duty and offering incentives to families with children, in order to try and motivate an increase in birth rates. Hungary, for example, has offered a lifelong income tax exemption to women who have four or more children. The income tax exemption, interestingly, applies only to these mothers, and not to the parents of the children together or to the main breadwinner. Of course, a woman who gives up her career to raise this many children will not benefit immediately from the income tax exemption – this, perhaps, is the reason that the promised exemption is lifelong, so that the reward may still be reaped later. (Witte, Griff. 2019. 'Hungary is so desperate for kids that mothers of four won't need to pay

income tax'. *Washington Post*, 11 February 2019. https://www.washingtonpost.com/world/europe/hungary-is-so-desperate-for-kids-mothers-of-four-wont-pay-income-tax/2019/02/11/04701764-2e01-11e9-ac6c-14eea99d5e24_story.html.)

5. Besides, it might be argued that comparing loves is a fool's errand, and (in this context) risks falling into an extrapolation of Velleman's 'naturalism' – that the 'best' love is for one's natural children. (Recall that in Chapter 5's discussion of Velleman, we concluded that it was perfectly possible, following an adoption, for parent and child to grow into a relationship together that was just as deep and loving.)
6. 'A state of the nation picture on adoption', published by Ofsted 22 November 2012. https://www.gov.uk/government/news/a-state-of-the-nation-picture-on-adoption. It is worth noting that 478 applications (11.5 per cent) were withdrawn prior to a decision being made by the relevant authority; no information is given on the breakdown of reasons for withdrawing an application, but such reasons may include frustration with the waiting time for assessment and approval, unexpected pregnancy, a change of heart about adoption or an applicant's belief that they might be rejected.
7. 'Fostering in England 1 April 2020 to 31 March 2021' published by Ofsted 11 November 2021. https://www.gov.uk/government/statistics/fostering-in-england-1-april-2020-to-31-march-2021/fostering-in-england-2020-to-2021-main-findings.
8. The UK Children Act 1989, Part 1, Section 1(1) states: "When a court determines any question with respect to: (a) the upbringing of a child; or (b) the administration of a child's property or the application of any income arising from it, the child's welfare shall be the court's paramount consideration."
9. Deboick, Sophia. 2012. 'Poland's "Baby Hatches" leave vulnerable mothers exposed'. *The Guardian*, 10 December 2012, sec. Opinion. https://www.theguardian.com/commentisfree/belief/2012/dec/10/poland-baby-hatches-vulnerable-mothers.
10. Again, we do not want to spend any time on the abortion debate, partly because (i) it is too complicated and would take us too far away from our main concerns; (ii) we assume that the arguments are already familiar to readers, and readers will have settled views; (iii) we're writing in the context of the UK, where there has been no serious political movement to repeal the 1967 Abortion Act.
11. Recall our discussion of testing and licensing parents in Chapter 1, where we considered different versions of how such a test might look. One version in the context of the present chapter would be an objective test to determine how well the new parents had 'risen to the task' of dealing with an unplanned baby after, say, the first six weeks. The testing regime would not need to be structured in punitive terms; it could involve a sensitive discussion that would allow the new couple to see for themselves that they were not up to it, and they could then agree to beginning the adoption process. Alternatively, if the new couple found themselves struggling not with motivation but with resources, the six-week assessment could unlock further state support.
12. There is a question of whether IVF should be treated like natural reproduction or like adoption. (i) If IVF is like natural reproduction, then applicants will not be assessed in terms of suitability to parent (but will only be assessed medically); (ii) if IVF is like adoption, then applicants will be assessed. The UK has chosen the first interpretation. The

argument in favour of the first interpretation is that in both IVF and natural reproduction, no child exists when the attempt is launched; IVF is 'merely' assisting the couple.

13. In the case of lesbian couples, this will apply to whichever partner intends to gestate the child.
14. https://www.abcivf.co.uk/blog/who-is-eligible-for-ivf-on-the-nhs accessed 5/12/2022.
15. As of 2022, the UK government recognised this inequality and changed the ART eligibility rules to allow NHS-funded donor insemination treatment for lesbian couples, lack of success of which can then be used as grounds for NHS-funded ART (Thomas, Tobi. 2022. '"A giant Step": Charities welcome plan to widen access to IVF on NHS'. *The Guardian*, 20 July 2022. https://www.theguardian.com/society/2022/jul/20/a-giant-step-charities-welcome-plan-to-widen-access-to-ivf-on-nhs).
16. One potential justification of these policies would again invoke the NHS's limited resources, such that priority should be given (i) to those who have no children at all, and (ii) to those who have always known they wanted children, as revealed by their avoidance of sterilization.
17. A related area of debate is that surrounding 'saviour siblings': this concerns the ethics of implanting embryos selected for their tissue-type match to an existing, sick child, for the purpose of providing 'donor' stem cells from their umbilical cord blood. We discussed this topic in Chapter 4.
18. Since abortion in the UK is available virtually upon request up until the twenty-fourth week, then there is nothing to prevent a woman from waiting until the sex is revealed in a scan and deciding accordingly.
19. Mitochondrial DNA donation/replacement allows a woman to pass on her nuclear DNA to a future child without passing on her mitochondrial DNA, by using another woman's egg (with healthy mitochondria) that has been enucleated and the nuclear DNA replaced by that of the first woman.
20. In the case of same-sex female couples whose desperation for a child drives them to continue trying (at great expense) after a number of failed IVF cycles, a particular worry might be about the influence of heteronormative models of both family life and 'proper' womanhood.
21. Actually, the 'selfish' accusation can go both ways. One can be 'selfish' for not having children, but also selfish for having children – as a 'mini-me' project, as well as selfish for putting all one's energies into one's children at the expense of one's neighbours. We suggest avoiding the word 'selfish' entirely!
22. Comparing surrogacy with sperm/egg donation highlights some asymmetry: those who contribute gametes to intending parents are called sperm/egg donors, rather than surrogate fathers or mothers. The term 'surrogate mother' is used only to refer to women who agree to carry a pregnancy to term and give birth to a child that someone else intends to raise in accordance with a pre-implantation contract. Depending on jurisdiction, the surrogate may be able to charge a market fee, or only claim compensation for reasonable expenses (the UK has chosen the latter).
23. This is the theory; however, in practice, significant sums (far beyond what could be considered 'reasonable compensation') have been approved by courts where the

alternative would mean removing the child from the custody of the commissioning parents (Baron 2023: 118–20).

24. Alternatively, she could give the child directly to the adoptive parents once screened and selected by that agency. Either way, the stance against private transfers implies the need for a third party whose actions and decisions are motivated primarily by the best interests of the child.
25. Co-parenting arrangements between same-sex male and female couples can likewise be legally processed as a custody matter between unmarried biological parents: the biological father and gestational mother will generally be legal parents, whilst their partners will play a parental role in the absence of a legal relationship to the child (Herbrand 2018). Given that in nearly all countries, a child can only have two legal parents, such arrangements leave the non-biological parents in a legally more precarious position regarding their parent-child relationship. This, together with the potential complexity of custodial arrangements, is a significant reason for the growing popularity of surrogacy and donor sperm use in place of co-parenting.
26. This is correct at the time of writing, but preparation for a proposed package of legal reforms to UK surrogacy law is underway, with a draft bill due to be presented to Parliament in spring 2023 by the Law Commission of England & Wales and Scottish Law Commission. See https://www.lawcom.gov.uk/project/surrogacy/.
27. This is not the only way in which such a contract can break down – the commissioning couple might also refuse the child, leaving the gestational mother with parental responsibility. This is morally ugly in the event that the child is born with the 'wrong' sex, or is disabled as in the infamous 'Baby Gammy' case (see Hibino 2020). Surrogacy contracts in some countries and states – for example, California and Greece – therefore preclude the commissioning parents' being able to simply refuse the baby.

Chapter 7

1. For reasons of space, there are two aspects of the Cline case that we will not be discussing. First, the risk of consanguinity (in-breeding) among the children created from Cline's sperm, and the associated risk of genetic birth defects in future generations. Second, we will not be speculating about Cline's character: according to the documentary, he was without empathy, he carried a gun, he tried to threaten Ballard into non-disclosure, he may have been a member of a racist cult – but these factors are not relevant enough to our philosophical discussion.
2. Todd Foster, another Sibling, described his response to the Cline paternity revelation thus: 'Someone just cut the tether to who I am. Because we're all taught our identity resides in our blood, right? That's why I took the damn DNA test. But yeah, this complete feeling like my whole identity, is that gone? Am I no longer a Foster?' This was taken from a podcast about the Cline case on the website *Sick*: https://sickpodcast.org/season1/rightinhisowneyes.
3. Ibid. This quotation was not mentioned in the Netflix documentary, and yet we would argue that it should have opened and framed the entire programme.

4. 'Constructing' and 'understanding' an identity is complex and ambiguous in various ways. One of the axes of complexity has to do with the on-going relation between the active and the passive: how much choice does the agent have in assembling the raw materials which she discovers? How much choice does she have in endorsing or repudiating the limits which she discovers? How self-conscious does the choice process have to be for the agent to claim ownership over the resulting identity? In a similar context, Daniel Groll uses the verb 'determine': when I determine my identity, I am engaged partly in an epistemic exercise and partly an agential exercise (see Groll 2021: 112).
5. Zhang, Sarah. 2019. 'The fertility doctor's secret'. *The Atlantic*, 18 March 2019. https://www.theatlantic.com/magazine/archive/2019/04fertility-doctor-donald-cline-secret-children/583249/

Chapter 8

1. In the UK there is also the legal option of a 'civil partnership', but these involve such small numbers and raise so few separate issues that we will ignore them.
2. Office for National Statistics 'Marriage in England and Wales: 2018'. https://www.ons.gov.uk/peoplepopulationandcommunity/birthsdeathsandmarriages/marriagecohabitationandcivilpartnerships/bulletins/marriagesinenglandandwalesprovisional/2018
3. Also see Chambers (2017) for a book-length argument against marriage. She argues that state-sponsored 'marriage regimes' violate core principles of liberalism, including value neutrality and non-discrimination. One function of matrimonial law, that of protecting vulnerable participants, could still be ensured by new legislation designed for *all* caring relationships.
4. Susan Mendus (1984) takes a more extreme position and argues that a 'true' marriage requires an unconditional promise, for only such a step can distinguish it from the myriad types of essentially temporary, essentially fallible relationships with 'lovers' and 'partners' and 'girlfriends' and 'boyfriends', not to mention all the other essentially temporary conditional relationships with neighbours and work colleagues.
5. As before, we are taking 'love' not as a mere feeling here, but as an orientation and a set of behaviours towards the other. See Chapter 2's discussion.
6. It could be argued that a marriage ceremony is an insufficient demonstration of commitment precisely because it is not more than *words*. A more reliable indicator of the seriousness of commitment would be the joint mortgage.
7. As one example out of thousands, consider George Bernard Shaw's 1913 play *Pygmalion*. The upper-class linguist Henry Higgins takes on the lower-class saleswoman Eliza Doolittle, partly as an extra servant, but mainly as an intellectual challenge: to teach her how to speak English with the 'proper' accent and accompanying behaviour to convince his upper-class friends that she is now one of them. All goes well, but the newly empowered Doolittle leaves Higgins in the end. When the play was first produced, it was a big success, but Shaw was so criticised for the ending that in the 1916 print edition he added a note entitled 'What happened afterwards', and explained exactly why Doolittle

could *not* marry Higgins. Notoriously, the 1938 film, the 1956 musical *My Fair Lady* and the 1964 film of the musical all ignored Shaw.

8. Most norms can be explained, and some children are particularly insistent about 'why?' questions, but the explanations for norms range from the straightforwardly pragmatic ('If people drive on either side of the road, there will be a lot more accidents') to the dogmatic ('girls climbing trees are unladylike').
9. Some workplaces insist on female employees wearing high-heeled shoes as part of formal office-wear; why is this not straightforward unjust discrimination?
10. Another symbol of oppressive norms is the skirt, designed to flatter the female body for the male customer's gaze. Only in 2016 did British Airways give female cabin crew the right to wear trousers (as their male colleagues were doing). See Topham G. 'Female British Airways cabin crew win the right to wear trousers', *The Guardian*, 5 February 2016. https://www.theguardian.com/business/2016/feb/05/female-british-airways-cabin-crew-win-the-right-to-wear-trousers.
11. For a more detailed argument regarding the normative identification of 'good' motherhood with self-sacrifice, even prior to conception, see Baron (2023: 63–70).
12. There is a separate question of whether divorce should be made *easier* or *harder*. Making it harder prolongs the agony of a bad marriage and postpones a clean start, but couples might be retrospectively grateful for being prevented from acting too impulsively during a rocky patch. On the other hand, we can ask: what possible business of the state it is to prevent two competent adults from formally separating when that is their wish? (This question would of course be avoided by avoiding marriage itself in the first place.) It is interesting that the UK only recognised no-fault divorce with the *Divorce, Dissolution and Separation Act* 2020; before that, one individual had to *justify* wanting to leave the other individual, and had to offer one of a few permitted reasons.
13. According to the *Marriage and Civil Partnership (Minimum Age) Act* 2022.
14. Leiper Gupta Family Lawyers, 'Marrying less and later: new marriage stats from the ONS' [Office of National Statistics]. https://lgfamilylawyers.co.uk/new-marriage-stats-from-ons/. Certain cultures might need to be granted an exemption to the pre-marital cohabitation requirement.
15. By definition, a *pre*-nuptial (or ante-nuptial) contract is signed before the wedding. A *post*-nuptial contract is signed after the wedding, and may well have the same content. There is an important difference in that a post-nuptial contract might place one or both parties under unfair pressure to sign, to the point of undermining the voluntariness – whereas a prenup allows each party to withdraw from the wedding if they don't like the deal. In what follows, therefore, we will speak only of prenups.
16. The Supreme Court case of *Radmacher v Granatino* [2010] UKSC 42. In 2014 the Law Commission then published *Matrimonial Property Needs and Agreements (Report no. 343) with further discussion and recommendations.*
17. Any commitment involves a strange kind of double-thinking. On the one hand we 'know' that any marriage can fail; on the other we resolve to make it work, whatever it takes. Such a resolve is incompatible with the conscious anticipation of failure; it is not that one *denies* the possibility of failure, rather than one does not *attend* to it. Someone making

the wedding vow, writes Mendus, 'cannot now envisage anything happening such as would make [her] give up that commitment' (1984: 247). While love may alter, '… love is not love which allows in advance that it will so alter' (250).

18. However, this seems to be something most couples don't grasp until they are actually struggling with infertility, and opinions change drastically during and after the process of diagnosis and fertility treatment (see Danilu 2001).
19. See the Marriage Care website on the preparation course: https://www.marriagecare.org.uk/marriage-preparation-2/preparing-together-catholic-church/.
20. This section has been adapted from Cowley (2020), and was originally inspired by the Guardian columnist Zoe Williams, who entitled her 2018 article 'I do, again: there is nothing as deadly serious as a second marriage'. https://www.theguardian.com/lifeandstyle/2018/may/05/i-do-again-there-is-nothing-as-deadly-serious-as-a-second-marriage.
21. There is a question of what Ruth thinks now, at forty, of the wedding vow she made when she was thirty, and it is important that she does not condemn it as naïve or ignorant. We will return to this issue of retrospective self-assessment later.
22. In his famous discussion of moral luck, Bernard Williams (1981) uses the example of Anna Karenina (Tolstoy's eponymous heroine), who abandons her husband and ten-year-old child for her lover Vronsky. At the time of the abandonment, writes Williams, it was not clear whether she was objectively justified or not; once the affair fails, however, the abandonment is retroactively 'unjustified' (Williams's word). We disagree with Williams here. That the original abandonment was unjustified is *Anna*'s conclusion, and we can certainly understand why she might conclude that. However, that does not mean that *Williams* or *we* have to accept that conclusion. All we can say, perhaps, is that she had serious reasons for leaving her husband and child.
23. It is true that the breakdown of a morally serious marriage need not be traumatic, and therefore need not result in transformation or disorientation, if both parties have the maturity and decency and self-confidence to admit that they no longer belong together. Again, I am limiting my discussion to *difficult* (but faultless) divorce cases such as Ruth's.
24. Harbin (2016: 155) stresses the importance of 'interpreters', close friends and family who can help the disoriented individual avoid being overwhelmed by the disorientation. As part of this, she adds, 'what feelings an individual can have depend to some extent on what feelings they are enabled to express to others' (156).
25. Note: Harbin's 'resolvism' should be distinguished from the 'resolve' which Mendus (1984) described as essential to marriage.
26. Harbin's main interest is less in disorientation as a process of useful self-discovery, but rather as a process of confidence-undermining leading to a healthy 'epistemic humility' in the person's encounters with others into the future; it can curb some of the arrogance she might have harboured in her married life, and, once 'tenderized' (119), allows her greater sensitivity to her own and others' vulnerabilities. Perhaps the self-discovery only begins in the reorientation phase, although there is hardly a clear dividing line between phases.
27. In passing, we are taking a not uncontroversial view of factual significance as shifting in time. Ruth remembers the facts of the first meeting with her husband. When she fell

in love, she blessed the day; during the divorce, she cursed the day; ten years after the divorce, she is bittersweet about the day – throughout, the remembered facts remain the same, but their significance changes. Importantly, we are taking such perspectival significance as objective in the sense of discoverable and serious. There is then a further question of whether the *final* significance of a fact in one's life, from the deathbed perspective, is somehow 'more accurate' than the earlier significance.

28. For a very recent exploration of this kind of 'biographical perspective', see Golub (2019). We are hoping that the reader will accept the loose Nietzschean spirit of our argument, without picking us up on the many assumptions we are making about causality. It can be notoriously difficult for therapists to identify causal influences on character change.

Chapter 9

1. The Domestic Abuse Act 2021 has recently been passed by the UK Parliament. This Act was a (much-delayed) response to the UK's support of the 2011 Istanbul Convention on Violence Against Women. The Act created the first statutory definition of domestic abuse 'to ensure that domestic abuse is properly understood, considered unacceptable and actively challenged across statutory agencies and in public attitudes'. It introduces new protective orders against abusers. At the time of writing this book, it is still too early to say how effectively the Act has been implemented. Here is a government factsheet about the aims of the original bill. https://www.gov.uk/government/publications/domestic-abuse-bill-2020-factsheets/domestic-abuse-bill-2020-overarching-factsheet. But note the criticism of the original bill: Maya Oppenheim 'Domestic abuse bill condemned for ignoring "gendered nature" of violence amid austerity cuts', *The Independent* 16 July 2019. https://www.independent.co.uk/news/uk/home-news/domestic-abuse-bill-parliament-criticism-theresa-may-women-men-violence-a9007151.html.
2. For the sake of clarity in the use of pronouns, we will speak in terms of a male abuser and a female victim, who are cohabitating in a sexually intimate relationship. Given the predominance men hold in all other areas of violent crime, gender symmetry in intimate/domestic violence would be noteworthy indeed. However, claims of gender symmetry here have been comprehensively disproved (see e.g. Johnson and Ferraro 2000; Kimmel 2005) and we therefore do not address this idea, focusing instead on the patterns characterizing the vast majority of domestic violence. Nevertheless, our focus should not be interpreted as playing down the very real abuse that can be suffered by males, by people in same-sex relationships, by non-intimate cohabitants, and by elderly parents cohabiting with their adult children.
3. Whilst some might speak of 'psychological violence', for our purposes we're taking 'violence' to be essentially physical.
4. We may, however, note Friedman's (1985) defence of the deferential wife and critique of Hill, where she argues that autonomy is more complicated than Hill realises. It is when the deferential wife defers *uncritically* to her husband's preferences that her moral integrity is diminished; this is because she then 'fails to utilize resources within her own person to make moral discriminations among the preferences which she acts to satisfy'

(Friedman 1985: 146). If, however, a wife holds certain traditionalist values, and upon reflection endorses these values, and these values lead her to a policy of deference – this can be autonomous in a more robust sense.

5. Domestic Violence, Crime and Victims Act 2004, s5.1(d). This section allows prosecution of household members who allow harm to vulnerable adults as well as children.
6. An amendment providing this kind of exemption was proposed by some members of the House of Lords, but was ultimately rejected on the grounds that it would leave the offence 'unprosecutable' (United Kingdom Hansard 2004c, col. 74).
7. Referring to Herring's (2007) argument, this point was made by the judge in *Khan (Uzuma)* [2009] EWCA Crim 2. In this case, following Shazan Khan's murder of his wife Sabia, a number of household members (including two of Khan's sisters) were convicted of allowing her death. The judge suggested that had either of the sisters been subjected to violence at Khan's hands themselves, 'the jury might have concluded that it would not have been reasonable to expect her to take any protective steps' (para. 33).
8. The distinction between justification and excuse is important; an abuser might believe that he was justified in his treatment of his wife, whilst knowing that a court would disagree, and thus seeking only to present legally acceptable excuses for his actions.
9. Common couple violence is 'not connected to a general pattern of control. It arises in the context of a specific argument in which one or both of the partners lash out physically at the other' (Johnson and Ferraro 2000: 949). Intimate terrorism refers to a pattern; here, violence is 'merely one tactic in a general pattern of control. The violence is motivated by a wish to exert general control over one's partner'. Violent resistance is the term Johnson and Ferraro use to refer to self-defence, though (going beyond the legal definition of self-defence) they also include actions such as the delayed-response actions of battered women who kill their husbands after years of abuse.
10. Maclean, R. (2022, November 30). *Domestic Homicide Sentencing Review* [Hansard]. (Vol. 723, Column 338WH). http://hansard.parliament.uk/commons/2019-03-27/debates
11. Column 395WH.
12. Challen, David. 2021. 'Lenient sentences for domestic abuse killings send a dangerous message'. Metro (blog), 23 February 2021. https://metro.co.uk/2021/02/23/lenient-sentences-for-domestic-abuse-killings-send-a-dangerous-message-14131994/.
13. There is also a 'concealed' partial defence for murder, which is also a specific offence: infanticide. This may be applied when a mother kills her baby before the baby is twelve months old, and whilst her balance of mind is disturbed. She may be either charged with the offence of infanticide, or charged with murder and plead infanticide as a partial defence (Infanticide Act 1938).
14. Women's Aid. 2017. 'Femicide Watch 2017: Republic of Ireland'. Dublin. https://www.womensaid.ie/assets/files/pdf/womens_aid_femicide_watch_2017.pdf.
15. *R v Ahluwalia* [1992] 4 All ER 889.

16. Hugh Lafollette's concern with child abuse was the main motivation for a parenting license (of some sort) to minimise the risk of harm before it happens (see our discussion in Chapter 1).
17. Though as discussed in more detail below, state perceptions of children's interests can often seriously frustrate a victim's ability to separate herself entirely from an abusive partner.
18. *Re H-N and Others (children) (domestic abuse: finding of fact hearings)* [2021] EWCA Civ 448, para.31. The acronym PD12J in this quote refers to Practice Direction 12J- Child Arrangements and Contact Orders: Domestic Abuse and Harm. This is a part of the Family Procedure Rules 2010 to which Judges must refer in any application relating to a child, involving allegations of domestic abuse, abandonment or controlling or coercive behaviour by one party against the other and/or against the children. If the accused party denies these allegations, and if the allegations would make a difference to the court's final decision, a fact finding hearing must take place; however, PD12J states that contact between the children and the alleged abuser cannot be mandated unless the court is satisfied that the children and alleged victim would not be exposed to an unmanageable risk of harm.
19. If we take a scenario where the father abuses the mother but does not abuse the child directly, the scenario will probably still involve *indirect* abuse. Even if the child does not witness the abuse, they will probably figure out what is going on, and they may even come to see it as *normal* couple behaviour, with ramifications for their own future relationships.
20. A particularly harrowing example given by one caseworker is that of a father who 'knew exactly how far he could take his abuse without giving [the social worker] grounds to terminate his parental rights' (Moody 2018: 15).
21. Re M (Children) [2017] EWCA Civ 2164.
22. The Court of Appeal adopted this definition in *Court of Appeal in Re S (Parental Alienation: Cult)* [2020] EWCA Civ 568, [2020] 2 FLR 263, and extended the definition such that the manipulation of the child need not be malicious or deliberate.
23. Whilst (in the UK) a child's preference in custody decisions must be given consideration (in proportion to their age), this preference is not legally decisive until the child is sixteen. Along with a number of other factors determining the best interests of the child, the court is required to take into account 'the ascertainable wishes and feelings of the child concerned (considered in the light of his age and understanding)'. However, the extent to which a child's age and (perceived) understanding are taken to strengthen or undermine their testimony will often be a subjective matter, and may be swayed by claims such as alienation. Commenting on one case of parental alienation, the court observed that 'To respond simply on the basis of what children say in this type of situation is manifestly superficial and naïve' *(Re A (Children) (Parental Alienation)* [2019] WLUK 445).
24. 'Parental alienation syndrome' (PAS) was devised by psychiatrist Richard Gardner forty years ago, and its use in family court 'essentially reversed the allegations of abuse,

implying that the abuse was, in effect, perpetrated by the custodial parent whose allegations alienated the child from the non custodial parent' (Adams 2006: 316). The 'syndrome' was explicitly based on negative stereotypes of women (and mothers particularly) as vengeful, frustrated, angry and as projecting their own desires for sexual attention when they alleged sexual abuse of their children by the father (Wood 1994: 1373). The use of testimony regarding PAS in custody hearings has been vociferously criticised as scientifically baseless.

Bibliography

Abraham N (1987) 'Notes on the Phantom: A Complement to Freud's Metapsychology'. Translated by N Rand, *Critical Inquiry*, 13 (2): 287–92.

Adams MA (2006) 'Framing Contests in Child Custody Disputes: Parental Alienation Syndrome, Child Abuse, Gender, and Fathers' Rights'. *Family Law Quarterly* 40 (2): 315–228.

Anderson ES (1990) 'Is Women's Labor a Commodity?' *Philosophy & Public Affairs* 19 (1): 71–92.

Anderson KL and D Umberson (2001) 'Gendering Violence: Masculinity and Power in Men's Accounts of Domestic Violence'. *Gender and Society* 15 (3): 358–80.

Archard D (1990) 'Child Abuse: Parental Rights and the Interests of the Child'. *Journal of Applied Philosophy* 7 (2): 183–94.

Archard D (2010) 'The Obligations and Responsibilities of Parenthood'. In *Procreation and Parenthood: The Ethics of Bearing and Rearing Children*, edited by David Archard and David Benatar, 103–27. Oxford; New York: Oxford University Press.

Archard D (2014) *Children: Rights and Childhood*. London: Routledge.

Asch A and D Wasserman (2005) 'Where Is the Sin in Synecdoche? Prenatal Testing and the Parent-Child Relationship'. In *Quality of Life and Human Difference*, edited by David Wasserman, Jerome Bickenbach and Robert Wachbroit, 1st ed., 172–216. Cambridge: Cambridge University Press.

Baker J (2008) 'All Things Considered, Should Feminists Embrace Basic Income?' *Basic Income Studies* 3 (3): 1–8.

Bancroft L (2003) *Why Does He Do That?: Inside the Minds of Angry and Controlling Men*. New York: Berkley Books.

Barnes E (2009) 'Disability, Minority, and Difference'. *Journal of Applied Philosophy* 26 (4): 337–55.

Baron T (2020) 'Gestationalism and the Rights of Adolescent Mothers'. *Moral Philosophy and Politics* 7 (2): 239–54.

Baron T (2023) *The Philosopher's Guide to Parenthood: Storks, Surrogates and Stereotypes*. Cambridge: Cambridge University Press.

Bellamy S (2005) 'Lives to Save Lives – the Ethics of Tissue Typing'. *Human Fertility* 8 (1): 5–11.

Bennett R (2009) 'The Fallacy of the Principle of Procreative Beneficence'. *Bioethics* 23 (5): 265–73.

Biblarz TJ and E Savci (2010) 'Lesbian, Gay, Bisexual, and Transgender Families'. *Journal of Marriage and Family*, 72 (3): 480–97.

Boniol M, M McIsaac, L Xu, T Wuliji, K Diallo and J Campbell (2019) 'Gender Equity in the Health Workforce: Analysis of 104 Countries'. WHO/HIS/HWF/Gender/WP1/2019.1. World Health Organisation.

Boyle K (2019) 'What's in a Name? Theorising the Inter-Relationships of Gender and Violence'. *Feminist Theory* 20 (1): 19–36.

Boyle RJ and J Savulescu (2001) 'Ethics of Using Preimplantation Genetic Diagnosis to Select a Stem Cell Donor for an Existing Person'. *BMJ* 323 (7323): 1240–3.

Brake E (2005) 'Fatherhood and Child Support: Do Men Have a Right to Choose?' *Journal of Applied Philosophy* 22 (1): 55–73.

Brake E (2010) 'Willing Parents: A Voluntarist Account of Parental Role Obligations'. In *Procreation and Parenthood: The Ethics of Bearing and Rearing Children*, edited by David Archard and David Benatar, 151–77. Oxford; New York: Oxford University Press.

Brake E (2011) 'Is Divorce Promise-Breaking?' *Ethical Theory and Moral Practice* 14: 23–39.

Brake E (2018) 'Paid and Unpaid Care: Marriage, Equality, and Domestic Workers'. In *Philosophical Foundations of Children's and Family Law*, edited by E Brake and L Ferguson, 1:75–94. Oxford: Oxford University Press.

Bramer M (2011) 'Domestic Violence as a Violation of Autonomy and Agency: The Required Response of the Kantian State'. *Social Philosophy Today: Poverty, Justice, and Markets* 27 (1): 97–110.

Brennan S and R Noggle (1997) 'The Moral Status of Children: Children's Rights, Parents' Rights, and Family Justice'. *Social Theory and Practice* 23 (1): 1–26.

Brighouse H and A Swift (2006) 'Parents' Rights and the Value of the Family'. *Ethics* 117 (1): 80–108.

Brighouse H and A Swift (2014) *Family Values: The Ethics of Parent-Child Relationships*. Princeton & Oxford: Princeton University Press.

Bucher J (2014) '"But He Can't Be Gay": The Relationship between Masculinity and Homophobia in Father-Son Relationships'. *The Journal of Men's Studies* 22 (3): 222–37.

Busch N (2015) 'When Work Doesn't Pay: Outcomes of a Deregulated Childcare Market and Au Pair Policy Vacuum in the UK'. In *Au Pairs' Lives in Global Context: Sisters or Servants?*, edited by R Cox, 53–69. Migration, Diasporas and Citizenship Series. London: Palgrave Macmillan UK.

Bywaters P (2015) 'Inequalities in Child Welfare: Towards a New Policy, Research and Action Agenda'. *British Journal of Social Work* 45 (1): 6–23.

Callaghan JEM, JH Alexander, J Sixsmith and LC Fellin (2018) 'Beyond "Witnessing": Children's Experiences of Coercive Control in Domestic Violence and Abuse'. *Journal of Interpersonal Violence* 33 (10): 1551–81.

Callahan D (2012) *The Roots of Bioethics: Health, Progress, Technology, Death*. Oxford: Oxford University Press.

Callan E (2006) 'Galston's Dilemmas and Wisconsin v. Yoder'. *Theory and Research in Education* 4 (3): 261–73.

Campbell JC, D Webster, J Koziol-mclain, C Block, D Campbell, MA Curry, F Gary, et al. (2003) 'Risk Factors for Femicide in Abusive Relationships: Results from a Multisite Case Control Study'. *American Journal of Public Health* 93 (7): 1089–97.

Campbell LD and A Martin-Matthews (2003) 'The Gendered Nature of Men's Filial Care'. *The Journals of Gerontology Series B: Psychological Sciences and Social Sciences* 58 (6): S350–58.

Camporesi S (2010) 'Choosing Deafness with Preimplantation Genetic Diagnosis: An Ethical Way to Carry on a Cultural Bloodline?' *Cambridge Quarterly of Healthcare Ethics* 19 (1): 86–96.

Cangiano A and I Shutes (2010) 'Ageing, Demand for Care and the Role of Migrant Care Workers in the UK'. *Journal of Population Ageing* 3 (1–2): 39–57.
Cannold L (2006) 'Women, Ectogenesis and Ethical Theory'. In *Ectogenesis: Artificial Womb Technology and the Future of Human Reproduction*, edited by Scott Gelfand and John R Shook, 12:47–58. Amsterdam: Editions Rodopi.
Card C (1996) 'Against Marriage and Motherhood'. *Hypatia* 11 (3): 1–23.
Carone N, R Baiocco, V Lingiardi and K Kerns (2020) 'Child Attachment Security in Gay Father Surrogacy Families: Parents as Safe Havens and Secure Bases during Middle Childhood'. *Attachment & Human Development* 22 (3): 269–89.
Cavaliere G and C Palacios-González (2018) 'Lesbian Motherhood and Mitochondrial Replacement Techniques: Reproductive Freedom and Genetic Kinship' *Journal of Medical Ethics* 44 (12): 835–42.
Chambers C (2017) *Against Marriage: An Egalitarian Defence of the Marriage-Free State*. Oxford: Oxford University Press.
Chase ND (1999) *Burdened Children: Theory, Research, and Treatment of Parentification*. New York: SAGE Publications.
Chojnacka B and R Iwański (2022) 'Young Carers and Parentification – between Support and Responsibility: Involving the Child in the Functioning of the Family'. *Journal of Family Issues* 43 (11): 2910–32.
Clayton M (2006) *Justice and Legitimacy in Upbringing*. Oxford: Oxford University Press.
Clayton M (2014) 'Anti-Perfectionist Childrearing'. In *The Nature of Children's Well-Being: Theory and Practice*, edited by Bagattini and Macleod, 123–40. Dordrecht: Springer Netherlands.
Coady CAJ (1986) 'The Idea of Violence'. *Journal of Applied Philosophy* 3 (1): 3–19.
Coleman L, S Shorto and D Ben-Galim (2022) 'Childcare Survey 2022'. *Coram Family and Childcare*, https://www.familyandchildcaretrust.org/sites/default/files/Resource%20Library/Final%20Version%20Coram%20Childcare%20Survey%202022_0.pdf.
Connell RW (2002) *Gender*. Cambridge: Polity Press.
Cowley C (2020) 'Divorce, Disorientation, and Remarriage' *Ethical Theory and Moral Practice* 23 (3–4): 531–44.
Danilu J (2001) '"If We Had It to Do Over Again … ": Couples' Reflections on Their Experiences of Infertility Treatments'. *The Family Journal: Counselling and Therapy for Couples and Families* 9 (2): 122–33.
Daum M (2015) *Selfish, Shallow, and Self-Absorbed: Sixteen Writers on the Decision Not to Have Kids*. London: Picador.
Davis DS (1997) 'Genetic Dilemmas and the Child's Right to an Open Future'. *Hastings Center Report* 27 (2): 7–15.
Decker B (2008) 'Violence and the Private: A Girardian Model of Domestic Violence in Society'. *University of Pennsylvania Journal of Law and Social Change* 11 (1): 105.
Dempsey MM (2009) *Prosecuting Domestic Violence: A Philosophical Analysis*. Oxford Monographs on Criminal Law and Criminal Justice. Oxford; New York: Oxford University Press.
Dickenson D (2017) *Property in the Body: Feminist Perspectives*. 2nd ed. Cambridge Bioethics and Law. Cambridge: Cambridge University Press.
Doan L and N Quadlin (2019) Partner Characteristics and Perceptions of Responsibility for Housework and Child Care. *Journal of Marriage and Family* 81 (1): 145–63.

Dobson R (2003) 'Review of Abortion Law Demanded after Abortion for Cleft Palate'. *British Medical Journal* 327 (7426): 1250.
Dorow SK (2006) *Transnational Adoption: A Cultural Economy of Race, Gender, and Kinship*. New York; London: New York University Press.
Douglas H and A Reed (2021) 'The Role of Loss of Self-Control in Defences to Homicide: A Critical Analysis of Anglo-Australian Developments'. *Northern Ireland Legal Quarterly* 72 (2).
Duncan S, A Ellingsæter and J Carter (2020) 'Understanding Tradition: Marital Name Change in Britain and Norway'. *Sociological Research Online* 25 (3): 438–55.
Edleson JL (1999) 'The Overlap between Child Maltreatment and Woman Battering'. *Violence Against Women* 5 (2): 134–54.
Ekman KE (2013) *Being and Being Bought: Prostitution, Surrogacy and the Split Self*. North Geelong, Australia: Spinifex Press.
Enoch D (2012) 'Being Responsible, Taking Responsibility, and Penumbral Agency'. In *Luck, Value and Commitment; Themes from the Ethics of Bernard Williams*, edited by Heuer & Lang. Oxford: Oxford University Press.
Epstein RA (1995) 'Surrogacy: The Case for Full Contractual Enforcement'. *Virginia Law Review* 81 (8): 2305.
Ergas Y (2013) 'Babies without Borders: Human Rights, Human Dignity, and the Regulation of International Commercial Surrogacy'. *Emory International Law Review* 27 (1): 117–88.
Featherstone B, S White and K Morris (2014) *Re-Imagining Child Protection: Towards Humane Social Work with Families*. Bristol: Policy Press.
Federici S (1975) *Wages against Housework*. Bristol: Falling Wall Press.
Feinberg J (1968) 'Collective Responsibility'. *Journal of Philosophy* 65 (21): 674–88.
Feinberg J (1992) 'The Child's Right to an Open Future'. In *Freedom & Fulfilment*, 76–97. Princeton, NJ: Princeton University Press.
Ferracioli L (2018) 'Procreative-Parenting, Love's Reasons and the Demands of Morality'. *The Philosophical Quarterly* 68 (270): 77–97.
Folbre N (2008) 'Reforming Care'. *Politics & Society* 36 (3): 373–87.
Forelit C (1990) 'Mandatory Arrest and Police Tort Liability for Failure to Assist Battered Women'. *Berkeley Women's Law Journal* 6 (2): 215–62.
Frankfurt H (1998) 'Duty and Love'. *Philosophical Explorations* 1 (1): 4–9.
Freiman C (2021) 'Against Parental Testing'. *Journal of Social Philosophy* 53 (1): 113–26.
Friedman MA (1985) 'Moral Integrity and the Deferential Wife'. *Philosophical Studies* 47 (1): 141–50.
Friedrich D (2013) 'A Duty to Adopt?' *Journal of Applied Philosophy* 30 (1): 25–39.
Gheaus A (2012) 'The Right to Parent One's Biological Baby'. *Journal of Political Philosophy* 20 (4): 432–55.
Gheaus A (2018a) 'Children's Vulnerability and Legitimate Authority Over Children'. *Journal of Applied Philosophy* 35 (February): 60–75.
Gheaus A (2018b) 'Biological Parenthood: Gestational, Not Genetic'. *Australasian Journal of Philosophy* 96 (2): 225–40.
Gheaus A (2020) 'The Feminist Argument against Supporting Care'. *Journal of Practical Ethics* 8 (1): 1–27.
Gheaus A and C Straehle (2024) *Debating Surrogacy*. Oxford: Oxford University Press.

Glantz MJ, MC Chamberlain, Q Liu, C Hsieh, KR Edwards, A Van Horn and L Recht (2009) 'Gender Disparity in the Rate of Partner Abandonment in Patients with Serious Medical Illness'. *Cancer* 115 (22): 5237–42.

Glover J (1977) *Causing Death and Saving Lives*. London: Penguin Books.

Golub C (2019) 'Personal Value, Biographical Identity, and Retrospective Attitudes'. *Australasian Journal of Philosophy* 97 (1): 72–85.

Gotlib A (2016) '"But You Would Be the Best Mother": Unwomen, Counterstories, and the Motherhood Mandate'. *Journal of Bioethical Inquiry* 13 (2): 327–47.

Gracia E and J Herrero (2006) 'Acceptability of Domestic Violence against Women in the European Union: A Multilevel Analysis'. *Journal of Epidemiology and Community Health* 60 (2): 123–9.

Grigoryeva A (2017) 'Own Gender, Sibling's Gender, Parent's Gender: The Division of Elderly Parent Care among Adult Children'. *American Sociological Review* 82 (1): 116–46.

Groll D (2021) *Conceiving People: Genetic Knowledge and the Ethics of Sperm and Egg Donation*. Oxford: Oxford University Press.

Groves JM and L Lui (2012) 'The "Gift" of Help: Domestic Helpers and the Maintenance of Hierarchy in the Household Division of Labour'. *Sociology* 46 (1): 57–73.

Hall M (1985) 'Rights and the Problem of Surrogate Parenting'. *The Philosophical Quarterly* 35 (141): 414–24.

Hammer R (2003) 'Militarism and Family Terrorism: A Critical Feminist Perspective'. *Review of Education, Pedagogy, and Cultural Studies* 25 (3): 231–56.

Harbin A (2016) *Disorientation and Moral Life*. Oxford: Oxford University Press.

Harris GW (1992) 'Surrogacy, Patriarchy, and Contracts'. *Public Affairs Quarterly* 6 (3): 255–69.

Harris LJ (2010) 'Failure to Protect from Exposure to Domestic Violence in Private Custody Contests'. *Family Law Quarterly* 44 (2): 169–95.

Haslanger S (2009) 'Family, Ancestry and Self: What Is the Moral Significance of Biological Ties?'. *Adoption and Culture* 2: 92–122.

Haslanger S (2012) *Resisting Reality: Social Construction and Social Critique*. Oxford: Oxford University Press.

Haslanger S and C Witt, eds (2005) *Adoption Matters: Philosophical and Feminist Essays*. Ithaca, NY: Cornell University Press.

Häyry M (2004) 'There Is a Difference between Selecting a Deaf Embryo and Deafening a Hearing Child'. *Journal of Medical Ethics* 30 (5): 510–2.

Heitmueller A and K Inglis (2007) 'The Earnings of Informal Carers: Wage Differentials and Opportunity Costs'. *Journal of Health Economics* 26 (4): 821–41.

Herbrand C (2018) Ideals, Negotiations and Gender Roles in Gay and Lesbian Co-parenting Arrangements. *Anthropology & Medicine* 25 (3): 311–28.

Herring J (1999) 'The Welfare Principle and the Rights of Parents'. In *What Is a Parent? A Socio-Legal Analysis*, edited by A Bainham, S Day Sclater, and Richards, 89–105. Oxford: Hart.

Herring J (2007) 'Familial Homicide, Failure to Protect and Domestic Violence: Who's the Victim?' *Criminal Law Review*, December 2007: 923–43.

Herring J (2009) 'The Shaming of Naming: Parental Rights and Responsibilities in the Naming of Children'. In *Responsible Parents and Parental Responsibility*, edited by Probert, Gilmore, Herring, 105–22. London: Hart.

Herring J (2013) 'The Power of Naming: Surnames, Children, and Spouses'. *Law and Language*, 15: 310–27.
Herring J (2014) *Caring and the Law*. London: Hart Publishing.
Herring J, R Probert and S Gilmore (2012) *Great Debates in Family Law*. London: Palgrave Macmillan.
Hibino Y (2020) 'Non-commercial Surrogacy in Thailand: Ethical, Legal, and Social Implications in Local and Global Contexts'. *Asian Bioethics Review* 12: 135–47.
Hill J (1991) '"What Does It Mean to Be a Parent?" The Claims of Biology as the Basis for Parental Rights'. *New York University Law Review* 66: 353–420.
Hill TE (1973) 'Servility and Self-Respect'. *The Monist* 57 (1): 87–104.
Hochschild AR (2006) 'The Nanny Chain'. In *Inequality Reader: Contemporary and Foundational Readings in Race, Class, and Gender*, edited by David B Grusky and Szonja Szelényi, 357–60. Boulder, Colorado: Westview Press.
Hohl S (2021) 'Fair Play, Coercion, and the Costs of Children: A Reply to Olsaretti'. *Philosophy & Public Affairs* 49 (1): 6–25.
Hopkins A and P Easteal (2010) 'Walking in Her Shoes: Battered Women Who Kill in Victoria, Western Australia and Queensland'. *Alternative Law Journal* 35 (3): 132–37.
Ilioi E, L Blake, V Jadva, G Roman and S Golombok (2017) 'The Role of Age of Disclosure of Biological Origins in the Psychological Wellbeing of Adolescents Conceived by Reproductive Donation: A Longitudinal Study from Age 1 to Age 14'. *Journal of Child Psychology and Psychiatry* 58 (3): 315–24.
Jadva V, T Freeman, W Kramer and S Golombok (2009) 'The Experiences of Adolescents and Adults Conceived by Sperm Donation: Comparisons by Age of Disclosure and Family Type'. *Human Reproduction* 24 (8): 1909–19.
Jaffe PG and CV Crooks (2004) 'Partner Violence and Child Custody Cases: A Cross-National Comparison of Legal Reforms and Issues'. *Violence against Women* 10 (8): 917–34.
Jeske D (1998) 'Families, Friends, and Special Obligations'. *Canadian Journal of Philosophy* 28 (4): 527–55.
Johnson D and L Scheuble (2002) 'What Should We Call Our Kids? Choosing Children's Surnames When Parents' Last Names Differ'. *The Social Science Journal* 39 (3): 419–29.
Johnson MP and KJ Ferraro (2000) 'Research on Domestic Violence in the 1990s: Making Distinctions'. *Journal of Marriage and Family* 62 (4): 948–63.
Jourdan L, dir (2022) *Our Father*. Documentary: Crime. Blumhouse Television.
Kant I (1996) *Practical Philosophy*. Edited by Mary J Gregor. Cambridge: Cambridge University Press.
Kant I (2015) *Critique of Practical Reason*. Translated by Mary J Gregor. Cambridge: Cambridge University Press.
Kant I (2017) *The Metaphysics of Morals*. Translated by Mary J Gregor. Cambridge: Cambridge University Press.
Keller S (2006) 'Four Theories of Filial Duty'. *The Philosophical Quarterly* 56 (223): 254–74.
Keller S (2016) 'Moral Blackmail and the Family'. *Journal of Moral Philosophy* 13 (6): 699–719.

Kimmel MS (2005) *The Gender of Desire: Essays on Male Sexuality*. New York: State University of New York Press.
Kingma E (2021) 'Harming One to Benefit Another: The Paradox of Autonomy and Consent in Maternity Care'. *Bioethics* 35 (5): 456–64.
Kittay EF (1999) *Love's Labor: Essays on Women, Equality, and Dependency*. New York: Routledge.
Kittay EF (2002) 'Love's Labor Revisited'. *Hypatia* 15 (3): 237–60.
Klier CM, C Grylli, S Amon, C Fiala, G Weizmann-Henelius, SI Pruitt and H Putkonen (2013) 'Is the Introduction of Anonymous Delivery Associated with a Reduction of High Neonaticide Rates in Austria? A Retrospective Study'. *BJOG: An International Journal of Obstetrics & Gynaecology* 120 (4): 428–34.
Kolodny N (2003) 'Love as Valuing a Relationship'. *Philosophical Review* 112 (2): 135–89.
Lafollette H (1980) 'Licensing Parents'. *Philosophy and Public Affairs* 9 (2): 182–97.
Le Sage L and D De Ruyter (2008) 'Criminal Parental Responsibility: Blaming Parents on the Basis of Their Duty to Control versus Their Duty to Morally Educate Their Children'. *Educational Philosophy and Theory* 40 (6): 789–802.
Lebell S (1988) *Naming Ourselves, Naming Our Children: Resolving the Last Name Dilemma*. Freedom, CA: Crossing Press.
Levy N (2002) 'Deafness, Culture, and Choice'. *Journal of Medical Ethics* 28 (5): 284–5.
Lewis H (1948) 'Collective Responsibility'. *Philosophy* 24: 3–18.
Lewis S (2019) *Full Surrogacy Now: Feminism against Family*. London: Verso Books.
Lewis S (2022) *Abolish the Family: A Manifesto for Care and Liberation*. London: Verso Books.
Lotz M (2006) 'Feinberg, Mills, and the Child's Right to an Open Future'. *Journal of Social Philosophy* 37 (4): 537–51.
Luppi M and T Nazio (2019) 'Does Gender Top Family Ties? Within-Couple and between-Sibling Sharing of Elderly Care'. *European Sociological Review* 35 (6): 772–89.
MacDougall P (1985) 'The Right of Women to Name Their Children'. *Law & Inequality* 3: 91–110.
MacKinnon CA (1989) *Toward a Feminist Theory of the State*. Cambridge, MA: Harvard University Press.
Mackinnon CA (2018) '3. Rape, Genocide, and Women's Human Rights'. In *Violence against Women: Philosophical Perspectives*, 43–54. Ithica, NY: Cornell University Press.
McColgan A (1993) 'In Defence of Battered Women who Kill'. *Oxford Journal of Legal Studies* 13 (4): 508–29.
McDonnell E and AA Ryan (2014) 'The Experience of Sons Caring for a Parent with Dementia'. *Dementia* 13 (6): 788–802.
McEwan I (2014) *The Children Act*. London: Jonathan Cape.
Meier JS (2020) 'U.S. Child Custody Outcomes in Cases Involving Parental Alienation and Abuse Allegations: What Do the Data Show?' *Journal of Social Welfare and Family Law* 42 (1): 92–105.
Mendus S (1984) 'Marital Faithfulness'. *Philosophy* 59 (228): 243–52.
Mills C (2003) 'The Child's Right to an Open Future'. *Journal of Social Philosophy* 34 (4): 499–509.
Millum J (2008) 'How Do We Acquire Parental Responsibilities?' *Social Theory and Practice* 34 (1): 71–93.

Ministry of Justice (2008) 'Murder, Manslaughter and Infanticide: Proposals for Reform of the Law'. Consultation Paper CP19/08.
Mitchell B (2011) 'Loss of Self-Control under the Coroners and Justice Act 2009: Oh No!' In *Loss of Control and Diminished Responsibility*, edited by Alan Reed and Michael Bohlander, 39–50. Farnham: Ashgate.
Moody A (2018) *The Children Money Can Buy: Stories from the Frontlines of Foster Care and Adoption*. Lanham, Maryland, USA: Rowman & Littlefield.
Moore MR (2008) 'Gendered Power Relations among Women: A Study of Household Decision Making in Black, Lesbian Stepfamilies'. *American Sociological Review* 73 (2): 335–56.
Muller and Perry (2001) 'Adopted Persons' Search for and Contact with Their Birth Parents I: Who Searches and Why?' *Adoption Quarterly* (4): 5–34.
Mullin A (2007) 'Children, Autonomy, and Care'. *Journal of Social Philosophy* 38 (4): 536–53.
Murphy TF (2009) 'Choosing Disabilities and Enhancements in Children: A Choice Too Far?' *Reproductive BioMedicine* Online 18 (January): 43–9.
Murphy TF (2018) 'Pathways to Genetic Parenthood for Same-Sex Couples'. *Journal of Medical Ethics* 44 (12): 823–4.
Newman AM (2019) 'Mixing and Matching: Sperm Donor Selection for Interracial Lesbian Couples'. *Medical Anthropology* 38 (8): 710–24.
Okin SM (1989) *Justice, Gender, and the Family*. New York: Basic Books.
Olsaretti S (2013) 'Children as Public Goods?' *Philosophy & Public Affairs* 41 (3): 226–58.
Olsaretti S (2022) 'Why Socializing the Costs of Children Is Fair to Parents: A Rejoinder to Hohl'. *Philosophy & Public Affairs* 50 (4): 413–29.
Oshana M (2006) 'Moral Taint'. *Metaphilosophy* 37 (3–4): 353–75.
Overall C (2012) *Why Have Children?: The Ethical Debate*. Cambridge, MA: The MIT Press.
Pain R (2014) 'Everyday Terrorism: Connecting Domestic Violence and Global Terrorism'. *Progress in Human Geography* 38 (4): 531–50.
Pande A (2010) 'Commercial Surrogacy in India: Manufacturing a Perfect Mother-Worker'. *Signs: Journal of Women in Culture and Society* 35 (4): 969–92.
Parfit D (1984) *Reasons and Persons*. Oxford: Clarendon Press.
Parks SH and M Pilisuk (1991) 'Caregiver Burden'. *American Journal of Orthopsychiatry* 61 (4): 501–9.
Parreñas RS (2000) 'Migrant Filipina Domestic Workers and the International Division of Reproductive Labor'. *Gender and Society* 14 (4): 560–80.
Parreñas RS (2005) 'Long Distance Intimacy: Class, Gender and Intergenerational Relations between Mothers and Children in Filipino Transnational Families'. *Global Networks* 5 (4): 317–36.
Paul LA (2014) *Transformative Experience*. Oxford: Oxford University Press.
Pearce A (2018) 'Väterliteratur'. In *Remembering the Holocaust in Educational Settings*, edited by A Pearce. London: Routledge.
Pedersen J and S Bøyum (2020) 'Inheritance and the Family'. *Journal of Applied Philosophy* 37 (2): 299–313.
Picoult J (2009) *My Sister's Keeper*. London: Hachette UK.
Połomski P, A Peplińska, A Lewandowska-Walter and J Borchet (2021) 'Exploring Resiliency and Parentification in Polish Adolescents'. *International Journal of Environmental Research and Public Health* 18 (21): 11454.

Porter L (2014) 'Why and How to Prefer a Causal Account of Parenthood'. *Journal of Social Philosophy* 45 (2): 182–202.
Protasi S (2018) '"Mama, Do You Love Me?": A Defense of Unloving Parents'. In *The Routledge Handbook of Love in Philosophy*, edited by A Martin, 35–46. London: Routledge.
Radziwinowiczówna A, A Rosińska and W Kloc-Nowak (2018) *Ethnomorality of Care: Migrants and Their Aging Parents*. London: Routledge.
Richards N (2010) *The Ethics of Parenthood*. Oxford: Oxford University Press.
Roberts D (2002) *Shattered Bonds: The Color of Child Welfare*. New Yorks: Basic Civitas Books.
Robeyns I (2001) 'Will a Basic Income Do Justice to Women?: A Contribution to the Symposium on P. Van Parijs's "Real Freedom for All." *Analyse & Kritik* 23 (1): 88–105.
Robinson B and M Thurnher (1979) 'Taking Care of Aged Parents: A Family Cycle Transition1'. *The Gerontologist* 19 (6): 586–93.
Rothman BK (1989) *Recreating Motherhood: Ideology and Technology in a Patriarchal Society*. New York: W. W. Norton.
Ruddick S (1980) 'Maternal Thinking'. *Feminist Studies* 6 (2): 342–67.
Ruddick S (1989) *Maternal Thinking: Towards a Politics of Peace*. Boston, MA: Beacon Press.
Rulli T (2016) 'Preferring a Genetically-Related Child'. *Journal of Moral Philosophy* 13 (6): 669–98.
Rutter J and K Stocker (2015) *Childcare Costs Survey 2015*. London: Family and Childcare Trust.
Salzberger M (2022) 'The Moral Harms of Domestic Violence'. *Journal of Social Philosophy* 53 (2): 168–84.
Sandberg J, U Lundh and M Nolan (2002) 'Moving into a Care Home: The Role of Adult Children in the Placement Process'. *International Journal of Nursing Studies* 39 (3): 353–62.
Sands P (2019) *The Rat Line: Love, Lies and Justice on the Trail of a Nazi Fugitive.* London: Weidenfeld & Nicolson.
Sarajlic E (2018) 'The Ethics and Politics of Child Naming'. *Journal of Applied Philosophy* 35: 121–39.
Satz D (1992) 'Markets in Women's Reproductive Labor'. *Philosophy & Public Affairs* 21 (2): 107–31.
Savulescu J (2001) 'Procreative Beneficence: Why We Should Select the Best Children'. *Bioethics* 15 (5–6): 413–26.
Schoeman F (1980) 'Rights of Children, Rights of Parents, and the Moral Basis of the Family'. *Ethics* 91 (1): 6–19.
Serrano R, R Saltman, and M Yeh (2017) 'Laws on Filial Support in Four Asian Countries'. *Bulletin of the World Health Organization* 95 (11): 788–90.
Shapira A (1998) '"Wrongful Life" Lawsuits for Faulty Genetic Counselling: Should the Impaired Newborn Be Entitled to Sue?' *Journal of Medical Ethics* 24 (6): 369–75.
Sheldon S and S Wilkinson (2004) 'Should Selecting Saviour Siblings Be Banned?' *Journal of Medical Ethics* 30 (6): 533–7.
Sherr L, J Mueller and Z Fox (2009) 'Abandoned Babies in the UK – a Review Utilizing Media Reports'. *Child: Care, Health and Development* 35 (3): 419–30.
Shiffrin SV (1999) 'Wrongful Life, Procreative Responsibility, and the Significance of Harm'. *Legal Theory* 5 (02): 117–48.

Sikora J, MDR Evans and J Kelley (2019) 'Scholarly Culture: How Books in Adolescence Enhance Adult Literacy, Numeracy and Technology Skills in 31 Societies'. *Social Science Research* 77: 1–15.
Singh S (2021) 'Punishing Mothers for Men's Violence: Failure to Protect Legislation and the Criminalisation of Abused Women'. *Feminist Legal Studies* 29 (2): 181–204.
Sloan-Lynch J (2012) 'Domestic Abuse as Terrorism'. *Hypatia* 27 (4): 774–90.
Solomon R (2002) 'Reasons for Love'. *Journal for the Theory of Social Behaviour* 32 (1): 1–28.
Solomon R (2003) 'On Fate and Fatalism'. *Philosophy East and West* 53 (4): 435–54.
Stark E and M Hester (2019) 'Coercive Control: Update and Review'. *Violence against Women* 25 (1): 81–104.
Stocker M (1976) 'The Schizophrenia of Modern Ethical Theories'. *The Journal of Philosophy* 73 (14): 453–46.
Stuifbergen MC and JJM Van Delden (2011) 'Filial Obligations to Elderly Parents: A Duty to Care?' *Medicine, Health Care and Philosophy* 14 (1): 63–71.
Sun F, R Ong, and D Burnette (2012) 'The Influence of Ethnicity and Culture on Dementia Caregiving: A Review of Empirical Studies on Chinese Americans'. *American Journal of Alzheimer's Disease & Other Dementias®* 27 (1): 13–22.
Swan SC, LJ Gambone, JE Caldwell, TP Sullivan and DL Snow (2008) 'A Review of Research on Women's Use of Violence With Male Intimate Partners'. *Violence and Victims* 23 (3): 301–14.
Swift A (2003) *How Not to Be a Hypocrite: School Choice for the Morally Perplexed Parent*. London: Routledge.
Takševa T (2017) 'Mother Love, Maternal Ambivalence, and the Possibility of Empowered Mothering'. *Hypatia* 32 (1): 152–68.
Taylor R (2015) 'Responsibility for the Soul of the Child: The Role of the State and Parents in Determining Religious Upbringing and Education'. *International Journal of Law, Policy and the Family* 29 (1): 15–35.
Tober D (2019) *Romancing the Sperm: Shifting Biopolitics and the Making of Modern Families*. New Brunswick, New Jersey: Rutgers University Press.
Tronto JC (2002) 'The "Nanny" Question in Feminism'. *Hypatia* 17 (2): 34–51.
United Kingdom Hansard (2004c) House of Commons Standing Committee E. 22 June.
Vallentyne P (2003) 'Rights and Duties of Childrearing'. *William & Mary Bill of Rights Journal* 11 (3): 991–1010.
Van Houtven CH, NB Coe and MM Skira (2013) 'The Effect of Informal Care on Work and Wages'. *Journal of Health Economics* 32 (1): 240–52.
Vehmas S (2002) 'Parental Responsibility and the Morality of Selective Abortion'. *Ethical Theory and Moral Practice* 5: 463–84.
Vehmas (Simo) (2002) 'Parental Responsibility and the Morality of Selective Abortion'. *Ethical Theory and Moral Practice* 5: 463–84.
Velleman D (2005) 'Family History'. *Philosophical Papers* 34 (3): 357–78.
Velleman D (2008a) 'II. The Gift of Life'. *Philosophy & Public Affairs* 36 (3): 245–66.
Velleman D (2008b) 'III. Love and Nonexistence'. *Philosophy & Public Affairs* 36 (3): 266–88.
Weinberg R (2008) 'The Moral Complexity of Sperm Donation'. *Bioethics* 22 (3): 166–78.

Williams B (1981) 'Moral Luck'. In *Moral Luck: Philosophical Papers 1973–1980*. Cambridge: Cambridge University Press.

Witt C (2014) 'Family, Self and Society: A Critique of the Bionormative Conception of the Family'. In *Family-Making: Contemporary Ethical Challenges*, edited by MacLeod and Baylis, 49–63. Oxford: Oxford University Press.

Wolf S (2004) 'The Moral of Moral Luck'. In *Setting the Moral Compass. Essays by Woman Philosophers*, edited by C Calhoun, 113–27. Oxford: Oxford University Press.

Wood CL (1994) 'The Parental Alienation Syndrome: A Dangerous Aura of Reliability'. *Loyola of Los Angeles Law Review* 27 (1): 1367–416.

Yeates N (2009) *Globalising Care Economies and Migrant Workers: Explorations in Global Care Chains*. Basingstoke: Palgrave Macmillan.

Youngs J (2015) 'Domestic Violence and the Criminal Law; Reconceptualising Reform'. *Journal of Criminal Law* 79 (1): 55–70.

Yu H, L Wu, S Chen, Q Wu, Y Yang and H Edwards (2016) 'Caregiving Burden and Gain among Adult-Child Caregivers Caring for Parents with Dementia in China: The Partial Mediating Role of Reciprocal Filial Piety'. *International Psychogeriatrics* 28 (11): 1845–55.

Index

www.ingramcontent.com/pod-product-compliance
Ingram Content Group UK Ltd.
Pitfield, Milton Keynes, MK11 3LW, UK
UKHW021907150926
475560UK00003B/228

9 781350 373624